Phenomenological Insights for the Classroom

A Book Series of Curriculum Studies

William F. Pinar
Series Editor

Vol. 67

Phenomenological Insights for the Classroom

Edited by
Oscar Koopman and Karen Joy Koopman

PETER LANG

New York · Berlin · Bruxelles · Chennai · Lausanne · Oxford

Library of Congress Cataloging-in-Publication Data

Names: Koopman, Oscar editor | Koopman, Karen J. editor
Title: Phenomenological insights for the classroom / edited by Oscar
   Koopman, Karen Joy Koopman.
Description: New York : Peter Lang, [2025] | Series: Complicated
   conversation, 1534-2816 ; vol. 67 | Includes bibliographical references
   and index.
Identifiers: LCCN 2025004126 (print) | LCCN 2025004127 (ebook) | ISBN
   9783034355285 paperback | ISBN 9783034355599 pdf | ISBN 9783034355605
   epub
Subjects: LCSH: Technical education—Africa | Computer-assisted
   instruction—Africa
Classification: LCC LB1028.3 .P47425 2025 (print) | LCC LB1028.3 (ebook)
   | DDC 371.33096—dc23/eng/20250521
LC record available at https://lccn.loc.gov/2025004126
LC ebook record available at https://lccn.loc.gov/2025004127

Bibliographic information published by the Deutsche Nationalbibliothek.
The German National Library lists this publication in the German
National Bibliography; detailed bibliographic data is available
on the Internet at http://dnb.d-nb.de.

Business strategy with a chess king
© istockphoto | Yutthana Gaetgeaw

Cover design by Peter Lang Group AG

ISSN 1534-2816 (print)
ISBN 9783034355285 (paperback)
ISBN 9783034355599 (ebook)
ISBN 9783034355605 (epub)
DOI 10.3726/b22803

© 2025 Peter Lang Group AG, Lausanne
Published by Peter Lang Publishing Inc., New York, USA
info@peterlang.com - www.peterlang.com

All rights reserved.
All parts of this publication are protected by copyright.
Any utilization outside the strict limits of the copyright law, without the permission of the publisher, is forbidden and liable to prosecution.
This applies in particular to reproductions, translations, microfilming, and storage and processing in electronic retrieval systems.

This publication has been peer reviewed.

To Rachmat Koopman (née Snyders), Oscar's mother. Your continued prayers, unwavering support and nurturing presence have been the bedrock of Oscar's journey. We are grateful for your continued love and guidance.

&

To Sheila de Mink (née Smith), Karen's mother. Though you are no longer with us, your spirit lives on in Karen. Your wisdom, strength, and love continue to guide and inspire her every day.

Your influence, Rachmat and Sheila, extends far beyond your roles as mothers. The values you instilled in us and the sacrifices you made have not only shaped our lives but have also, in turn, shaped this book. We are forever grateful for the foundation you provided, allowing us to pursue our passions and contribute to the field of education.

This work stands as a testament to your enduring impact on our lives and careers.

With love and eternal gratitude, Oscar and Karen

CONTENTS

	Foreword	ix
	Preface	xv
	Acknowledgements	xxi
Chapter 1.	Introduction and Overview: Phenomenology in the Classroom: Foundations for Teaching and Research *Karen J. Koopman, Oscar Koopman & Jeffrey Beyer*	1
Chapter 2.	Approaching Phenomenological Understanding: Positionality and Reflexivity in Education and Education Research *Russ Walsh*	21
Chapter 3.	Phenomenology and Music: A New Path for 21st Century Education *Chatradari Devroop*	37

Chapter 4.	Towards Reclaiming the Primacy of Lived Experience in an Artificial Intelligence-Centred World of Teaching and Learning in South Africa *Oscar Koopman & Karen Joy Koopman*	61
Chapter 5.	Critical Phenomenological Perspectives of Reflective Entrepreneurial Learning Through Mini-Enterprise Projects *Gosaitse E. Solomon & Suriamurthee M. Maistry*	83
Chapter 6.	Insights into the Lived Experiences of a South African Black High School Principal in Leading the School Towards a Learning Organisation *Karen J. Koopman, Juliana M. Smith & Keith Long*	103
Chapter 7.	Unveiling Power Dynamics in South African Classrooms: A Critical Phenomenological Exploration into Student Teachers' Teaching Practicum Schooling Placements *Clive Jimmy William Brown & Sarasvathie Reddy*	125
Chapter 8.	Conclusion: Towards Education and Educational Research: As an "Act of Caring" for the African Learner *Oscar Koopman & Karen Koopman*	149
	Biographies of Authors	171
	Index	175

FOREWORD

Oscar Koopman's reputation as a science teacher and practitioner emerged in the early 2000s', flourishing amidst challenging circumstances. He taught science at schools situated in communities grappling with poverty, limited resources, broken communities, and a curriculum still carrying the burden of a regime lingering under the "shadow burdens" of coloniality and an inhuman apartheid system that left deep scars, not only on the education system but on people of colour across the country.

In this era, teachers were reduced to mere "deliverers" of the curriculum and constrained by a rigid technocratic managerial system—the very system that had shaped Oscar's own education from primary school through to university. It was when he joined the Cape Peninsula University of Technology (CPUT) in 2008 that I came to know Oscar. At the time I was teaching philosophy and psychology, amongst other subjects, in the Faculty of Education, which led to our intellectual journeys as academics. At CPUT, Oscar faced a new and different challenge: he had to prepare science teachers for the same schooling system in which he taught. It was then that I met him as a serious and resolute lecturer and an emerging scholar. His scholarly journey, I believe, required him to reinvent himself, as he ventured from the structured world of natural science to the humanities. I think his quest for personal authenticity drew him to the work of phenomenological thinkers—from Husserl, Heidegger, Merleau-Ponty, and later curriculum scholars that draws extensively on the ideas of existential phenomenologists like Aoki, Greene, and Pinar, amongst others.

My history with Karen is remarkably similar, like with Oscar, I made my acquaintance with her at CPUT. She brings a rich history and broad experience spanning multiple educational context—from her own business ventures to colleges, high school, the technical university (CPUT), and the University of the Western Cape (UWC) where she currently works.

Her experience even extends internationally, including a teaching position at a primary school in South Korea. This varied background provides her with a Birdseye view on learners' lived experiences across different educational settings. Throughout her career she has always been engaged in innovative work and served on key committees as well as mentoring peers in these institutions. She brings this richness and breadth of experience to inform her research publications. She is well placed both experience-wise and as an astute academic as a guest co-editor of journals. Like Oscar, her commitment to education and care for students and learners resonates with a culture of care and a focus on lived experience as explored from a phenomenological stance in this book.

It was inevitable that their common concern for the legitimisation of human development and reclaiming of the authentic self would result in a book like this. They are prolific authors as they published in highly respected journals and have authored books and functioned as guest editors of accredited journals of the academic esteem. I raise this as context to this very book. A novel and courageous response to the educational research and teaching challenges facing the African continent. They have managed to gather experts in the field of phenomenology from South Africa and Botswana, countries representing a broad perspective and a rich lived experience as well as two experts from the United States. In this way, this book, "Phenomenological Insights for the Classroom," bridges a current gap in the literature that students and scholars of education and research battle to bridge.

The book opens with an introductory chapter by Karen Koopman, Oscar Koopman and Jeffrey Beyer. That examines the crucial role of phenomenology in educational research and teaching and learning. The authors establish a fundamental premise that the learners' lived experiences underpin and inform all forms of learning. Through a researcher's lens, they demonstrate how phenomenological approaches can unveil subtle yet significant insights into educational complexities. This opening chapter establishes phenomenology as a powerful analytical framework through which to examine education, offering sharp focus on the lived experiences of its key participants—insights that prove essential for meaningful educational improvement and transformation.

In Chapter 2, Russ Walsh, discusses "Positionality and Reflexivity in Education and Educational Research". This he does by engaging seminal thinkers like Giorgi, Husserl, Heidegger, Gadamer, and Betti among others by exploring relational aspects of phenomenological understanding and competing methodological positions. He then discusses different forms of reflexivity and the concomitant implications for education and education research.

Chapters 3 and 4 employ phenomenology to engage with two contrasting worlds as their intersection with education, namely, Music education on the one hand and artificial intelligence on the other. In Chapter 3, Chatradari Devroop challenges conventional educational models, rooted in rationalist-empiricist thinking, arguing they inadequately prepare learners/students for the modern world. Devroop concludes by redefining the role of educators as facilitators of lived experiences and navigators of ambiguity, guiding students from mere knowing towards being and becoming in an increasingly complex world.

In Chapter 4, "Towards Reclaiming the Primacy of Lived Experience in an Artificial Intelligence Driven World of Teaching and Learning," Oscar Koopman and Karen Joy Koopman, examine AI's impact on students' lived experiences. They contrasts authentic bodied experience with AI-driven approaches, metaphorically describing their contest for shared teaching and learning space as "dancing on a moving carpet." They make a compelling case for the irreplaceable value of embodied experience and call for a more holistic approach to education that honours the inherently interactive and complex nature of learning. Thus, they conclude advocating for engaging learning spaces that forge generative relationships with technological innovations utilised to advance the teaching and learning agenda keeping the authentic human experience at its core.

Chapters 5, 6 and 7 follow the empirical path focusing on the work done on phenomenology in the opening chapters. These chapters take phenomenology into a practical research application. Gosaite Solomon and Suriamurtee Maistry, in Chapter 5 titled, "Critical Phenomenological Perspectives of Reflective Entrepreneurial Learning through Mini-Enterprise Projects", show how phenomenology has made it possible for them, as qualitative researchers, to suspend personal bias when using principles and techniques of bracketing, more commonly known in phenomenological language as the *epoché* and phenomenological reduction. They employed a hermeneutic phenomenological case study design to explore students' entrepreneurial learning experiences with an up-close perspective guided by a pragmatist orientated phenomenological theoretical framework, drawing on Heidegger, Merleau-Ponty and Dewey. The outcome of the research shows both positive and negative experiences, made possible by this approach. The research also suggested a curriculum design and implementation that is insensitive to student realities. They could consequently challenge curriculum designers and teachers to be more conscious of students' lived experiences.

Chapter 6, authored by Karen Koopman, Juliana Smith and Keith Long, examines the lived realities of a Black African high school principal in a township school, chronicling his journey to transform the institution into a learning organisation. Through his narrative, we witness firsthand the complexity, messiness, and structured chaos that unfolds both within and beyond the school gates. The chapter reveals the existential challenges this principal faces daily and his strategic navigation toward organisational learning objectives despite numerous obstacles.

What profound insights emerge from this principal's experience? As researchers, we often presume we can accurately map the inner landscapes of school leadership through our engagement with theoretical literature. However, it is only when we allow his story to emerge organically that we truly comprehend the complex reality in which he operates. This principal's narrative powerfully demonstrates the value of phenomenology as a research methodology—offering intimate insights into the everyday lived world as people experience it in real time. In Chapter 7, Unveiling Power Dynamics in South African classrooms: A Critical Phenomenological Exploration into Student Teachers' Reaching Practicum Schooling Practices, Clive Brown and Sara Reddy explore the lived experiences of two student-teachers from an insider-perspective as narrated by themselves, taking ownership of the primary meaning-making requiring the researchers to the mechanisms of this process. Brown and Reddy point out that individual meaning-making is influenced by its socio-political embeddedness. This is a dynamic study that is located at the intersection of personal and social dimensions of lived experiences navigating the lingering shadows of social inequalities and racial tensions still endemic to our broader society and its schooling system. Finally, they argue that the phenomenological approach adopted has broadened the paradigm to incorporate a "critical phenomenological" perspective.

This book closes with Chapter 8, *Towards Education and Education Research as an Act of Care*, by Oscar Koopman and Karen Koopman, reframing both as "acts of care" for the African child—a direct response to the persistent "shadow burdens" of colonialism, Apartheid, and systemic poverty that continue to traumatise African learners. The authors knit together the book's central theme by drawing on Aoki's concepts of, "the teacher as care" and "dwelling humanly together," alongside Patočka's, philosophy of, "care for the human soul." This synthesis brings all the strands together culminating in a proposed framework that transcends traditional pedagogical and research approaches to address the scourge of lingering and pervasive "shadow burdens" that manifests in human trauma. Finally, by incorporating insights from trauma theory and psychological concepts, they introduce this proposed transcendental framework to redefine education and research as acts of care, capable of shattering the shadow burdens and drawing a new and self-actualised generation of African learners into the light of human dignity, becoming and just being their authentic selves hovering in the winds of the African skies.

This book arrives at a critical juncture in our history, with the potential to exorcise the ghosts of the past and release a future long dormant within the African consciousness. It opens the way for children to dream dreams and reach out and embrace a future promised but withheld, and we may well have cause to reflect in the future on how important its contribution really was.

I am blessed to have been afforded this opportunity to write this foreword. The editors hold a special place in my heart and their tireless work is a blessing to our children, our nation, the continent and all those who are still groping in the shadow burdens that will not go away.

Dr Vince C. Bosman
29th October, 2024
Cape Town, South Africa

PREFACE

In recent years, we have witnessed an unprecedented surge in the use of digital tools in education. Some schools and universities have embraced these technologies to the point of near-exclusive reliance for content delivery. As Sian Bayne (2018) astutely observes, technology has become the dominant lens through which public discussions envision the future of education. This technological turn has been further accelerated by global events, as we observed during the COVID-19 pandemic how digital technologies moved from the periphery to the centre of education systems around the world.

As experienced academics who are preparing teachers, over the last few years we have consistently been encouraged through university and faculty policies to integrate technology into our lectures, ostensibly to familiarise our students with its use in the classroom. While we acknowledge the potential benefits of this approach, the COVID-19 pandemic forced an abrupt and widespread shift to digital tools. As schools and universities closed their physical doors, teachers and lecturers found themselves with no choice but to rely entirely on these platforms to complete their curricula.

During this period, we were compelled to use Learning Management Systems such as Blackboard and iKamva to upload course materials, make announcements, develop online discussion threads, use digital textbooks, and deliver lectures via synchronous live streaming that were recorded. We even turned to social media platforms like Facebook and WhatsApp to maintain regular communication with our students, addressing their questions and concerns. This rapid transition to technology-led teaching created a frenzied atmosphere, sparking concerns among many academics about the risks of over-reliance on technology in education.

I vividly recall one colleague expressing his frustration: "This shift to technology has made me sick to my core. It feels like I no longer know what I'm doing in my classroom. Now I'm talking to a computer like a madman, and I can't see or hear my students. What is happening to us?" Tragically, this colleague passed away during the pandemic, and I often can't help but wonder how he would have responded to the emergence of ChatGPT just a year later, in November 2022.

The concerns about technology's impact on education are real. Jonathan Crary (2022) describes generative artificial intelligence tools like ChatGPT as being inextricably linked to "the catastrophic operations of global capitalism" and functioning as part of a "global apparatus for the dissolution of society" (p. 5). Within the field of educational scholarship, Neil Selwyn (2023) highlights how digital technology has been shown to extend and entrench the privatisation of public education, increase corporate control over key educational processes, and exacerbate oppressive conditions such as individualisation, standardisation, and surveillance. Both Crary and Selwyn emphasise not only the internet's harmful social consequences but also its complicity in ecological destruction.

In this era of increasing technological dominance, we believe it is imperative for teachers to critically reflect on their approaches to teaching and learning. Rather than becoming dependent on these digital tools that is continuously evolving, we advocate for a deeper engagement with lived experience. This is the central motivation behind our decision to produce this book. We call for academics and researchers to slow down and reimagine their learning environments beyond the confines of traditional institutions, fostering an education rooted in open dialogue and direct encounters with the world around us.

This approach aligns naturally with the principles of phenomenology, which prioritises first-hand, subjective embodied lived experience in understanding and making meaning of our world. As van Manen (2007, p. 12) eloquently puts it, "Phenomenology is a project of sober reflection on the lived experience of human existence—sober, in the sense that reflecting on experience must be thoughtful, and as much as possible, free from theoretical, prejudicial and suppositional intoxications." By embracing these insights, we believe teachers can transform their practices and offer students a richer, more meaningful educational experience.

Our journey into phenomenology began during our doctoral studies when we first encountered the works of scholars like Edmund Husserl, Martin Heidegger, and Maurice Merleau-Ponty. Their thinking challenged the foundations of our beliefs about education—particularly regarding teaching, learning, assessment, and curriculum. This transformative experience can be understood through Ted Aoki's (2005) metaphor of a bridge. Crossing a bridge symbolises the movement from one worldview to another, but it also invites us to pause, linger, and reflect. A bridge, should encourage us not to rush but to meditate, critique, and question deeply, allowing new insights to emerge until we find our through essence. The bridge opens up possibilities for openness and dialogue to embrace tension and multiple perspectives leading to a richer understanding of the world.

This reflective crossing was essential for us, as we had been trained in a Western educational tradition that positioned the teacher as an authoritative figure—a wellspring of knowledge—and the learner as a passive recipient. We realised how this positivistic tradition in which we were trained did not allow us to reflect deeply, to critique and question as we were always in a rush to deliver our curriculum and to assess its effectiveness through testing and examination protocols. What we did not know was how we reduced our students to mere objects in the educational process, shaping them for predetermined roles in society. These ideas were not just theoretical but shaped by our own lived experiences and what we had come as learners and students, to believe as truth.

Phenomenology, however, became the bridge that opened our eyes to a more humanising perspective. It encouraged us to break through our self-imposed walls, to question our assumptions, unlearn much of what we had been taught, and reimagine our roles as teachers in a more meaningful and compassionate way. As Heidegger (1967, p. 58) reminds us, "The way in which the entity we are ourselves is, in its very Being, that Being which is an issue for it, is to see it in terms of authenticity and inauthenticity."

In our initial teacher training, the focus was largely on cold facts, outcomes, and measurable results. As science and commerce teachers, respectively, we once believed that success in the classroom meant producing students who could achieve good test scores. This belief narrowed our view of education to transactional exchanges of information, where knowledge was treated as a commodity to be delivered. What we failed to realise in those initial stages of our careers was that this approach alienated us from our learners. By doing so, we also limited their ability to think critically and engage deeply with their respective subjects and associated material.

Our pedagogical practices were shaped by the likes of Ralph Tyler and Franklin Bobbitt, whose educational philosophies viewed the learner's mind as an empty vessel waiting to be filled. The focus was on efficient delivery and measurable outcomes, with little regard for the emotional, social, and intellectual needs of the students. Phenomenology changed all of that for us. It shifted our focus from seeing learners as objects to be moulded into future resources for the country, to seeing them as complex human beings with needs, desires, and potential.

The works of Husserl, Heidegger, and Merleau-Ponty unsettled our thinking, encouraging us to consider the lived experiences of our students. We came to realise that education is not just about transferring knowledge, but it is about nurturing human beings to develop and grow holistically. The classroom became a space where we could help students see their own worth, understand their place in the world, and develop into individuals who could contribute meaningfully to society—not just as workers, but as whole human beings.

Unlearning the Western ideals that had dominated our thinking for so long was both a liberating and challenging process. For the first time, we began to understand that the student, not the teacher, should be at the centre of the learning experience. The more we immersed ourselves in phenomenology, the more we saw the importance of building deep relationships with our students, rooted in mutual respect, trust, and care. We learned that to truly understand our students, we had to open ourselves to them—allowing them to see that we cared not just about their grades, but about their growth as individuals.

This is no easy task. It involves patience, humility, and sometimes even letting go of the teacher's role entirely to allow the students to become the teachers. However, the reality of our educational system in South Africa presents challenges to this kind of deep engagement. The curriculum is often so densely packed with content that there seems to be no time to foster meaningful relationships with students. But phenomenology taught us that making time for these relationships is crucial. It also showed us that teaching is not about delivering information in a production-line fashion, but about creating spaces for authentic learning experiences.

As teachers, we needed to unlearn the idea that efficiency and outcomes are the most important aspects of education. Instead, we learned to embrace the unpredictability and richness that comes from truly engaging with our students' lived experiences. As van Manen (1990) suggests that the end of human science research for teachers is a critical pedagogical competence in knowing how to act tactfully in pedagogic situations on the basis of a carefully edified thoughtfulness.

As we started to delve deeper into the works of curriculum scholars like William Pinar (1998; 2005), and Maxine Greene (1988), we found further affirmation that education should not be a rigid, one-size-fits-all system. These scholars pushed us to think beyond the traditional boundaries of teaching and learning, challenging the notion that knowledge is something to be passively received. They encouraged us to view education, in particular the curriculum as a living and complicated conversation that is an ever-evolving, dynamic process that is shaped by the experiences, cultures, and identities of both the teacher and the learner. The modernist lineage of these scholars represents a radical shift away from the positivistic view of education. It emphasises autonomy, pluralism, and the idea that intelligence and knowledge are not fixed commodities, but rather fluid and diverse. This shift was crucial in helping us rethink our roles as curriculum scholars and reimagine what the classroom could be. We began to see the classroom as a space where the teacher and students co-create knowledge, where the rigid hierarchies of traditional curriculum dissolve, and where freedom, care, kindness, and creativity flourish.

This book, "Phenomenological Insights for the Classroom," was written with one purpose, that is, to invite teachers, academics, postgraduate students, and researchers to reassess, recalibrate, and reposition their understanding of education. It challenges the overinflated and often devalued expectations placed on teachers and learners alike. It calls for a more humane, compassionate, and thoughtful approach to teaching—one that recognises the learner as an individual with unique needs and potential.

Phenomenology has been a transformative force in our teaching careers, and we hope this book will inspire others to embark on a similar journey. Our hope is that by sharing our experiences and insights, as well as those of each contributor, we can contribute to a broader movement toward a more reflective, engaged, and humane education system. We envision an education that sees the learner not as an empty vessel, but as a whole person, full of potential, waiting to be nurtured and guided on their journey of self-discovery and growth.

As you read the chapters that follow, we invite you to reflect on your own experiences as a teachers or learner. Consider how the phenomenological insights presented here might reshape your understanding of teaching and learning. Challenge yourself to question long-held assumptions and to embrace the complexity and richness of human experience in the classroom.

This book is not meant to provide easy answers or quick fixes. Instead, it offers a lens through which to view education anew—a lens that brings into focus the humanity, the lived experiences, and the potential for growth that exist in every educational encounter. We hope that it will spark conversations, inspire new approaches, and ultimately contribute to a more thoughtful, empathetic, and effective educational practice.

As we face an uncertain future, where the role of technology in education continues to evolve and expand, the insights offered by phenomenology become even more crucial. They remind us of the irreplaceable value of human connection, of the importance of presence and authenticity in teaching, and of the transformative power of education when it is approached with care, curiosity, and openness.

We invite you to join us on this journey of unlearning and relearning, of moving from authority to authenticity, and of rediscovering the potential of education to shape not just minds, but lives. Welcome to "Phenomenological Insights for the Classroom." Let the exploration begin.

References

Bayne, S. (2018). Teacherbot: Interventions in automated teaching. Apertura (Guadalajara, Jal.), 10(2), 140–154. https://doi.org/10.32870/ap.v10n2.1342

Crary, J. (2022). *Scorched earth: Beyond the digital age to a post-capitalist world.* London: Verso.

Greene, M. (1988). *The dialectic of freedom.* New York: Teachers College Press.

Heidegger, M. (1967). Being and time (J. Macquarrie & E. Robinson, Trans.). Harper & Row.

Pinar, W. (2005). A lingering note: An introduction to the collected works of Ted T. Aoki. In W. Pinar & L. Irwin (Eds.), *Curriculum in a new key: The collected works of Ted T. Aoki.* London: Lawrence Erlbaum and Associates Publishers.

Pinar, W. (1998). *The passionate mind of Maxine Greene. 'I am . . . not yet.'* London: Falmer Press.

Selwyn, N. (2023). "Digital degrowth: Toward radically sustainable education technology." *Learning, Media and Technology*, 49(2), 186–199.

Van Manen, M. (1990). Researching lived experience: Human science for an action sensitive pedagogy. State University of New York Press.

Van Manen, M. (2007). Phenomenology of practice. *Phenomenology & Practice*, 1(1), 11–30.

Oscar Koopman (Stellenbosch University) &
Karen Joy Koopman (University of the Western Cape)
10th October, 2024

ACKNOWLEDGEMENTS

We extend our heartfelt gratitude to all contributors who helped bring this book to life. We are deeply grateful to our anonymous reviewers for their thoughtful critiques and shared wisdom, which have not only improved the quality of scholarship but also enriched our understanding of phenomenology and its application in education. A special word of thanks goes to our colleague and friend, Dr Vince Bosman, who, without hesitation and despite his busy schedule, always made room to assist us. Whether it was critically reviewing a chapter, acting as a critical reader, or serving as a clearance reader, you never declined. We also thank you for taking Oscar's classes, allowing him the time needed to complete his duties related to the book. To our families, whose unwavering love, patience, and support provided the foundation upon which this project was built, we offer our sincere appreciation. Finally, we acknowledge the scholars whose work has profoundly influenced our thinking and shaped the direction of this book. To all, we offer our deepest gratitude.

· 1 ·

INTRODUCTION AND OVERVIEW: PHENOMENOLOGY IN THE CLASSROOM: FOUNDATIONS FOR TEACHING AND RESEARCH

Karen J. Koopman, Oscar Koopman & Jeffrey Beyer

In the planning phase of this chapter, we were confronted with a crucial question: *How should we craft an opening chapter for a book that promises to provide phenomenological insights for the classroom?* Our challenge was to capture the reader's interest despite the complex and abstract nature of phenomenological thinkers and the complex and dense nature of the language they use to frame their ideas.

This question not only addresses the book's purpose but also raises concerns about how researchers, postgraduate students, and teachers—as drivers of teaching, learning, and assessment—will perceive the relevance of phenomenology to their daily work. Moreover, we recognised that this introductory chapter serves as the reader's gateway into the world of phenomenology in education. Consequently, we needed to make a strong first impression. Our collective aim in writing this chapter is threefold, this is to capture interest, establish credibility, and provide a clear roadmap for the content that follows in the book. By achieving these goals, we hope to create a solid foundation for readers to understand the rich intersection of phenomenology and educational practice.

This question aligns with the phenomenological tradition of questioning our assumptions and experiences, of being open as much as possible to how a phenomenon is lived, how it presents itself, how it is structured and how it resonates with the lived realities of others in the world. We learn this from existential-phenomenological scholars like Heidegger and Merleau-Ponty who emphasised that the primary importance of examining the presuppositions implied and always present in our explorations of immediate, lived experience. By carefully considering these opening elements, we (the authors of this chapter) aspire to embody this phenomenological approach in the very structure of our work here, holding to our commitment to self-reflection, being ever mindful of our assumptions. This is central to phenomenological thought and sets the stage for a collaborative exploration of phenomenology's potential in the classroom.

Education, at its very core, can be thought of as some form of intertwining encounter of transference and countertransference between teachers and learners. But teaching and learning, strictly speaking, are only a moment of a subset of the larger category of the ongoing life paths of their individual subjectivities and experiences. This more inclusive range of the whole of the encounter resonates with what psychoanalysts like Freud (1933) and Lacan (2006) would describe as a psychological storm. The prescribed content to be taught and learned is not a singular circumscribed thread of information delivered unidirectionally from teacher to learner, like a load of potatoes being dumped into a bin or water poured from a pitcher into a waiting glass. Rather, in every instant it is a reciprocating experiential event bathed in a dynamic and multi-determined matrix of meaning, one that includes overlapping contexts for the subjectivity of the teacher and the subjectivity of the learner. This storm description is apt because even though teaching and learning can appear superficially to be a simple transfer-of-information event that takes place within the four walls of a school building, a more nuanced look reveals that it is a complex, unfolding horizon of intermingling subjectivities, a historically situated, meaning laden event in which multiple subjects with individual personalities and life circumstances meet to share knowledge, to deepen understanding, and, more fundamentally, to seek and nurture the development and integration of meaning.

Whether in a school or university classroom, what too often makes this an unnecessarily turbulent psychological storm is the surplus pressure placed on both teachers and learners—pressure from the educational institutions themselves, from family, community, and the social milieu, as well as from the more insidious pressure already internalised by both the teachers and the students. Learners are expected to perform well on standardised tests, their future careers and social standing seeming to depend on it. Teachers are expected to produce good results and thereby demonstrate their competence, intelligence, and work ethic even while rushing through the lessons at a competitively driven, often ill-advised pace towards prescribed goals. Speed is an asset to surfers, it keeps them moving forward and on the surface, out of the depths; speed for learners can be a detriment, keeping them on the surface, out of the depths of understanding. Depthful moments of reflection, contemplation, and integration are among the casualties in the unrelenting rush forward. In this hurried storm we easily and often lose sight of the valuable depths of the lived experiences that pulse beneath the surface of every classroom at every moment.

So what if, instead of asking what learners know, we begin by asking how they live and experience the world? We should be clear that a shift in paradigm like this cannot be simply an add-on to an already full and overflowing teaching day. Instead, it requires a deliberate and carefully crafted shift in *how* one approaches the teaching day. This shift in approach, however, is not what curriculum planners and policymakers anticipated when they made predetermined decisions about what learners should know, how much time is needed to learn it, presumably, and how teachers should teach it. It is no wonder Freud (1933) called teaching the "impossible profession" (p. 149).

A phenomenological approach offers us the much needed opportunity to slow down, to listen more attentively, and to reflectively sink into the depths of the subjective, embodied realities of both teachers and learners. These embodied depths are always already there in any case, whether we attend to them and take them into account or not. In a demanding world that increasingly prioritises efficiency and outputs, phenomenology allows us to rediscover or reclaim the authentic human essence of learning and teaching by valuing the lived world experiences of both teachers and learners. At the heart of phenomenology lies the radical assertion that all knowledge begins with subjectivity—the lived-through and embodied experience of being-in-the-world. Hannah Arendt (1968) writes:

> I have always believed that no matter how abstract our theories may sound or how consistent our arguments may appear, there are incidents and stories behind them, which at least for ourselves contain in a nutshell the full meaning of whatever we have to say. Thought itself, to the extent that it's more than a technical logical operation, which electronic machines may be better equipped to perform than the human brain, arises out of the actuality of incidents, and incidents of living experience must remain the guidepost which thinking soars into the depths into which it descends. (p. 3)

Arendt emphasises here the primacy of lived experience as the foundation for abstract philosophising and theorising. She reiterates that our understanding of the world, and with it, of course, our learning in the classroom, is inherently shaped and coloured by our subjective, embodied interactions with people and objects in the world. She avers that behind every theory or argument lie "incidents and stories" that contain and embody the ever unfolding full meaning of our ideas. In the classroom, this translates to recognising, valuing, and welcoming into the setting the unique lived experiences that each learner brings. These experiences form the "guidepost", the subjective matrix of the personally meaningful contact surface of relating, the fertile soil from which all learning and understanding emerge and grow. Teachers who embrace this phenomenological perspective appreciate that effective education is not just about transmitting information, it is not like dumping a load of potatoes into a bin or the pouring of water into an awaiting glass; rather, it is about a subjective "intertwining with," a mutual engaging with and building upon the richness of the learners' lived experiences. This approach acknowledges that students are not blank slates or passive recipients of knowledge (Koopman & Koopman, 2023). Instead, they are active participants in the ever reciprocating learning process, constantly interpreting and making meaning from their experiences in the dynamic learning context. Their personal histories and cultural backgrounds, their individual perspectives, inclinations and dreams, and their habitual ways of being all contribute to how they engage with and understand new information.

By recognising the critical importance of "incidents of living experience," teachers can take these into account to create more meaningful and impactful learning environments. This might involve encouraging learners to reflect on and share their personal experiences, using real-world examples that resonate with learners' lives, or designing learning activities that engage learners' embodied, sensory experiences. Ultimately, this phenomenological approach to teaching and learning recognises that learning is not just a cognitive process but a holistic, embodied experience. It acknowledges that our most profound insights and understandings often arise not from abstract theorising but from the clarity of deep engagement with the lived world. This perspective invites us to consider the learner as a being-in-the-world, inseparable from their context and experiences. It recognises that knowledge is not simply acquired but emerges through the intricate dance between self and world, body and mind, perception and reflection. The learner's lifeworld—their unique tapestry of experiences, emotions, cultural background, and bodily sensations—becomes the fertile ground from which understanding grows.

In this light, the classroom transforms into a space of intersubjectivity, where the horizons of teacher and student merge and expand. Learning becomes a co-constitutive act, with meaning emerging through dialogue, shared experiences, and the fusion of different perspectives. The teacher, rather than being a mere transmitter of information, becomes a guide in the exploration of lived experience, helping students uncover the rich layers of meaning embedded in their everyday encounters with the world.

This approach also acknowledges the role of the body in learning. It recognises that our understanding is not just conceptual but is deeply rooted in our corporeal being. The way we move, perceive, and physically interact with our environment shapes our understanding in profound ways. In embracing this embodied dimension of learning, we open up new avenues for engagement and comprehension that go beyond traditional cognitive approaches.

Moreover, this phenomenological stance invites us to embrace the ambiguity and open-endedness of the learning process. It acknowledges that our understanding is always partial, always in flux, always open to new interpretations and perspectives. This recognition of the inherent incompleteness of knowledge creates a space for wonder, curiosity, and continuous exploration.

If all of this happens in the classroom, it indeed makes us wonder if Freud (1933) would reconsider his statement of teaching as an "impossible profession." The impossibility that Freud spoke of perhaps stemmed from a view of education as a unidirectional transmission of fixed knowledge, a task that indeed seems Sisyphean in its futility.

But when we embrace this phenomenological approach, the seeming impossibility transforms into a field of endless possibility. The classroom becomes a space of perpetual becoming, where both teacher and learner are constantly evolving, constantly discovering new dimensions of themselves and the world. The "impossibility" is not a barrier but an invitation—an invitation to continually explore, question, and reimagine. In this light, we might indeed rephrase teaching as a "profession of possibilities." It becomes a calling that celebrates the inexhaustible depth of human experience and the boundless potential for growth and understanding. The teacher, far from being trapped in an impossible task, becomes a facilitator of wonder, a co-explorer in the vast landscape of lived experience.

This reframing doesn't negate the challenges of education, but it recontextualises them. The difficulty lies not in the futile attempt to fill empty vessels with knowledge, like dumping potatoes in a bin or water into an awaiting glass, but in the complex, nuanced work of nurturing each learner's unique way of being-in-the-world. It's a profession that demands constant reflection, adaptation, and a willingness to embrace the unknown. In embracing teaching as a profession of possibilities, we open ourselves to the transformative power of education—not just in shaping minds, but in enriching lives, fostering empathy, and expanding our collective understanding of what it means to be human in this complex, interconnected world.

As we transition now to a discussion of the phenomenological researcher, it will become clear that the application of phenomenology in education extends beyond the issues of pedagogy in the classroom. The researcher adopting a phenomenological stance embodies many of the same principles we have discussed for teachers. Just as teachers must attune themselves to the lived experiences of their students and engage them accordingly, phenomenological researchers must cultivate a heightened sensitivity to the nuanced, subjective realities of their research participants. This approach demands a level of engaging receptivity and openness that parallels the posture we have advocated in the classroom. In the following section, we will explore how phenomenological researchers position themselves to best take up the complex terrain of lived experience, employing methods that honour and remain faithful to the richness and complexity of human subjectivity. We will examine how the phenomenological researcher, like the phenomenologically-oriented teacher, must learn to bracket their assumptions, engage in deep, attentive listening, and strive to capture the essence of lived experiences just as they present themselves. It is hoped that this exploration will begin to illuminate the potential of phenomenology not just as a teaching philosophy, but as a robust framework for educational research that can inform and enrich classroom practice.

Phenomenological Philosophy Guiding the Researcher

How do phenomenologists nose dive into the depths of lived experiences to contextualise, and conceptualise phenomena related to teaching and learning, thereby articulating their precise nature? To address this question, we turn to the philosophical writings of canonical phenomenological thinkers such as Husserl (1970), Heidegger (1967), Merleau-Ponty (1962), and Jean-Paul Sartre (1956). To be sure, the writings of these great thinkers are notoriously difficult—not surprising since they attempt to articulate the complex fundamental aspects of existence. For a general orientation to the ideas, we present here a brief overview of some of the relevant aspects of their careful and sophisticated working of the issues in general.

These philosophical cannons, to mention here only a few from amongst many others, provided phenomenological researchers, scholars, and postgraduate students with the theoretically grounded conceptual tools necessary to articulate, describe, and narrate the essence of the phenomena of lived experience. Explorations such as these reveal the intentionality, representation, and constitution underpinning an individual's lived experiences as they engage the world. Husserl (1970) provides insight into the seminal idea of intentionality, that is, that a person's consciousness does not stand alone as such but is always directed towards an object or experience; consciousness is always consciousness *of* something. Representation, for Husserl, involves the way in which consciousness grasps, interprets, and assigns meaning to the objects of consciousness. Constitution is the term used to describe how the individual's consciousness actively shapes and structures (more precisely, co-constitutes or co-creates) their lived experiences within the world. Merleau-Ponty (1962) employs the term "conditions of satisfaction" to signify a description that is deemed the "accurate" interpretation or revelation of a phenomenon as it is subjectively encountered. Conditions of satisfaction, he argues, support or satisfy one's expectations or anticipations, suggesting that the way things appear in the world carries some inherent sense or significance as one experiences changing perspectives. For example, when observing a television screen from the front side, although only the front side is visible in this perception, the implication is that it must have a back side that would be perceived as the embodied perspective shifts, and that this anticipated perspective is given in the original perception from the front. These concepts (intentionality, representation, constitution, conditions of satisfaction) serve as foundational tools for the phenomenological researcher by providing a framework to examine how a teacher's thinking and conscious experience shapes their teaching. They provide insight into what happens beneath the surface of what people might superficially observe, including those invisible forces behind the scenes, those perhaps just below awareness for the subject, as well as those forces situated deep in the unconscious. By considering the intentionality behind a teacher's engagement with the phenomenon, the mental representations they form of it, and the way their consciousness constitutes the meaning and structure of the experience, the researcher can develop a rich understanding of the essence of the phenomenon as it is lived and perceived by the individual. From Husserl's perspective, revisiting and remaining faithful to the "things in themselves" in this way is crucial for the researcher in gaining a satisfactory grip on a phenomenon under investigation (1970, p. 252).

According to Husserl (1970), when a phenomenologically oriented researcher undertakes the task of describing an experience, they embark on a journey of "reduction," necessitating the suspension of personal biases through the application of what he called the phenomenological epoché. Instead of being unreflectively subject to the influence of their own assumptions, the researcher deliberately brings them into awareness, recognises them and takes note of them, in order to "set them aside," as it were. In this way the phenomenological researcher does their best to divest themselves of all preconceived notions about the phenomenon under investigation thus attaining greater clarity and focus in their pursuit of remaining true to the "things in themselves" (Husserl, 1970, p. 252). It also provides the transparency of method needed for other researchers who wish to reproduce or validate the results.

By being guided by and integrating the concepts of description, reduction, and essence, the phenomenologist arrives at the centre of an individual's experience of any given phenomenon—intentionality. Intentionality denotes the subjectively internal, imperceptible system of thought and meaning that underlies human consciousness for that particular situated subject (Merleau-Ponty, 1962). In the simplest terms, intentionality constitutes the complete meaning of an object in the ever-unfolding horizon of experience, an essence that can only be unearthed and explicated within the subjective space of consciousness. Husserl asserts that consciousness remains grounded in the subject yet also extends beyond the inner, skin-bounded world of the subject, the whole of its reach thus pushing outward and extending into the world. It follows that "being" is more accurately understood therefore as "being-in-the-world". Through phenomenology, we gain access to a systematic and reliably reproducible method of comprehending this most important aspect of human subjective existence.

In the context of teaching and learning, the phenomenological toolbox, nicely stocked with an assortment of those specialised tool sets from the respective phenomenological scholars, provides a solid and useful framework for researchers to understand the experiences of teachers and learners. By adopting a phenomenological approach, researchers can explore the deeply connected layers of teaching and learning, revealing their deeper meanings and implications. These deeper layers are often severed from the whole and left untouched in many other, more traditional natural scientific quantitative research approaches. As a method, it allows for a more nuanced and profound grasp of educational phenomena, ultimately enhancing both teaching practices and learning outcomes.

Therefore, as an individual, the research participant—whether a learner, student or teacher—stands at the epicentre of the classroom, the situated, embodied subject at the focal point of an entire world of interrelated meanings. It thus becomes imperative for researchers to shift their focus towards understanding the subjective world of the individual at the level of perception as lived. By "level of perception," we refer to what Merleau-Ponty (1962) terms the deployment of the "crypto-mechanism," that routine inclination found in unreflective perception in which the act of perceiving itself is skipped over and replaced by the object perceived in the "natural attitude." Here we experience skipping over the context-rich, relational act of "perceiving a table" (which includes the all-important created meanings and perspectives that we bring into the relating) and say simply "I see a table," an object in the world that exists independent of our relating with it. Instead, in the phenomenological attitude, the researcher endeavours to elucidate the whole of the relational event, which encompasses their own underlying structures of meaning-making as well as the visible elements that shape the researcher's perception. Nothing observed or felt in that experiential space is taken for granted—it is all part of the relational ecology of the meanings. The researcher's natural attitude is thus recognised and bracketed, set aside (the epoche). Far from attempting to study subjectivity from a traditional objective attitude (a move which effectively annihilates the very matter under investigation as it approaches and attempts to study it) phenomenological scholars encourage us to enter into the subjective consciousness of the subject with our own, recognising, and bracketing our own presuppositions as we do, and engage it on its own terms. It is a "joining with" posture (as opposed to, say, a "looking at from a distance" posture), more like engaging in a dance with a subject than engaging in a transactional task with an object. The researchers thus explicate the subject's experience, thoughts, feelings, etc., from within the subject's own system of meaning, aiming toward a maximum fidelity to that lived system of meaning, thereby developing a deeper and more integrated understanding of their actions and their being as lived. We turn now to Heidegger to help us understand the being—teacher and/or learner—in-the-midst-of-the-world (classroom) during a lesson.

Heidegger seeks to understand the person by asking, "What is the 'is-ness' of the experience?" This question involves both the "existential structure" and the "pre-understanding" as referential points. The existential structure links the individual to their interconnectedness with beings (others) and Being (existence as such) in a complex web of encounters, creating a mostly unconsciously held rhythm tied to the totality of their experiences. To say that the subject is situated is to say that experience is always already a system within a system within an even broader system. This reminder provides contextual insight into the perceptions an individual holds with specific experiences as they make sense of the phenomenon. The pre-understanding refers to the background knowledge the person holds about the world, their subjective history, which they always in some way bring to an experience while they are making sense of it. Appreciating the contribution of this historically loaded aspect of experience, informed as it is by an enormous store of prior knowledge, is crucial in teaching, learning, and research since it significantly shapes teacher decision-making.

We can see that addressing these questions can potentially significantly enhance the quality of teaching and learning in general, and also in South African schools and universities in particular. Could our failure to adequately take up these questions be one reason behind the multitude of curriculum revisions witnessed over the last three decades in the South African educational context? As educational researchers, we must devise means to comprehend our teachers, students, and learners more profoundly—they play crucial roles in the education system. Given the complexity of the ever-evolving human psyche, the world of subjectivity moulded and influenced by lived experiences, its impact on teaching, learning, and assessment, we argue that a greater emphasis on phenomenological research is needed. This approach does not replace but is instead complementary to the contributions to be found in the vast sea of quantitative research. Phenomenological research not only illuminates the concealed dimensions of subjective life for both teachers and learners but also grants access to the dynamic structural relationships of their inner landscapes. Enabling an understanding of their reasoning, perceptual frameworks, behaviours, emotions, and passions. These elements collectively enrich our comprehension of the human being in the education system.

Returning to the initial question posited within this chapter—"How do phenomenologists nose dive into the depths of lived experiences to conceptualise and contextualise phenomena such as teaching and learning, thereby elucidating the precise nature of these experiences?"—we now pivot our focus towards the terrain of what the phenomenological methodology entails.

Researcher Positionality

The phenomenologist's task is to carefully and skilfully unpack and explore the experience as described by the subject, to uncover the implicit and latent meanings, to reveal what else was there, as it was lived, adjacent to and beyond the first descriptive expression by the subject. Like the automotive novice taking apart the engine of a car, the phenomenological researcher must take great care to recognise and preserve the relationships among the emerging constituents of the structure of the experience; these meaning systems are embedded within the whole and find their true lived meaning in that context. This process, referred to as breaking down lived experience, involves meticulously peeling away and climbing through the layers of meaning that at once constitute, obscure, and lead to deeper levels of meaning in a person's conscious experience (Merleau-Ponty, 1962).

Giorgi (2008) states that the researcher must peel away all layers until they obtain an accurate description of a phenomenon as lived through by the person. In educational research, this means exploring the meaning of certain phenomena (things, experiences) to identify in context the constituents and structure of a research participant's consciousness and ways of being as they present themselves in this situation. The goal is to better understand what affects teachers' and students' thoughts, actions, behaviours, decision-making processes, etc. Phenomenological research in education thus seeks to provide a deeper understanding of the vast, influential, but mostly invisible lived experiences of teachers and learners, offering valuable insights into their awareness, motivations, and—like the novice auto mechanic—to see how the whole interrelated system works.

Phenomenologists draw from an array of existential and hermeneutical phenomenological approaches which are deeply rooted in the insights of eminent phenomenological thinkers such as Edmund Husserl (1970), Martin Heidegger (1967), Maurice Merleau-Ponty (1967), Jean-Paul Sartre (1955), mentioned above, and also Simone de Beauvoir (1948/2015), Henri Lefebvre (1991), Paul Ricoeur (1984), and Patrick Heelan (1983). Their theories and methodologies, ranging from transcendental phenomenology to diverse hermeneutical traditions, guide the quest for understanding the consciousness of research participants. The basic tenets of phenomenology allow for creativity of method, and a great variety of ways to proceed have been put forward. These distinct research paradigms serve as methodological lenses to scrutinise how individuals co-constitute their lived experiences.

In order to ensure research rigour, scholars often adhere to Husserl's principle of "bracketing the self" at each stage of the data construction process. This practice of "bracketing" enables the researcher to return to the pure essence of the subject matter as it was lived and described. Consequently, each participant's data must remain as free as possible from elements not essential to the phenomenon. It must be revealed in its unique history and constitution in relation to its own circumstances, environment, interpersonal interactions, and ideologies. For example, the concept of time, or temporality, according to Van Manen, referred to as phenomenological time, is perceived through the myriad experiences one encounters daily. These experiences are termed a succession of now moments. These clusters of "now moments" significantly mould and influence an individual's thoughts and ways of being, shaping beliefs and values and explaining the past, present, and future over time. Phenomenologists strive to accurately capture these moments. These "now moments" render each experience unique, and interviews are employed to capture these fleeting yet profound instances.

In phenomenological research, time is conceived not merely as a linear progression of events, but as a rich tapestry of lived experiences. Here Van Manen's concept of phenomenological time offers insight into how individuals perceive and internalise their temporal existence. Unlike the rigid structure of clock time, phenomenological time is fluid, subjective, and deeply intertwined with an individual's unique life circumstances. Central to Van Manen's notion of the concept of "now moments" are not uniform increments of time, but rather significant instances of lived experience that punctuate our consciousness. Each "now moment" is imbued with its own significance, coloured by the research participants personal history, cultural context, and immediate environment. These moments cluster together, forming the fabric of our temporal experience in shaping an individual's cognitive and emotional landscape. They mould our thoughts, influence our ways of being, and contribute to the formation of our beliefs and values. Through this lens, we can understand how our interpretation of past events, our engagement with the present, and our anticipation of the future are all intimately connected to these lived experiences.

Importantly, phenomenological time is not experienced uniformly. A single moment might stretch into what feels like an eternity during times of stress or pain, while hours might slip by unnoticed when we're deeply engaged in a meaningful activity. This non-linear nature of experienced time is a key focus for phenomenologists, who strive to capture and understand these nuanced temporal perceptions. The challenge for researchers lies in accurately documenting these fleeting yet profound "now moments." Interviews and field notes serve as a primary tool in this endeavour, providing a means to delve into the intricate details of an individual's lived experience. Through careful and empathetic questioning, researchers aim to uncover the rich temporal texture of their subjects' lives, revealing how each unique constellation of "now moments" contributes to the individual's overall being-in-the-world. By embracing this phenomenological approach to time, we gain a deeper understanding of how individuals construct meaning from their experiences. It allows us to move beyond simplistic, linear narratives and engage with the complex, multifaceted nature of human temporal experience. This perspective not only enriches our research methodologies but also offers profound insights into the nature of human consciousness and the intricate ways in which we navigate our temporal existence.

In concluding this section of the phenomenological researcher a question that often pops up is what are the most effective data construction instruments? Some often ask is document analysis allowed in phenomenological research? The answer to this question is very simple, "the subject matter of phenomenological research is lived experience." Therefore the first method entails semi-structured, face-to-face, one-on-one in-depth phenomenologically-oriented interviews, meticulously crafted to explore the phenomenon—including any and all concerns, challenges, successes, potential fears—whatever presents itself as part of the experience. It's crucial to note that these interviews often take on a conversational tone, creating a comfortable space for the research participant to share their lived experiences. The researcher's role is to guide the conversation gently, allowing the participant's narrative to unfold naturally while probing deeper into areas of particular interest. This approach helps to uncover rich, nuanced descriptions of the participant's lifeworld.

The second method involves field notes, invaluable for documenting observations and insights gleaned from the research context. Field notes capture not just what is said, but also non-verbal cues, environmental factors, and the researcher's immediate reflections. They serve as a complement to the interview data, providing context and depth to the researcher's understanding of the participant's lived experience. Field notes might include descriptions of the interview setting, the participant's demeanour, or sudden insights that occur to the researcher during or immediately after the interview. By employing these robust data collection methods, it becomes possible to comprehensively grasp the multifaceted dimensions of lived experiences within the context of education. Next we introduce the organisational layout of the book, which systematically unpacks these phenomenological insights and their implications for educational practice.

Organisational Layout of the Book

This book "Phenomenological Insights for the Classroom" explores the value and application of phenomenology in educational settings. This book offers rich and dynamic perspectives on how phenomenological approaches can boost our understanding of teaching and learning processes in the classroom as well as its use as a research approach. By entering into the philosophy and theories of lived experiences as well as the everyday lived realities of teachers and learners, the authors in this book provide valuable insights into the complex dynamics of education in various contexts.

The book addresses critical issues in education, including the philosophy behind artificial intelligence and its impact on teaching and learning and the nuances of power dynamics in the classroom. It also examines specific educational domains such as music improvisation and entrepreneurship education and looks into the diverse roles of a Black principals in leading his schools towards a learning organisations. Throughout, the authors emphasise the importance of embodied experience, intersubjectivity, and critical reflection in educational practice.

By bringing together diverse phenomenological approaches—from Husserl's transcendental phenomenology to Heidegger's hermeneutical phenomenology—this book offers a multifaceted examination of educational phenomena. It provides teachers, academics, post graduate students, researchers, and policymakers with new tools for understanding and improving educational experiences across different levels and disciplines.

The book is organised into eight chapters, each focusing on a specific aspect of phenomenology in education.

Chapter 2, by Russ Walsh, titled "Approaching phenomenological understanding in teaching and learning", examines various aspects of positionality, or approach, with respect to phenomenological understanding, drawing specifically from the works of Amedeo Giorgi, Edmund Husserl, Martin Heidegger, Hans-Gorge Gadamer, and Emilio Betti, among others. Beginning with explication of the concepts of the *epoche* and bracketing, the author discusses the relational aspects of phenomenological understanding and the competing methodological stances advocated by Gadamer and Betti. In light of Heidegger's characterisation of modes of being, the challenge of discerning one's position in understanding is discussed, and forms of reflexivity will be elaborated. The author then discusses the implications of these for the classroom.

Chapter 3, by Chatradari Devroop, titled "Embodiment and Intersubjectivity in the Teaching of Music Improvisation" explores the transformative potential of a phenomenological approach to teaching music improvisation in the university classroom. Drawing on key concepts from phenomenology, such as lived experience, embodiment, and intersubjectivity, we argue that by shifting the focus of improvisation pedagogy towards the lived, in-the-moment creative process, educators can foster a more authentic, engaging, and meaningful learning experience for students. The chapter begins by examining the phenomenology of music improvisation, highlighting the pre-reflective, embodied, and intersubjective nature of the improvisatory experience. He then critiques traditional approaches to teaching improvisation, which often prioritise theoretical knowledge and technical skill over the lived experience of improvising. In contrast, he proposes a phenomenological approach that emphasises embodied learning, collaborative improvisation, and reflective practices. Through a series of case studies, he demonstrates how this approach has been successfully implemented in various university music education contexts, drawing on student perspectives to illustrate its transformative impact. The chapter also addresses the challenges and strategies for overcoming obstacles in implementing a phenomenological approach to teaching improvisation. He concludes by discussing the implications of this approach for improvisation pedagogy in higher education and its potential relevance to other areas of music education, as well as identifying avenues for future research and exploration. Ultimately, this chapter contributes to the growing discourse on phenomenology in music education and offers a valuable resource for university music educators seeking to enrich their teaching practice and enable their students to develop a deeper, more embodied understanding of improvisation as a lived creative experience.

Chapter 4, by Koopman and Koopman, examines the role of embodied experience in education within the context of increasing artificial intelligence (AI) integration. Drawing on postphenomenological insights, it advocates for a renewed focus on students' lived experiences in learning environments. The chapter proposes reconceptualising the body not as a technological object, but as an integral component of the learning process. This perspective fosters authentic educational experiences where teaching and learning unfold as ontological phenomena within the shared classroom environment. By emphasising the irreplaceable value of embodied experiences, the research suggests a more holistic approach to education that honours the complexity of human cognition and interaction. The chapter concludes by stressing the importance of balancing technological advancements with human-centred pedagogical approaches. This work contributes to the ongoing dialogue about technology's role in education, offering a critical perspective on AI-centred approaches and advocating for a renewed focus on the experiential aspects of teaching and learning. It aims to foster more engaging and effective learning environments that leverage both technological innovations and fundamental human experience

Chapter 5, by Gosaitse and Maistry, reports on a study that deploys phenomenology to study the experiences of entrepreneurial learning by Botswana junior secondary school students. Although mini companies or mini-enterprise projects are a common pedagogical vehicle to teach entrepreneurship globally, very little attention has been paid to students' learning experiences with an up-close critical perspective of how learning occurs in these contexts from a phenomenological perspective. Therefore this study employs a hermeneutic phenomenological case study design to explore students' experiences of entrepreneurial learning in the mini-enterprise projects. Guided by a pragmatism oriented phenomenological theoretical framework, it draws from the philosophies of Heidegger, Merleau-Ponty, and Dewey to consider the cognitive, embodied, enactive, affective, social, and context-embeddedness aspects of entrepreneurial learning. The findings reveal that learning experientially has educational benefits that are cognitive and non-cognitive. The findings also reveal that the mini-enterprise experience is fraught with challenges that sometimes manifest in students experiencing unpleasant embodied experiences and poor curriculum design and implementation issues. Whereas the challenges may not turn off some students from entrepreneurship, due to these frustrations other students may develop negative attitudes towards entrepreneurship as a possible career choice. These challenges reveal a curriculum design and implementation that may be too aloof and insensitive to students' realities, and they suggest that designers and educators be more conscientious and responsive to learners' experiences.

In Chapter 6, Koopman, Smith and Long investigates the lived experiences of a South African Black principal in carrying out his strategic leadership responsibilities in leading a "township" school towards becoming a learning organisation. The rationale of the study is to deepen our knowledge about the lived experiences of black high school principals in South Africa and the challenges they face in turning their schools into learning organisations through strategic leadership. Theoretically the chapter draws on the foundational principles of Husserl's transcendental (descriptive) phenomenology and Heidegger's hermeneutical (interpretive) phenomenology infused with Senge's five disciplines, namely, personal mastery, shared vision, mental models, team learning, and systems thinking in search of understanding whether a school is truly a learning organisation, or on the pathway of becoming such an organisation. Methodologically the chapter adopted a phenomenological research approach to the data construction process. An in-depth one-on-one semi-structured interview was conducted with a black high school principals who teaches in a "township" school, that were augmented with fieldnotes to elicit rich descriptions of the teachers' experiences. The findings by integrating Senge's five disciplines with Heidegger's hermeneutical phenomenology illustrate the, the ongoing challenges he faced. These are a lack of a well-established shared vision among staff and the difficulties in fostering open communication highlight areas where the school falls short of fully embodying a learning organisation. These challenges align with Senge's emphasis on the importance of mental models and shared vision in organisational learning.

Chapter 7, by Clive Brown and Saras Reddy, investigates the lived experiences of student teachers undertaking work-integrated learning placements, with a particular focus on uncovering the typologies of power that shape their practicum encounters. Methodologically, the chapter recruited two final-year Intermediate Phase student teachers based within the Intermediate Phase Studies Department at a university of technology in South Africa. To elucidate rich descriptions of the student teachers' lived realities, interviews and field notes were utilised as the main sources of data. The data construction process focused on student teachers' descriptions of their teaching practicum in diverse post-apartheid, democratically informed South African classrooms during their final year. The findings illuminate how student teachers navigate and perceive power structures within their practicum settings, shedding light on the complex interplay between identity, agency, and pedagogical practices.

Chapter 8, the concluding chapter, examines the enduring impact of historical traumas on African learners, proposing a phenomenological approach to education and research grounded in the philosophies of Ted Aoki and Jan Patočka. The concept of "shadow burdens"—persistent challenges rooted in colonialism, apartheid, and systemic poverty—is introduced to frame the complex realities facing African children in educational settings. To this purpose the chapter advocates for a paradigm shift in education and research, emphasising it as an act of care for the soul of the African learn as a guiding principle. Drawing on Aoki's notions of "the teacher as care" and "dwelling humanly together" as well as Patočka's philosophy of care for the human soul, it proposes a framework that transcends traditional pedagogical and research approaches to address the lingering effects of historical trauma. By integrating phenomenological insights with trauma theory and psychoanalytic concepts, the chapter offers a nuanced understanding of the psychological dynamics at play in post-colonial educational contexts. It argues for the creation of transformative educational experiences that not only address academic needs but also contribute to healing historical traumas and fostering critical consciousness among African learners. The chapter concludes by outlining practical pedagogical and research principles for transcending historical burdens, emphasising the importance of authentic engagement, reflective practice, and ethical research methodologies. This approach aims to redefine education and research as acts of care, capable of shattering shadow burdens and empowering a new generation of African learners.

Conclusion

This structure of the book allows readers to engage with a wide range of phenomenological applications in education, from broad theoretical discussions to specific case studies across various educational contexts and levels. In perceiving the chapters, one discerns multiple educational queries or concerns at their core. Each author traverses unique paths, delving into the enriching contributions of phenomenology for educational endeavours, showcasing phenomenology as a living, breathing movement, vibrant with diversity and creativity. The chapters exhibit a kaleidoscope of theories and concepts sourced from various phenomenological wellsprings. By engaging education issues with the essence and insights of phenomenology, this tome unveils vistas of understanding across an array of educational inquiries. Beyond specific queries, these chapters exemplify a spectrum of phenomenological inquiry methods, unveiling the manifold ways through which one may phenomenologically probe into the depths of educational phenomena.

References

Arendt, H. (1968). Men in dark times. New York: Harcourt, Brace & World.

Beauvoir, S. de. (2015). *The Ethics of Ambiguity*. (B. Frechtman, Trans.). New York: Open Road Media (Original work published 1948).

Freud, S. (1933). Lecture XXXIV: Explanations, applications and orientations. In J. Strachey (Ed.), *The standard edition of the complete psychological works of Sigmund Freud* (Vol. XXII (1932–36), pp. 136–57). Lonvdon: Vintage

Heelan, P. A. (1983). *Space-perception and the philosophy of science*. Berkeley: University of California Press.

Heidegger, M. (1967). *Being and time* (J. Macquarrie & E. Robinson, Trans.). New York: Harper & Row. (Original work published 1927).

Husserl, E. (1970). *The crisis of European sciences and transcendental phenomenology: An introduction to phenomenological philosophy*. Northwestern University Press.

Koopman, O., & Koopman, K. J. (2023). *Decolonising the South African university: Towards curriculum as self authentication*. New York: Palgrave Macmillan

Lacan, J. (2006). The mirror stage as formative of the I function as revealed in psychoanalytic experience. (B. Fink, Trans.). In *Écrits: The first complete edition in English* (pp. 75–81). W. W. Norton & Company. (Original work published 1949)

Lefebvre, H. (1991). *The production of space*. (D. Nicholson-Smith, Trans.). Oxford: Blackwell.

Merleau-Ponty, M. (1962). *Phenomenology of perception*. (C. Smith, Trans.). London: Routledge & Kegan Paul. (Original work published 1945)

Ricoeur, P. (1984). *Time and narrative*. (K. McLaughlin & D. Pellauer, Trans.). Chicago: University of Chicago Press.

Sartre, J.-P. (1956). *Being and nothingness: An essay on phenomenological ontology*. (H. E. Barnes, Trans.). New York: Washington Square Press.

· 2 ·
APPROACHING PHENOMENOLOGICAL UNDERSTANDING: POSITIONALITY AND REFLEXIVITY IN EDUCATION AND EDUCATION RESEARCH

Russ Walsh

Approaching Phenomenological Understanding

What does it mean to approach understanding phenomenologically, and what are the implications of this for education and education research? In the paragraphs that follow, I will explore the notion of approach and its relevance for phenomenological theory and practice. Beginning with an introduction to the origin and definition of the term, approach, I will discuss the contributions of numerous phenomenological scholars regarding the conceptualisation and explication of positionality with respect to phenomenological understanding. I will then introduce the term, reflexivity, and consider the methodological forms it can take as means for discerning the features of one's approach. The challenges to reflexivity posed by recent considerations of intersectionality, and the promise of guidelines recently put forth by the Canadian Psychological Association will then be discussed. The implications of approach, reflexivity, and intersectionality for education and education research will then be explored.

Historical Background of Approach

In his endeavour to introduce a phenomenological method to the field of psychology, Amedeo Giorgi emphasised the importance of *approach*:

> By establishing the category of approach we mean to take into account the researcher himself in the enterprise of science. By approach is meant the fundamental viewpoint toward man and the world that the scientist brings, or adopts, with respect to his work as a scientist, whether his viewpoint is made explicit or remains implicit (1970, p. 126).

Giorgi's intention here was to call attention to the implicit assumptions that underlie any effort to understand, particularly those that are characterised as objective or scientific. The above quote is noteworthy not only for its explication of the term approach, but also for the implicit features of the definition itself—what we can now see as exclusionary language (man; himself) that at the time of Giorgi's writing was simply the dominant, taken for granted framework within which academic scholarship was presented. Hence Giorgi both defined and demonstrated the indelible role of one's approach in both how one sees and interacts with others, as well as how one conducts research.

As articulated by Giorgi (1983), phenomenological research seeks "to bend back upon or take up again what we have experienced, lived through, or acted upon prereflectively ... by making as explicit as possible hidden assumptions and implicit perspectives" (p. 142–143). The phenomenological method, in other words, aims to address the interplay between one's presuppositions and the objects of one's attention. Giorgi (1986) characterised this as the "putting out of play of what we know about things in order experience them freshly" (p. 6).

The empirical phenomenological method was developed by Giorgi at Duquesne University (Giorgi, 1970; 1985), who adapted the phenomenology of Edmund Husserl (1913/2001) by applying what was a method for discerning the features of one's own lived experience to the investigation of experiential accounts by research participants. As a result, the practice of empirical phenomenology grapples with two forms of reflexive awareness: that of research participants, who reflect on some aspect of their own lived experiences, and that of researchers, whose task is to reflect on their own presuppositions in order to better understand participants' experiences.

Husserl's method employed what he termed the epoche, a stance of trying to set aside one's taken for granted assumptions to observe freshly "the things themselves" (1913/2001, p. 168). Giorgi proposed that this stance, achieved through the process of "bracketing" one's preconceptions, could be the foundation for a qualitative psychological method that sought to describe and summarise participants' accounts of their lived experiences free from the imposition of researchers' assumptions and expectations. Over time, the apparent similarities between this stance and that of engaged, non-judgmental listening in helping relationships contributed to models in psychotherapy, nursing, and education characterised as a phenomenological attitude (Gustin, 2018; Morse & Blenkinsop, 2020; Snyder, 1982; Spiegelberg, 1972; Thomas & Pollio, 2002; Varghese, 1988).

Across a growing number of research and relational applications, notions of the phenomenological attitude and bracketing came to be seen as a straightforward process of setting aside one's assumptions to bear witness to others' experiences. However, at the same time numerous scholars (Colaizzi, 1973; Wertz, 1984; Halling & Leifer 1991; Churchill, 1984; Walsh, 1995; Salner, 1996) began to discuss bracketing and the phenomenological attitude as a much more complex and necessarily ongoing process. Colaizzi (1973) employed the terms *fundamental description* and *fundamental structure* to note an important distinction between participants' self-reflections and researchers' interpretations of those reflections. *Fundamental description* refers to the participants' initial accounts of their experiences, as well as a basic descriptive summary of those accounts carried out by researchers. *Fundamental structure* denotes a more depthful analysis, wherein researchers attempt to discern implicit features of the participants' accounts. By integrating the fundamental description and the fundamental structure, Colaizzi suggested that the phenomenological researcher can examine participants' views of their experiences as well as the broader viewpoints through which those experiences were made meaningful. In other words, discerning fundamental structure entails moving beyond a summary of what participants said to an interpretation of the horizon of meanings, or organising assumptions, implicit in participants' accounts.

With respect to the concept of approach, Colaizzi's proposed levels of analysis can be equally applied not just to participants' descriptions of their experience, but to researchers' qualitative analyses as well. Hence, we can distinguish between a researcher's (fundamental) description of participants' experiences and the researcher's perspective through which those experiences were understood (fundamental structure). Churchill (1984) applied this distinction in his study of psychodiagnostic seeing to explore the viewpoints through which clinicians understood client experiences via psychological assessment. Drawing upon Colaizzi and Churchill, I proposed that bracketing in phenomenological research could entail the sequential processes of

(1) acknowledging a priori assumptions at the start of a project, (2) recording throughout data gathering and analysis one's experiences and associations, (3) discerning the presence of assumptions and associations evident in one's research findings, and (4) documenting these implicit features in the presentation of one's results (Walsh, 1995). Hence, a phenomenological attitude is now seen to encompass both efforts to understand the lived experience of another and a thorough examination of the implicit assumptions through which that understanding occurs.

The more complex view of bracketing holds implications for how a researcher engages with participants. Salner (1996) argued that "methodological self-management" (p. 19), in the form of a so-called neutral or nondirective stance, was more likely to foster researcher self-deception rather than self-awareness. Instead, recognizing that any stance is one within the context of a relational encounter, Salner advocated an explicitly conversational approach in which the researcher gets "caught up in the ongoing social interaction" with participants while also engaging in "systematic critique" of that interaction via "reflection—after the fact" (p. 22).

Salner's argument is similar to one made by Gadamer (1960/1989) in his debate with Betti (1962/1980) regarding how to seek interpretative understanding. Gadamer saw method, or what we might better conceptualise as rigidly defined procedure, as inimical to understanding in that it constrains the natural "play of language itself" through efforts at precision and eliminating bias (p. 490). For Gadamer, formal research procedures that strive for objectivity run the risk of eliciting from participants "statements" concerned with "exactness", and "meaning thus reduced to what is stated is always distorted meaning" (1989, p. 469). In contrast, Betti argued that without disciplined procedures one's understanding would default to an "apparently easily accessible meaning" (p. 79) that minimises the ways in which presuppositions can obscure understanding. Salner's model suggests a compromise, whereby the benefits of natural conversation are balanced with retrospective scrutiny to discern the implicit dimensions of those conversations. Churchill (2012) characterised this compromise, which he called the second-person perspective, as "*experiencing the other within the we*" (p. 2, emphasis in original).

The Challenges of Disclosing One's Approach

Discerning one's implicit suppositions, even after the fact, is by no means straightforward. Hence, bracketing is perhaps best conceptualised as a process of making problematic our taken for granted assumptions *as they are manifested in our efforts to understand*. Here it may be useful to consider Heidegger's (1927/1962) characterisation of human modes of engagement, in particular the ready-to-hand (Zuhandenheit) and unready-to-hand (Unzuhandenheit) modes. When one is engaged in an activity, it is often without awareness of the implicit features of that engagement. It is only when our ready-to-hand engagement is interrupted, when something doesn't work, that the implicit features of our engagement become noticed. Hence, the task of bracketing is to look for instances of misunderstanding or miscommunication, and to scrutinise these for what they reveal about the researcher's presuppositions.

Viewed in this way, bracketing is not the setting aside of presuppositions, but rather placing them alongside the researcher's account of participants' experiences. It is in other words similar to the grammatical function of parentheses, or brackets, in writing. The parenthetical phrase is both set aside from, and underscored in relation to, the central proposition of the sentence. The ideas presented in parentheses are both distinct from and contingent on the sentence in which they are embedded. Hence, in bracketing phenomenological researchers aim to set aside presuppositions, not in the sense of discarding them but rather as placing them alongside their findings regarding participants' lived experiences.

Phenomenology and Reflexivity

Both within and outside of the field of phenomenology, the epoche and bracketing have more recently been subsumed by the broader term, reflexivity. However, the broad use of this term is such that the precise focus of reflexive awareness can vary widely across different studies employing the term. As one way of organising these differing procedures, I distinguished between personal, interpersonal, methodological, and contextual reflexivities (Walsh, 2003; 2024). Personal reflexivity is focused on the researcher's attitude and expectations that inform a given study. Interpersonal reflexivity is concerned with dimensions of the relationships that unfold between researcher and participants, and their implications for the conclusions drawn by the researcher. Methodological reflexivity examines the theoretical and procedural commitments that shape a research project. And contextual reflexivity aims to situate a particular study in its cultural and historical milieu.

In practical terms, personal reflexivity documents that the phenomenon studied was understood from a particular standpoint, and that this *limitation* of the findings is not one in the sense of shortcoming, but rather a demarcation of the horizon through which the phenomenon came into view. As I've suggested elsewhere (Walsh, 2024), this is best accomplished by showing through several examples how one's presuppositions regarding the phenomenon studied were evident in the analysis and conclusions. Personal reflexivity should bring friction to the researcher's initial conclusions, and allow for the "object (of study) to object" (Camic et al., 2003, p. 7). While this ensures rigour with respect to the methods employed, it also provides a way to move researchers beyond what Colaizzi (1973) would call a fundamental description of their approach to a thoughtful examination of the fundamental structure or viewpoint with which the findings were found.

Interpersonal reflexivity calls for ongoing reflection throughout the research process that looks at the ways in which the researcher's presence shapes participants' responses. Salner's (1996) critique of purportedly neutral stance is particularly relevant here: deferring to a so-called neutral stance under the guise of objectivity is likely to ignore the influence that is unavoidable. Instead, the goal of interpersonally reflexivity is to make the researcher's indelible presence in interactions with participants a "central focus of one's concern" (p. 9).

The researcher's reactions to participants and their stories can also be important sources of information. As with patients' reports in psychotherapy, one should keep in mind that participants' accounts are stories being told to an audience, with some expectation of how those stories will be received. As those stories will have an impact on the listener, discerning this impact, and interpreting its potential meanings, is a valuable function of interpersonal reflexivity.

Methodological reflexivity entails careful reflection on, and disclosure of, the epistemological and ontological claims embedded in a research project. Although, as Giorgi (1970) noted, this is ultimately an "inexhaustible" process, it is nonetheless our obligation as researchers "to make explicit whatever one can" (p. 126). The growing prominence of qualitative research has resulted in a vast range of methods and procedures from which researchers may draw. As a consequence, it is at times quite difficult to discern the theoretical commitments and assumptions that are imbedded in a given study. As my colleague Lori Koelsch and I have argued elsewhere, "for an audience ... to be capable of evaluating a research project, it must be made aware of researchers' positions: what they tried to do, how they tried to do it, and what admixture of ideals and procedures seemed reasonable to accomplish these goals." (Walsh & Koelsch, 2012, p. 388). Methodological reflexivity aims to disclose the horizon through which a researcher posed questions and found answers regarding the phenomena studied.

Methodological reflexivity also calls to mind a longstanding debate as to whether phenomenology is best seen as descriptive or interpretative. While Giorgi (1986) argued that phenomenology is descriptive, Colaizzi and others (cf., Smith, 2004) have emphasised the interpretative aspects of understanding. It is, however, useful to consider that these alternatives follow from differing yet complementary emphases in qualitative research. As a method, bracketing can focus on two kinds of presuppositions: the natural attitude and theoretical abstraction. The natural attitude, or the taken-for-granted assumptions that shape our everyday understandings of things, can eclipse both immediate lived experience and the broader web of meaning through which that understanding is made possible. This was Husserl's primary concern, and why he directed phenomenology to turn back to things themselves. However, while a researcher's presuppositions may indeed include the natural attitude, they are far more likely to veer in the direction of theoretical abstraction. Consequently, while bracketing with respect to the natural attitude requires a move of detachment, bracketing abstract conceptualisation calls for attention to the concrete and practical aspects of the phenomenon as lived. As I see it, moving back and forth between these polarities is what makes phenomenology a hermeneutical enterprise.

Contextual reflexivity aims to consider how a given topic and the researcher's approach are products of their time and place. To some extent, the literature review that precedes a study accomplishes this task. However, the rhetorical function of a review which is to make a strong case for the particular study, often entails winnowing rather than widening one's view. The background of any research is complex, comprised of multiple trajectories. The challenge of contextual reflexivity is to document this complexity in a reasonably concise way.

As with each of the categories of reflexivity, the primary focus of contextual reflexivity should be implicit factors that would otherwise remain opaque to researchers and their audience. The orienting question is, what set of assumptions and practices are necessary for this specific topic and research question to be meaningful? Contextual reflexivity is also an opportunity to look carefully at dominant discourses and their impact on the experiences and perspectives of minority or otherwise minimised others. The quotation from Giorgi (1970) that began this chapter is one example of how norms of a dominant culture can silence or eclipse others (in that case, the others being other than men).

While many studies employ only one of the four categories of reflexivity, there is a growing tendency in qualitative research to include all four dimensions. In doing so, it is possible to address each with the multistep process of acknowledging explicit assumptions at the start of a project, recording throughout the project one's experiences and associations, and discerning the assumptions and associations evident in one's research findings (Walsh, 1995). The objective throughout each stage is to "to make explicit whatever one can" (Giorgi, 1970, p. 126).

Reflexivity and Intersectionality

The elements that comprise one's approach are of course myriad and overlapping. The understanding of approach, therefore, can be informed by more recent considerations of *intersectionality* (Crenshaw, 1989; Carastathis, 2016), which highlight how our ways of knowing include a complex interplay of cultural values, historicity, and geographical locations. Intersectionality also calls attention to the impact of power and privilege on the (in)visibility of ways of knowing that are minimised or ignored by dominant cultures. Hence, thoughtful consideration of approach requires acknowledging the oppressive potential of dominant discourses, and the ways in which researchers may—without sufficient reflection—silence voices and experiences different from than their own.

Martin Heidegger used the term horizon (Horizont) to describe the culturally-based framework or boundary (Grenze) that both allows for and constrains one's perspective (1927/1962). Using the metaphor of a forest, Heidegger spoke of the clearing (Lichtung) that is one's area of focus—as with the saying that one "can't see the forest for the trees", an individual's clearing opens up a space for understanding, but in doing so necessarily excludes other clearings, or approaches. This was presented not as a flaw to be corrected, but as an unavoidable feature of human knowledge. Indeed, Heidegger's student Hans-Georg Gadamer (1960/1989) carried these ideas further, arguing that one's historically and linguistically situated prejudice (Vorurteil) is the lens through which any understanding is made possible. However, neither Heidegger nor Gadamer gave sufficient attention to the oppressive potential of dominant ways of knowing. It is for this reason that the future of phenomenology "must pay particular attention to the rich diversity of lived experiences that have heretofore been silenced or otherwise neglected" (Walsh, 2024, p. 8).

The implications of intersectionality call for a more detailed explication of bracketing that recognises the risk of neglecting experiences deemed other than dominant ways of knowing. Relevant in this regard are recent efforts in Canada to acknowledge and atone for policies and practices that neglected the experiences and rights of Indigenous peoples. While elaborating the longstanding abuse and neglect suffered by Canadian Indigenous groups is beyond the scope of this chapter, the horizon through which these practices were imposed—one that presumed to understand Indigenous experiences through the lens of dominant values and judgements—demonstrates the oppressive potential of an approach that is hegemonic and believed to be self-evident.

The Truth and Reconciliation Commission of Canada was established in 2008 with the charge to document the experiences and traumatic consequences of the Canadian residential school system, which for decades forcibly removed Indigenous children from their homes with the goal of imposing dominant, non-Indigenous language and values under the banner of education. In response to the report of the Commission (2015) and its calls to action, the Canadian Psychological Association articulated "recommendations and guiding principles that acknowledge and respect Indigenous concepts of the person, health, family, and ways of knowing" (2018, p. 6). These concerns were echoed by the American Psychological Association, which concluded that we "should elevate psychology's understanding of and regard for Indigenous epistemologies and ontologies and research centred on Native persons, peoples, and communities" (American Psychological Association, APA Indigenous Apology Working Group, 2023, p. 3).

The CPA's guiding principles—*cultural allyship, humility, collaboration, critical reflection, respect, and social justice*—were proposed as benchmarks for psychologists' work in education, research, or applied psychology (2018, p. 12). While these guidelines were framed as being explicitly for psychologists, their application to education and research suggests a breadth of relevance beyond the field of psychology. And, as these guidelines also follow from an acknowledgement that the term Indigenous in Canada refers to a group comprised "hundreds of culturally distinct groups" varying in language spoken, spirituality and religion, education, and urban or rural setting, "as well as all the variability that is in the population at large" (p. 6), these guidelines also seem relevant to concerns for intersectionality. Hence, these guidelines may provide some useful elaborations for the practices of bracketing and reflexivity from within a phenomenological attitude.

The guiding principles of *cultural allyship, humility, collaboration, critical reflection, respect, and social justice*, although not framed in phenomenological terms, seem quite appropriate to a phenomenological attitude. Indeed, a phenomenological method that strives to recognise the complicated, overlapping, and implicit features of understanding would seem to require at a minimum humility and critical reflection. Moreover, to the extent that phenomenology is concerned with faithfully engaging with and discerning the lived experience of another, collaboration and respect seem of paramount importance. And, if considering intersectionality and difference are believed to be crucial aspects of understanding, as well as for rectification of collective misunderstanding, neglect, and oppression, cultural allyship and social justice seem valuable corollaries to the practice of phenomenology.

Implications for Education and Education Research

To consider issues of positionality and reflexivity, a phenomenological attitude requires openness and curiosity towards both the experiences of those with whom we're engaged and the implicit assumptions and expectations we bring to those encounters. This holds important implications for education researchers as well as for educators.

Phenomenological education research can benefit from incorporating the broad view of bracketing as a multistep process undertaken throughout all stages of a research project. Qualitative research along these lines affirms the indelible role of presuppositions, both explicit and implicit, in the accounts of participants as well in the researcher's engagement with and understanding of those accounts. Seen in this way, Husserl's dictum "to the things themselves" (1913/2001, p. 168) refers not to a pristine set of circumstances freed from bias but rather to a complex, contextual view of meaningful experiences that are understood relationally.

Openness to the relational nature of phenomenological research allows for the "play of language" (Gadamer, 1960/1989, p. 490) to unfold in conversations between researchers and participants, and for those conversations to be scrutinised via "reflection after the fact" (Salner, 1996, p. 22) to discern the co-constitution of results and conclusions. This seems particularly appropriate for education research, which by its very nature recognises the relational, co-constituted nature of teaching and learning.

Considering the multiple areas of focus for reflexivity can also enhance education research. The dimensions of reflexivity identified as personal, interpersonal, methodological, and contextual each point to important factors that situate research questions, procedures, participants, and their broader context. Acknowledging and documenting these features can allow the audience of research, and the stakeholders of research findings, to make sense of and meaningfully draw from each study's conclusions. In this way, our research can also demonstrate that Giorgi's notion of approach is a distinguishing feature of phenomenological education research.

Education research can also benefit from a phenomenological attitude that incorporates the guidelines drawn from the efforts by the Canadian Psychological Association to address longstanding neglect of Indigenous voices and experiences. While it can be argued that humility, collaboration, critical reflection, and respect follow directly from a phenomenological standpoint, cultural allyship, and social justice demand more from researchers. To strive for these latter goals, we must critically examine past practices and current initiatives to ensure that our future trajectory is inclusive and advocates for those whose voices and experiences have been neglected. This calls for both contextual and methodological reflexivity attuned to the oppressive impact of longstanding assumptions regarding what count as valid sources of knowledge, and what becomes privileged in academic and educational worlds. And to the extent that these assumptions implicitly shape one's approach to research topics and interactions with participants, diligent personal, and interpersonal reflexivity can bring these to our attention.

A phenomenological attitude interwoven with the CPA guidelines also has much to offer the practice of education itself. To approach education phenomenologically, we must recognise the many forms of diversity that our students express in and outside of the classroom. *Cultural allyship* in an educational context applies to the unique experiences and practical wisdom of our students. While there is much that students do not know, they bring a diversity of life experiences and acquired knowledge that can inform and even challenge the canons of education. Openness to what students bring to the classroom enriches the learning experiences of educators and students alike. Cultural allyship affirms this openness, and adds a particular sensitivity to those students from historically and currently oppressed communities, whose voices can even now be minimised or silenced by dominant cultures and discourses. Hence, listening for, inviting, and affirming these perspectives is especially important for contemporary teaching and learning.

Humility in education entails recognising the limits of our knowledge, both individually and collectively, as well as striving to complement our bodies of knowledge with the wisdom of other forms of knowing. Although epistemology may be an intimidating term for both students and educators, we must affirm that all knowledge claims are situated in a horizon of assumptions—the approach underscored by Giorgi—and that becoming aware of those assumptions contextualises what we know. *Critical reflection*, a corollary or concomitant of humility, requires looking at the ways in which our own perspectives have fostered or perpetuated exclusionary and oppressive practices. To the extent that these practices have marginalised particular cultures and peoples, this reflection is necessary if *social justice* is to be attained.

Respect and *collaboration* cultivate a classroom atmosphere wherein educators and students learn together. In showing respect to our students, we communicate an interest in who they are as persons, and a belief that the perspectives they bring to learning are valued. This invites collaboration, engaging students in a process of learning that is participatory rather than passive.

Applying each of the CPA's guiding principles to educational practice can facilitate reflexivity on the part of both educators and students. Phrased differently, a phenomenological attitude shaped by cultural allyship, humility, collaboration, critical reflection, respect, and concern for social justice can inform both the practices of education and the practices of learning. For educators, this attitude calls attention to the approach implicit in our interactions with students, particularly those aspects that might neglect the lived experiences of students whose backgrounds are nontraditional or different. For students, introduction to a phenomenological attitude with respect to learning can foster greater awareness of the horizon of assumptions and past experiences that frame their understandings of, and openness to, new areas of knowledge. By acknowledging this indelible presence of approach in all aspects of teaching and learning, a phenomenological attitude can "slacken the intentional threads which attach us to the world and thus bring them to our notice" (Merleau-Ponty, 1945, cited in Aanstoos, 1983, p. 253).

Conclusion

This chapter began with the questions, what does it mean to approach understanding phenomenologically, and what are the implications of this for education and education research? To approach understanding phenomenologically is to thoughtfully consider one's approach—the horizon, or fundamental structure, through which understanding occurs. Over the past several decades, numerous scholars (cited above) have explored the challenges in "making explicit whatever one can" (Giorgi, 1970, p. 126), and made recommendations for conceptualising and discerning positionality in the processes of engaging with others and seeking understanding of their lived experiences. These recommendations suggest that bracketing, or reflexivity, is not a discrete procedure of setting aside one's presuppositions, but rather an ongoing and complex process of recognising one's indelible presence in acts of understanding. This process can be informed by distinguishing multiple categories of reflexivity (personal, interpersonal, methodological, and contextual), as well as considering the implications of intersectionality, particularly for those whose perspectives have been minimised or neglected.

The guidelines proposed by the Canadian Psychological Association to address longstanding neglect and devaluing of Indigenous experiences offer useful benchmarks for phenomenological research and practice. Through cultural allyship, humility, collaboration, critical reflection, respect, and concern for social justice, phenomenology can facilitate understanding that is mindful of intersectionality and the oppressive potential of dominant discourses and ways of knowing.

The implications of positionality, reflexivity, and intersectionality for education and education research are many. For education research, acknowledging the indelible presence of researchers in the co-constitution of research results can demonstrate the relational nature of phenomenological research. Considering the multiple areas of focus for reflexivity and the guidelines put forth by the Canadian Psychological Association can assist researchers in discerning and documenting the multiple dimensions of their approach.

A phenomenological attitude informed by the CPA guidelines also has much to offer the practice of education itself. By recognising and affirming the many forms of diversity that our students bring to the classroom, showing respect and humility, engaging collaboratively and demonstrating critical reflection, and modeling concern for social justice, educators can enhance students' learning experiences and invite them, via phenomenology, to become phenomenologists themselves.

References

Aanstoos, C. (1983). The think aloud method in descriptive research. *Journal of Phenomenological Psychology, 13*, 243–266.

American Psychological Association, APA Indigenous Apology Working Group (2023). Report on an offer of apology, on behalf of the American Psychological Association, to the First Peoples in the United States. https://www.apa.org/pubs/reports/indigenous-apology.pdf

Betti, E. (1980). Hermeneutics as the general methodology of the human sciences. In J. Bleicher (Ed.), *Contemporary hermeneutics: Hermeneutics as method, philosophy, and critique* (pp. 51–94). Boston: Routledge & Kegan Paul. (Original work published 1962).

Camic, P. M., Rhodes, J. E., & Yardley, L. (2003). Naming the stars: Integrating qualitative methods into psychological research. In P. M. Camic, J. E. Rhodes, & L. Yardley (Eds.), *Qualitative Research in psychology: Expanding perspectives in methodology and design* (pp. 3–16). Washington, DC: American Psychological Association Press.

Canadian Psychological Association & Psychology Foundation of Canada. (2018). *Psychology's response to the Truth and Reconciliation Commission of Canada's Report: A report of the Canadian Psychological Association and the Psychology Foundation of Canada.* https://cpa.ca/docs/File/Task_Forces/TRC%20Task%20Force%20Report_FINAL.pdf

Carastathis, A. (2016). *Intersectionality: Origins, contestations, horizons.* University of Nebraska Press.

Churchill, S. (1984). Forming clinical impressions: A phenomenological study. In C. Aanstoos (Ed.), *Exploring the lived world: Readings in phenomenological psychology.* Carrollton: West Georgia College.

Churchill, S. (2012). Teaching phenomenology by way of "second-person perspectivity" (From my thirty years at the University of Dallas). *Indo-Pacific Journal of Phenomenology*, 12, 1–14.

Colaizzi, P. (1973). *Reflections and research in psychology.* Dubuque: Kendall Hunt.

Crenshaw, K. (1989) *Demarginalizing the intersection of race and sex: a black feminist critique of antidiscrimination doctrine, feminist theory, and antiracist politics.* University of Chicago Legal Forum, 139.

Gadamer, H. (1989). *Truth and Method* (J. Weinsheimer & D.G. Marshall, Trans.). New York: Crossroad (Original work published 1960).

Giorgi, A. (1970). *Psychology as a human science: A phenomenologically based approach.* New York: Harper and Row.

Giorgi, A. (1983). Concerning the possibility of phenomenological psychological research. *Journal of Phenomenological Psychology*, 13, 129–169.

Giorgi, A. (1985). *Phenomenology and psychological research.* Pittsburgh: Duquesne University Press.

Giorgi, A. (1986). Theoretical justifications for the use of descriptions in psychological research. In P. Ashworth, A. Giorgi, & A. DeKonig (Eds.), *Qualitative research in psychology.* Pittsburgh: Duquesne University Press.

Gustin, L.W. (2018). Being mindful as a phenomenological attitude. *Journal of Holistic Nursing*, 36(3), 272–281.

Halling, S., & Leifer, M. (1991). The theory and practice of dialogical research. *Journal of Phenomenological Psychology*, 22, 1–15.

Heidegger, M. (1962). *Being and time* (J. Macquarrie & E. Robinson, Trans.). Oxford: Blackwell Publishing. (Original work published 1927).

Husserl, E. (2001). *Logical investigations* (J. Findlay, Trans.). New York: Routledge. (Original work published 1913).

Merleau-Ponty, M. (1945). Phenomenology of perception (C. Smith, Trans.). London: Routledge.

Morse, M., & Blenkinsop, S. (2020). Educational possibilities: Teaching toward the phenomenological attitude. In *Phenomenology and educational theory in conversation* (pp. 197–209). Routledge.

Salner, M. (1996). Researcher self-reflexivity, illusion, and self-deception in qualitative research. *Methods*, 3–27.

Smith, J. A. (2004). Reflecting on the development of interpretative phenomenological analysis and its contribution to qualitative research in psychology. *Qualitative Research in Psychology*, 1, 39–54.

Snyder, D. M. (1982). Perspective and engagement in counseling and psychotherapy: The phenomenological approach. *International Journal for the Advancement of Counselling*, 5(2), 95–107.

Spiegelberg, H. (1972). *Phenomenology in psychology and psychiatry: A historical introduction*. Evanston: Northwestern University Press.

Thomas, S. P., & Pollio, H. R. (2002). *Listening to patients: A phenomenological approach to nursing research and practice*. Springer Publishing Company.

Truth and Reconciliation Commission of Canada (2015). *Honouring the truth, reconciling for the future: Summary of the final report of the Truth and Reconciliation Commission of Canada*. Government of Canada.

Varghese, F. T. (1988). The phenomenology of psychotherapy. *American Journal of Psychotherapy*, 42(3), 389–403.

Walsh, R. (1995a). The approach of the human science researcher: Implications for the practice of qualitative research. *The Humanistic Psychologist*, 23, 333–344.

Walsh, R. (2003). The methods of reflexivity. *The Humanistic Psychologist*, 31(4), 51–66.

Walsh, R., & Koelsch, L. E. (2012). Building across fault lines in qualitative research. *The Humanistic Psychologist*, 40(4), 380.

Walsh, R. (2024). Revisiting reflexivity. *The Humanistic Psychologist*. Advance online publication. https://doi.org/10.1037/hum0000357

Wertz, F. (1984). Procedures in phenomenological research and the question of validity. In C. Aanstoos (Ed.), *Exploring the lived world: Readings in phenomenological psychology*. Carrolton: West Georgia College.

· 3 ·

PHENOMENOLOGY AND MUSIC: A NEW PATH FOR 21ST CENTURY EDUCATION

Chatradari Devroop

Introduction: The Crisis in Modern Education and the Role of Ambiguity

In a rapidly evolving era, education is at a crossroads. Traditional learning models rooted in rationalist and empiricist philosophies are increasingly being questioned for their relevance and effectiveness in preparing students for the complex demands of the 21st century (Antunes, 2021; Şentürk & Baş, 2020; Masethe et al., 2017). As we stand on the cusp of a new educational paradigm, phenomenology appears as a beacon of hope that offers a new perspective on how we engage with the world, and thus how we learn and teach.

This chapter shows that phenomenology, especially when applied to the field of music education, offers a solid framework for reshaping education in the 21st century. By emphasising immediate, lived experience and the primacy of perception, phenomenology offers a way to bridge the gap between abstract knowledge and concrete reality, between theory and practice, and between the individual and the world.

Central to this reinterpretation is the concept of ambiguity, especially in music. The tension between the desire for precise notation and the inherent ambiguity in musical performance serves as a powerful metaphor for the broader challenges in education (McKay, 2021). This spectrum from unambiguity to ambiguity provides a framework for understanding the limitations of traditional pedagogical approaches and the potential of phenomenological methods.

The crisis of modern education is multifaceted (Krishnan, 2020). Standardised tests and rigid curricula are often unable to foster creativity, critical thinking, and adaptability—skills that are crucial for navigating an increasingly complex world. Furthermore, the rapid pace of technological change renders much of what is taught in schools obsolete as students enter the workforce (Antunes, 2021). This disconnect between education and the demands of the real world requires a fundamental rethink of our approach to learning and teaching.

Phenomenology, centred on lived experience, offers a compelling alternative. (Devroop, 2022; Smith, 2022). By grounding education in direct, embodied experiences rather than abstract concepts, it can create more engaging, relevant, and meaningful learning experiences. Music education, with its inherent blend of theory and practice, mind and body, provides an ideal model for exploring how phenomenological approaches can be applied in educational contexts.

This chapter will explore how phenomenology in music education can inform 21st century education. I will examine how embracing ambiguity, prioritising direct experience, and focusing on the process of meaning-making can create more holistic and effective educational practices. Through this exploration, I aim to chart a new course for education—one that prepares students not to know, but to be and to become, and equips them with the tools to navigate the complexity and uncertainty of our rapidly changing world.

The Historical Context of Education: From Certainty to Ambiguity

In order to understand the potential of phenomenology in education, it is essential to examine the historical development of the philosophy of education. Western education has long privileged abstract thought over embodied experience, reflecting a persistent quest for certainty and unambiguous knowledge, often at the expense of lived experience and contextual understanding (Coetzee, 2018, p. 1).

In ancient Greece, Plato's Theory of Forms argued that true knowledge lies in the understanding of abstract, unchanging ideals rather than the fluctuating physical world (Sedley, 2016). This philosophical stance profoundly influenced Western education and established a tradition that prioritised theoretical knowledge over practical experience (Roy, 2022). The Middle Ages, with its emphasis on religious teachings and scholasticism, reinforced this trend by emphasising memorisation and the interpretation of authoritative texts (Maurer, 2023).

The Enlightenment era brought with it a turn towards reason and empiricism, but still maintained a focus on abstract, generalisable knowledge. Thinkers such as John Locke and Jean-Jacques Rousseau began to reflect on the nature of learning itself, but their approaches still attempted to systematise education into clear, unambiguous methods. (Bristow, 2010; Locke & Daniel, 1913; Rousseau, 1912).

The Industrial Revolution marked a significant turning point as it reshaped education to meet the needs of an industrialised society. Schools were modelled on factories and emphasised standardisation, efficiency, and measurable outcomes. While this approach was effective in producing labour for the industrial economy, it moved education from embodied, contextual learning experiences (Carl, 2009).

The historical trend in education described above mirrors the development of music notation. Just as traditional education aimed to convey unambiguous knowledge, musical notation evolved to convey specific pitches, rhythms, and other elements with increasing precision (Cromleigh, 1977; Williams, 1903).

However, the quest for certainty and precision in both education and music faced increasing challenges. Just as philosophy faced a crisis in the face of rapid social change in the 20th century (Gilbert, 2019), education has also struggled to adapt to the needs of a globalised, digital world. The call for educational reform is reminiscent of the phenomenologists' critique of traditional philosophy: the need to return to "things themselves" and base learning on lived experience rather than abstract concepts (Zahavi, 2008).

In music, this parallels the realisation that even the most precise notation cannot capture the full complexity of musical performance (Grier, 2021; Holder et al., 2015). The nuances of interpretation, the physicality of playing an instrument, the emotional engagement of the performer—all of these crucial elements defy complete notational capture. Similarly, in education, we increasingly recognise that standardised curricula and tests do not do justice to the richness of individual learning experiences and the complexity of the real-world application of knowledge (Hinchman, 2019; Rubin & Kazanjian, 2011).

The shift from certainty to ambiguity in educational thinking reflects a broader philosophical and cultural shift. Postmodern thinking has challenged the notion of absolute truths (Muhamba & Francis, 2023), while globalisation has exposed us to different ways of knowing and being. In this context, the rigid, one-size-fits-all approach of traditional education seems increasingly inadequate.

At this educational crossroads, phenomenology offers a way to understand the ambiguity of human experience and learning. By focusing on direct, lived experience, and the process of meaning-making, it provides a framework for education that better accommodates the complexities and nuances of learning in the real world.

Phenomenology: A New Educational Paradigm Embracing Ambiguity

Phenomenology, as developed by thinkers such as Husserl, Heidegger, and Merleau-Ponty, offers a radical reorientation of the way we understand human consciousness and its relationship to the world. This philosophical approach provides a framework for education that is inherently more holistic and engaging than traditional models. (Devroop, 2022; Käufer & Chemero, 2021).

At its core, phenomenology prioritises immediate experience over abstract knowledge (Chaplin, 2013). For example, in a science class, students might first observe and interact with natural phenomena before learning theoretical explanations. This approach grounds learning in lived experience and makes it more meaningful and memorable.

Phenomenology also emphasises intersubjectivity and the co-creation of meaning. This could manifest itself in collaborative projects where students work together to develop understanding and recognise that knowledge is not individually acquired but socially constructed. The role of perception in shaping understanding is central to phenomenology.

Context and situated learning are crucial in this paradigm. For example, a history class might include immersive experiences that place students in the historical context they are studying rather than simply memorising facts.

Finally, phenomenology views ambiguity as a source of richness in learning. Rather than looking for definitive answers, students are encouraged to explore different interpretations and possibilities and become comfortable with complexity and uncertainty. The use of a phenomenological approach is in line with contemporary educational theories such as constructivism and experiential learning, but provides a deeper philosophical foundation (Creely, 2018). By recognising the inherent ambiguity of human experience and knowledge, it prepares students for a world of complexity and change.

Music as a Model for Phenomenological Education: Navigating Ambiguity

Music, as an art form that engages the whole person—body, mind and emotions—is an ideal model for understanding how phenomenology can be applied to education. The experience of music, whether as listener, performer, or creator, embodies many key principles of phenomenology as discussed in the works of Husserl (1982, 1970), Heidegger (1996), Merleau-Ponty (1996), and others (see Devroop, 2022). This holistic engagement through music education offers far-reaching benefits for cognitive, emotional, and social development. Recent studies have shown that it enhances cognitive skills and promotes personal growth (Xu & Liu, 2024), improves adolescent development in terms of the Five Cs: competence, confidence, caring, character, and connectedness (Morris et al., 2018) and the development of emotional skills while improving cognitive performance (Campayo-Muñoz & Cabedo-Mas, 2017).

Here I present some of these principles of phenomenology and explain their relationship to music. These principles are taken from Robert Sokolowski's *Introduction to Phenomenology* (1999):

1. Immediacy of Experience (p. 2–7): Music is experienced directly, without the mediation of language or abstract concepts. For example, when listening to a symphony, one does not need to understand music theory in order to be moved by the swell of the orchestra.
2. Embodiment (p. 152): Music involves the body through rhythm, movement and physical sensations. Remember that a drum circle involves not only auditory perception, but also physical coordination and visceral sense of rhythm.
3. Intersubjectivity (p. 152–155): Music is inherently social and involves shared experiences and co-created meanings. A jazz improvisation session is an example of this: the musicians react to each other in real time, creating a collective musical experience.
4. Temporality (p. 215): Music unfolds in time, emphasising the fluid nature of experience. The way a piece of music develops over its

duration reflects how our understanding evolves through the learning process.
5. Intentionality (pp. 216–220): Musical experience involves a directed awareness of sound and meaning. When a violinist concentrates on producing a particular sound, his or her consciousness is focused on that specific listening goal.
6. Ambiguity (p. 6): Music exists on a spectrum between precise notation and ambiguous interpretation. A classical score contains specific instructions, but each performance is unique and emphasises the richness of human interpretation.

The tension between unambiguous notation and ambiguous performance in music is therefore a powerful metaphor for the broader pedagogical challenges. Just as a musical score cannot capture the full complexity of a performance—the subtle variations in tempo, the emotional allusions, the interplay between musicians—traditional education often fails to capture the richness of human learning and experience (Holder et al., 2015, p. 107). This parallel emphasises the need for educational approaches that embrace both structure and flexibility, recognising that true understanding emerges from the interplay between defined knowledge and personal interpretation.

1. Lessons from Phenomenological Music Education: Embracing the Spectrum of Ambiguity

The application of phenomenological principles to music education offers valuable insights that can be applied to the broader field of education. By examining how these principles manifest themselves in music education, we can draw lessons that are applicable to other disciplines and pedagogical approaches. This section explores five key areas where phenomenological music education provides clues for a more holistic and engaging educational paradigm.

Prioritising Direct Experience

In traditional music education, theory, notation and technical skills are often overemphasised at the expense of direct musical experience. A phenomenological approach reverses this priority and emphasises immersive musical experiences from the outset. This shift can be achieved through a variety of strategies, by starting with listening and responding to music before introducing notation. For example, young learners could be encouraged to move or draw to respond to different pieces of music before learning to read music notation. This approach allows learners to develop a personal, embodied relationship with music before engaging with its abstract representations. Empirical evidence supports this approach and emphasises the cognitive benefits of early engagement with music through listening and physical response.

Encouraging improvisation and creative expression alongside the development of technical skills, rather than focusing solely on reproducing existing pieces, will give students the opportunity to create their own music from the outset. This could include simple improvisation on percussion instruments or vocal explorations to encourage a sense of musical agency and creativity. Stark (2020) emphasises the importance of direct, immersive experiences in music education, which align with Dewey's (2018) experiential theory.

Using body movement and dance to internalise musical concepts such as rhythm, tempo, and dynamics can be taught through physical movement. For example, students can walk or clap to different beat patterns to physically experience the structure of the music. Studies (Castro-Alonso et al., 2024; Nijs & Bremmer, 2019; Juntunen, 2016) have shown that such embodied learning strategies promote cognitive development and musical understanding.

By exploring the ambiguities in musical interpretation and performance, thereby comparing different performances of the same piece, students can discover how music allows for personal interpretation within structural constraints. This approach not only deepens understanding of music, but also encourages critical thinking and interpretative skills.

These approaches can also be applied to other subjects. In science lessons, for example, practical experiments and direct observations could precede theoretical explanations in order to recognise the ambiguity and complexity of real phenomena. In literature, students could look at the emotional impact of a text before analysing its formal structures.

Embodied Learning

Music inherently involves the body, from the physical act of sound production to the bodily response to rhythm and melody. A phenomenological approach to music education explicitly recognises and cultivates this embodied dimension of musical experience. This principle can be applied by incorporating movement and dance into music lessons: students might develop choreography to express musical phrases or explore concepts such as musical form through dance; using physical gestures to represent musical concepts: for example, rising and falling arm movements could represent pitch changes and help students internalise melodic contours; exploring the physical sensations associated with different sounds and rhythms: students would feel the vibrations of different instruments or learn how different rhythms affect heart rate and breathing; investigating how different physical interpretations can arise from the same musical notation: Students could experiment with how changing their physical approach (e.g. posture, breathing) affects the sound produced, even when following the same written music.

Empirical evidence (Nijs & Bremmer, 2019) supports these strategies and emphasises the benefits of embodied musical activities in enhancing learning by linking sound and movement in meaningful ways. Studies (Van Zijl & Luck, 2013; Schutz & Lipscomb, 2007; Davidson, 2009) have shown that physical gestures can effectively support the understanding and internalisation of musical concepts and that sensory experiences are crucial for the development of a deeper understanding of music. Furthermore, the role of physical participation in shaping musical perception and performance is well documented.

In other subjects, this principle could be applied to more kinesthetic approaches to learning. In maths lessons, abstract concepts could be illustrated using physical objects, while in history lessons, role play could be used to illustrate historical perspectives.

Intersubjectivity and Co-creation

Music is inherently social and involves shared experience and creation. Phenomenological music teaching emphasises this aspect in several ways. Group improvisation and composition allows students to create new pieces together, negotiate musical ideas, and learn to respond to each other in real time. Studies have shown that collaborative music improvisation fosters an intersubjective connection that requires mutual trust and dialogue qualities. Lähdeoja & Montes De Oca (2021), for example, show that improvisational practices in electronic music promote a heightened intersubjective awareness that facilitates non-verbal communication and reciprocal responsiveness among participants. In collaborative performance projects, or ensemble work, students learn to listen to each other, adapt their playing, and create a cohesive whole that is greater than the sum of its parts. Vass (2018) illustrates that collaborative music making, exemplified by the Kokas pedagogy, facilitates deep learning and creative dialogue through physical, interactive experiences. Kokas's method involves students physically responding to music through free movement, encouraging personal interpretation and emotional connection to the music. Her approach aims to develop musical understanding, creativity, and self-expression through embodied experiences and collaborative activities.

Exploring how musical meaning is culturally constructed and shared, could include examining how different cultures interpret similar musical elements or how musical traditions evolve over time through collective creativity. Research by Schutz & Lipscomb (2007) shows that visual cues and physical movements in musical performance can influence the perception and interpretation of sounds, suggesting that cultural factors play a role in shaping musical understanding.

The investigation of how different performers interpret the same score, by comparing different recordings or live performances, could enhance students' understanding of how individual and cultural contexts influence musical interpretation. Davidson (2009) argues that body movements and gestures during musical performances are crucial to collective learning and interpretation, emphasising the impact of both cultural contexts and personal variations.

This focus on intersubjectivity can also be brought to bear in other areas of education, encouraging collaborative approaches to learning and recognising the social construction of knowledge. In language learning, for example, students could develop stories or dialogues together, emphasising communication and co-creation of meaning over memorisation.

Perception and Meaning-Making

Phenomenology emphasises how our perceptions shape our understanding of the world. In music education, this means focusing on the development of perceptual skills and exploring how individuals construct musical meaning. This approach includes ear training exercises that focus on the quality of sound rather than pitch and rhythm: Students might describe the timbre of different instruments or explore how different acoustic environments affect sound perception. Silverman (2020) notes that emphasising sound quality in instrumental music education can lead to more meaningful musical engagement.

Exploring how different people and cultures perceive and interpret the same piece of music, could include discussions about personal associations with particular songs or exploring how cultural background influences musical preferences. Schiavio et al. (2023) show that an individual's cultural background and personal experiences have a significant impact on how they perceive and give meaning to music.

Students could be encouraged to articulate their personal responses to music. Regular reflective exercises, such as keeping a diary of musical experiences, can help them become more aware of their perceptual processes. Nijs & Bremmer (2019) argue that personal reflection and embodied experiences are fundamental to developing a comprehensive understanding of music within the framework of embodied music cognition.

This approach also recommends exploring ambiguities in musical perception and interpretation: students could explore optical illusions in visual art as a parallel to auditory illusions in music and understand how subjective and malleable perception can be. Nijs & Bremmer (2019) further explain how sensory impressions and physical movement can influence the perception and interpretation of music.

This approach can be applied more broadly to develop students' critical thinking skills and awareness of their own perceptual processes. In literature, for example, students could explore how their personal experiences influence their interpretation of a text.

Contextual and Situated Learning

Phenomenology recognises that every experience is situated in a specific context. In music education, this principle encourages the study of music in its cultural and historical context: rather than studying pieces in isolation, students should learn about the social, political, and cultural factors that influenced their creation and reception. White (2021) shows that immersive, real-world learning experiences enhance students' understanding and appreciation of music.

Recognising how the physical environment affects the musical experience, could include playing or listening to music in different spaces and thinking about how the acoustic properties affect the experience. Barrett (2014) shows that acoustic environments have a significant impact on how music is perceived and performed, and that they alter the listening experience.

By encouraging students to consider how personal experiences influence the interpretation of music, they could explore how their own life experiences and emotions influence their response to music and its performance. Creech et al. (2020) argue that individual emotional experiences and personal contexts are key factors in musical interpretation and engagement.

The investigation of how different contexts can lead to different interpretations of the same piece of music, could include performing the same piece in different settings (e.g. formal concert hall vs. outdoor venue) and discussing how context influences interpretation. Research by Anderson et al. (1996) demonstrates that situational knowledge and contextual learning can lead to different understandings of a single piece of music

This emphasis on context can also be brought to bear in other subjects by encouraging a more interdisciplinary approach to learning and recognising how knowledge is anchored in a particular cultural and historical framework. In history lessons, for example, this could mean looking at historical events through the lens of different cultural perspectives or examining how our current context influences our interpretation of the past.

By considering these phenomenological principles, music education becomes a model for a more holistic, engaging, and meaningful approach to learning. This model recognises the spectrum of ambiguity inherent in human experience and knowledge, viewing it not as an obstacle to be overcome, but as a rich source of depth and complexity to be explored. When we apply these lessons to broader educational contexts, we open up new possibilities for learning that is more attuned to students' lived experiences and better prepared for the complex challenges of the 21st century.

Challenges and Opportunities: Navigating the Spectrum of Ambiguity

Implementing a phenomenological approach in education is not without its challenges. It requires significant rethinking by both educators and policy makers, as well as changes in curriculum design and assessment methods. However, these challenges also present opportunities for innovation in education. By addressing these issues, we can develop more holistic and effective educational practices that better meet the needs of 21st century learners. The spectrum from unambiguity to ambiguity provides a framework for addressing these challenges, recognising that different educational contexts may require different approaches along this spectrum.

Resistance to Change by Traditionalists in Education

Many educators and administrators are deeply entrenched in traditional models of education and view phenomenological approaches as too radical or impractical. This resistance often stems from concerns about maintaining academic standards and preparing students for standardised tests. As Annamalai et al. (2022) have highlighted, resistance to change is a significant obstacle that has been particularly evident in the transition to online teaching during the COVID-19 pandemic. However, this challenge presents an opportunity to engage in meaningful dialogue about the purpose of education and to demonstrate the effectiveness of phenomenological approaches through pilot programmes and research studies. By addressing these concerns and demonstrating the potential of phenomenological methods to improve learning outcomes, educators can begin to shift perspective and adopt more innovative educational practices

Difficulties in Assessing Learning Outcomes Through Experience

Traditional assessment methods such as multiple-choice tests are poorly suited to assess the type of learning that is at the forefront of phenomenological education. The development of new assessment tools that can capture the depth and nuance of experiential learning is critical. Saevi (2014) emphasises that traditional methods are inadequate to capture the depth of experiential learning and highlights the importance of developing holistic assessment tools that align with phenomenological principles. This challenge offers an opportunity to completely rethink assessment and move towards more holistic methods such as portfolios, project-based assessments, and self-reflection exercises. By introducing these innovative assessment strategies, educators can better evaluate their students' learning outcomes and provide a more comprehensive understanding of their learning progress.

The Need to Train Teachers in Phenomenological Approaches

Most teachers have been trained in traditional pedagogical methods and may not feel prepared to implement phenomenological approaches. This requires considerable investment in professional development and teacher training programmes. Implementing phenomenological approaches requires significant investment in teacher training programmes. A study by Han & Ellis (2019) highlights the need for professional development programmes that equip educators with the skills to integrate phenomenological methods into their teaching practices. This challenge also presents an opportunity to revitalise the teaching profession by providing educators with new opportunities to engage with their subject matter and their students, thereby increasing their teaching effectiveness and professional satisfaction.

The Balance Between Experiential Learning and the Need for Standardised Knowledge

Even though phenomenological education emphasises direct experience and individual sense-making, students still need to acquire certain standardised knowledge and skills. Finding the right balance between these two aspects of education is a major challenge. Kolb's (2014) experiential learning theory (ELT) supports this integration by providing a framework that blends experiential and traditional learning methods.

Allowing for Ambiguity While Still Providing Clear Pedagogical Guidance

Phenomenological pedagogy acknowledges and embraces ambiguity, but students and parents often desire clear goals and expectations. Managing this tension requires careful communication and the development of flexible learning pathways. This challenge provides an opportunity to teach students valuable skills in dealing with uncertainty and complexity, preparing them for a world in which such skills will become increasingly important. Brinkmann & Friesen (2018) argue that phenomenological education values multiple perspectives and meanings, encourages imaginative application while requiring adaptable approaches to learning to meet the diverse needs and expectations of students.

Adapting to Different Learning Environments and Student Needs

Phenomenological approaches are easier to implement in some subjects (such as art) than others (such as maths). In addition, different students may respond differently to these methods. This challenge presents an opportunity to develop more personalised and adaptable approaches to learning that can move along the spectrum of ambiguity to meet different needs. According to Sanger (2020), inclusive pedagogy and Universal Design for Learning (UDL) emphasise the importance of anticipating and incorporating students' diverse backgrounds, abilities and interests into instruction to support personalised and adaptive learning.

Meaningful Integration of Technology

While phenomenology emphasises immediate, embodied experiences, integrating technology in a way that enhances rather than detracts from these experiences is essential. This challenge provides an opportunity to explore innovative technologies that support experiential learning, such as virtual reality simulations and interactive digital storytelling. Cilesiz (2011) shows that phenomenology provides a framework for seamlessly integrating technology into the classroom while preserving direct, embodied learning experiences that allow educators to create immersive, meaningful learning environments based on students' lived experiences.

Cultural Differences and Multicultural Contexts

Implementing phenomenological approaches in a multicultural context, such as South Africa, adds another layer of complexity. Cultural differences can affect how phenomenological methods are perceived and accepted. For example, in South Africa's diverse educational landscape, students come from different cultural backgrounds with different learning styles and expectations. This diversity can be both a challenge and an opportunity. Educators need to be culturally sensitive and adaptable, recognising that what works in one cultural context may not be effective in another. Olivier (2023) argues that phenomenological approaches in South Africa need to engage with the country's unique cultural and historical contexts. This presents an opportunity to develop inclusive, culturally responsive educational practices that honour diverse perspectives and foster a deeper appreciation of the country's rich cultural heritage.

Consideration of Equity and Access Issues

Experiential learning often requires resources that are not equally available to all schools or students. It is important to ensure that phenomenological education does not exacerbate existing inequalities. This challenge provides an opportunity to rethink the allocation of resources in education and to develop creative, cost-effective approaches to experiential learning. Some studies that address this issue include those by Omoeva et al. (2021), which emphasise equitable resource allocation in education; Nichols et al. (2004) highlight the role of experiential education in mediating social stratification; Rose & Paisley (2012) critique its potential to perpetuate inequalities; and Cowart (2010) offers strategies for funding experiential education in challenging economic times.

By addressing these challenges and capitalising on the opportunities they present, we can work towards an educational paradigm that truly prepares students for the complexities of the 21st century. The spectrum from uniqueness to ambiguity provides a flexible framework for this change and allows for customised approaches that can meet the needs of different learners and educational contexts.

The Future of Education: From Theory to Lived Experience

As we look to the future of education, the insights of phenomenology and their application to music education offer a compelling vision. This new paradigm sees education not as the transmission of unambiguous knowledge, but as the cultivation of the whole person—body, mind and spirit—through immediate, meaningful experiences that embrace the inherent ambiguities of human existence.

In this vision, schools would become spaces of exploration and discovery, not just places of information transmission. Learning would be understood as an active, embodied process of meaning-making rather than a passive reception of facts. Studies such as Barrett's (2014) have shown that the application of Interpretative Phenomenological Analysis (IPA) in music education has shown how active, embodied learning processes can be better understood and enhanced through phenomenological methods. The boundaries between subjects would become blurred and the interconnectedness of knowledge and experience would be recognised.

Based on our research into music education, we can imagine a future educational landscape in which immersive learning environments enable direct, multi-sensory experiences. History classes could include virtual reality simulations of historical events, while science labs could take students beyond the classroom and into nature preserves or community spaces. These environments would emphasise embodied learning and give students the opportunity to physically engage with the subject matter.

Collaborative knowledge building would be emphasised, mirroring the model of musical ensembles. Classrooms would emphasise interdisciplinary projects in which students from different grade levels and subject areas work together to solve real-world problems that reflect the complexity and intersubjectivity of the human experience. The Prism Project (Kohli et al., 1987), which brings together scientists, K–8 students and teachers in the United States, is an example of this approach as it creates a learning community that goes beyond the usual classroom. By fostering partnerships between students, educators, and scientists, the Prism Project provides opportunities for collaborative, hands-on learning experiences that are both interdisciplinary and highly engaging. This model not only enhances students' understanding of scientific concepts, but also promotes inclusion and equity in education by ensuring that all students have access to high-quality learning opportunities.

By recognising each student's unique perceptual world, education would become more personalised. AI-powered adaptive learning systems could help tailor experiences to individual learning styles and interests while maintaining a balance between collaborative and standardised elements. Students would be encouraged to reflect on their own learning processes and develop an awareness of how they perceive and give meaning to their experiences. This metacognitive approach, guided by the self-awareness cultivated in musical practice, would help students become lifelong learners.

The artificial separation between the arts and sciences would dissolve as it is recognised that both involve creative problem solving and abstract thinking. Music, visual arts, dance, and theatre would be integrated into the curriculum and used as tools for exploration and expression of ideas in all subjects.

Assessment would evolve into an ongoing dialogue between students, teachers, and peers and move away from standardised testing. This could include portfolio assessments, project presentations, and reflection journals that reflect the way musicians continually refine their performances through practice and feedback. Case studies (Crawford, 2019) in music education research highlight the potential of phenomenological approaches to improve assessment methods, emphasising continuous feedback and reflective practices.

The role of the teacher would shift from an authority figure to a facilitator of experiences and a co-learner. Teachers would design learning environments, guide explorations, and participate alongside students in the discovery process.

Expanding the Role of Technology

While the focus remains on direct, embodied experience, education would carefully integrate technology. AI could simulate complex systems and provide interactive models for students to explore and manipulate. This aligns with the findings of Cilesiz (2011), who emphasises the importance of phenomenological approaches to understanding experiences with technology. Augmented reality (AR) could overlay information onto the physical world to enhance real-world learning experiences. For example, AR could transform a simple nature walk into an interactive biology lesson, as suggested by Valentine et al. (2018) where students can see detailed information about plants and animals in their natural habitat—emphasising the role of phenomenological methods in educational technology.

Virtual reality (VR) could provide immersive experiences that bring abstract concepts to life. Imagine a history lesson where students can virtually walk through ancient cities, or a science lesson where they can explore the human body at a cellular level. These technologies can make learning more engaging and accessible, especially for students who struggle with traditional methods (Valentine et al., 2018).

Biofeedback devices could help students understand their own physical and emotional responses to learning experiences. By monitoring heart rate, skin conductance, and other physiological indicators, these devices can provide real-time feedback that helps students develop self-awareness and emotional regulation skills. This approach is supported by pilot studies that emphasise the importance of real-world testing before scaling up educational initiatives (IES Institute of Education Science, 2021).

This approach fits well with the skills needed in the 21st century: Creativity, critical thinking, collaboration, and adaptability. By grounding learning in immediate experience and emphasising the meaning-making process, the phenomenological approach to education prepares students not to know, but to be and become, in order to navigate the ambiguities of a complex world (Valentine et al., 2018; Cilesiz, 2011).

Furthermore, this future of education recognises that learning goes beyond the classroom and encompasses all of life. It seeks to instil a love of learning and the capacity for continuous growth, preparing students for a world where the ability to adapt, create, and find meaning in new experiences is paramount.

However, realising this vision will require significant changes in education policy, teacher training and societal attitudes towards learning. It requires a re-evaluation of what we consider to be valuable knowledge and skills, and a willingness to accept the uncertainty and complexity that comes with an open-ended, experiential approach to education.

As we move into this future, music education can serve as both a model and a laboratory for developing and refining these approaches. Through its inherent blend of theory and practice, individual expression and collective harmony, precision and ambiguity, music offers a microcosm for the broader educational transformation we envision.

By addressing these challenges and capitalising on the opportunities they present, we can work towards an educational paradigm that truly prepares students for the complexities of the 21st century. We must prepare them for the complexity of the 21st century. The spectrum from unambiguity to ambiguity provides a flexible framework for this change and allows for customised approaches that meet the needs of different learners and educational contexts.

Conclusion: The Educator as Facilitator of Experience and Navigator of Ambiguity

To conclude our exploration of phenomenology and music as a new path for 21st century education, we return to the crisis of modern education described in our introduction. The rapid technological advances and changing social paradigms of our time have revealed the limitations of traditional educational models based on rationalist and empiricist philosophies. These models, with their emphasis on standardisation and measurable outcomes, are often unable to prepare students for the complexity and ambiguity of our rapidly changing world.

Phenomenology, with its emphasis on direct, lived experience and the primacy of perception, offers a compelling alternative. By grounding education in embodied, contextualised learning experiences, we can bridge the gap between abstract knowledge and concrete reality, between theory and practice, and between the individual and the world. As we have seen, music education provides an ideal model for how these phenomenological principles can be applied to educational.

In this chapter, I have traced the historical journey of education from the search for certainty to the recognition of ambiguity. We have seen how the industrial model of education, reflecting the development of precise musical notation, has sought to eliminate ambiguity in favour of standardisation. However, as we recognise that even the most precise score cannot capture the full complexity of a performance, we now understand that traditional approaches to education are often unable to capture the richness of human learning and experience.

The lessons we learn from phenomenological music education provide a roadmap for transforming education in all disciplines. By prioritising direct experience, we can create more engaging and meaningful learning environments. Embodied learning recognises the role of the whole person—body, mind and emotions—in the educational process. Intersubjectivity and co-creation of meaning reflect the social nature of learning, while a focus on perception and sense-making recognises the unique way in which each learner engages with the world. Contextualised and situated learning anchors knowledge in the real world, making it more relevant and applicable.

These principles, if applied comprehensively, can reshape our educational landscape. We envision schools as spaces of exploration and discovery, where learning is an active, embodied process of meaning-making. The boundaries between subjects become blurred as knowledge is interconnected. Assessment becomes an ongoing dialogue and teachers evolve into facilitators of experience and co-learners on the educational journey.

However, realising this vision is not without its challenges. Resistance to change, difficulties with assessment, the need for teacher training and concerns about maintaining academic standards are all obstacles. But these challenges also present opportunities for innovation. They force us to rethink our assumptions about education, develop new assessment tools, reinvigorate teacher training and create more personalised and adaptive approaches to learning.

The future of education, as I have already outlined, is one in which immersive learning environments, collaborative knowledge building, and personalised learning journeys become the norm. It is a future where the artificial divide between the humanities and sciences is dissolved, where metacognition is emphasised and where technology is thoughtfully integrated to enhance, not replace, direct experience.

This vision is closely related to the skills needed in the 21st century: Creativity, critical thinking, collaboration, and adaptability. By embracing ambiguity as a source of richness and depth of learning, we prepare students not to know, but to be and to become. We equip them with the tools to navigate the complexity and uncertainty of our rapidly changing world.

In this new paradigm, the role of the educator is changing dramatically. The teacher is no longer the wise man on the stage, but a facilitator of experience, a guide in the process of exploration and discovery. Much like the musicus of the Middle Ages, who was intensely concerned with the philosophical and practical aspects of music, the modern pedagogue is both a thinker and a doer (Smith, 1979, pp. 45–46). He shapes learning experiences and participates in the learning process by bridging the gap between theory and practice.

Furthermore, the educator becomes a navigator of ambiguity, helping students to recognise and embrace the complexities and uncertainties inherent in knowledge and experience. Just as a musician must navigate between precise notation and ambiguous interpretation, educators, and students must learn to navigate the rich, complex landscape of human knowledge and experience.

Faced with the challenges of the 21st century—from technological disruption to climate change to social inequality—we need an approach to education that cultivates not knowledge but wisdom; not skills but understanding; not individual achievement but collective harmony. Phenomenology, with its emphasis on direct experience, embodied learning and the co-creation of meaning, offers us a path to this goal.

To summarise, the lessons of phenomenological approaches to music education provide a roadmap for this pedagogical shift. By embracing the spectrum from unambiguity to ambiguity, we can create educational experiences that are richer, more engaging, and more responsive to the complexities of the modern world. In doing so, we may find that education is not just a preparation for life, but a fuller, richer way of living itself. And in doing so, we may discover the true power of learning—not as an accumulation of unambiguous facts, but as a deepening of our engagement with the world and with each other, in all its beautiful complexity and ambiguity.

References

Anderson, J. R., Reder, L. M., & Simon, H. A. (1996). Situated Learning and Education1. *Educational Researcher, 25*(4), 5-11. https://doi.org/10.3102/0013189X025004005 (Original work published 1996)

Annamalai, N., Rashid, R. Ab, Saed, H., Al-Smadi, O. A., & Yassin, B. (2022). A phenomenological study of educators' experience after a year of the COVID-19 pandemic. *Frontiers in Psychology, 13*, 869687. https://doi.org/10.3389/fpsyg.2022.869687

Antunes, S. (2021). Education in a technology-shaped world: Which learning model helps preparing for the knowledge-based societies? In D. Raposo, J. Neves, J. Silva, L. Correia Castilho & R. Dias (Eds.), *Advances in design, music and arts* (Vol. 9, pp. 111–125). Springer International Publishing. https://doi.org/10.1007/978-3-030-55700-3_8

Barrett, J. R. (2014). Case study in music education. In C. M. Conway (Ed.), *The Oxford handbook of qualitative research in American Music Education* (1st ed.). Oxford University Press. https://doi.org/10.1093/oxfordhb/9780199844272.013.007_update_001

Brinkmann, M., & Friesen, N. (2018). Phenomenology and education. In P. Smeyers (Ed.), *International handbook of philosophy of education* (pp. 591–608). Springer International Publishing. https://doi.org/10.1007/978-3-319-72761-5_46

Bristow, W. (2010). Enlightenment. In *Stanford Encyclopedia of Philosophy*. https://plato.stanford.edu/eNtRIeS/enlightenment/ [Accessed 23 September 2024].

Campayo–Muñoz, E., & Cabedo–Mas, A. (2017). The role of emotional skills in music education. *British Journal of Music Education, 34*(3), 243–258. https://doi.org/10.1017/S0265051717000067

Carl, J. (2009). Industrialization and public Education: Social cohesion and social stratification. In R. Cowen & A. M. Kazamias (Eds.), *International handbook of comparative education* (pp. 503–518). Springer Netherlands. https://doi.org/10.1007/978-1-4020-6403-6_32

Castro-Alonso, J. C., Ayres, P., Zhang, S., de Koning, B. B., & Paas, F. (2024). Research avenues supporting embodied cognition in learning and instruction. *Educational Psychology Review, 36*(10). https://doi.org/10.1007/s10648-024-09847-4

Chaplin, A. D. (2013). Phenomenology: Merleau-Ponty and Sartre. In B. Gaut & D. Lopes (Eds.), *The Routledge companion to aesthetics* (0th ed., pp. 148–158). Routledge. https://doi.org/10.4324/9780203813034-20

Cilesiz, S. (2011). A phenomenological approach to experiences with technology: Current state, promise, and future directions for research. *Educational Technology Research and Development, 59*, 487–510.

Coetzee, M.-H. (2018). Embodied knowledge(s), embodied pedagogies and performance. *South African Theatre Journal, 31*(1), 1–4. https://doi.org/10.1080/10137548.2018.1425527

Cowart, M. R. (2010). Growing and funding experiential learning programs: A recipe for success. *New Directions for Teaching and Learning, 2010*(124), 63–68. https://doi.org/10.1002/tl.422

Crawford, R. (2019). Using interpretative phenomenological analysis in music education research: An authentic analysis system for investigating authentic learning and teaching practice. *International Journal of Music Education, 37*(3), 454–475.

Creech, A., Varvarigou, M., & Hallam, S. (2020). *Contexts for music learning and participation: Developing and sustaining musical possible selves*. Springer International Publishing. https://doi.org/10.1007/978-3-030-48262-6

Creely, E. (2018). 'Understanding things from within'. A Husserlian phenomenological approach to doing educational research and inquiring about learning. *International Journal of Research & Method in Education, 41*(1), 104–122. https://doi.org/10.1080/1743727X.2016.1182482

Cromleigh, R. G. (1977). Neumes, notes, and numbers: The many methods of music notation. *Music Educators Journal, 64*(4), 30–39.

Davidson, J. W. (2009). Movement and collaboration in musical performance. *The Oxford Handbook of Music Psychology*, 364–376.

Devroop, C. (2022). Phenomenology: Where is it and what is in it for us? *African Perspective of Research in Teaching and Learning*, 6(3), 16–28.

Dewey, J. (2018). *Democracy and education by John Dewey: With a critical introduction by Patricia H. Hinchey*. Myers Education Press

Gilbert, A. S. (2019). Hannah Arendt: Crisis as modernity's choice. In A. S. Gilbert, *The crisis paradigm* (pp. 105–151). Springer International Publishing. https://doi.org/10.1007/978-3-030-11060-4_4

Grier, J. (2021). *Musical notation in the West*. Cambridge University Press.

Han, F., & Ellis, R. A. (2019). Using phenomenography to tackle key challenges in science education. *Frontiers in Psychology*, 10, 1414. https://doi.org/10.3389/fpsyg.2019.01414

Heidegger, M. (1996). *Being and Time: A Translation of Sein und Zeit* by Joan Stambaugh. Albany, NY: SUNY

Hinchman, T. (2019). Expanding the Curriculum With Creativity. In *Critical Literacy Initiatives for Civic Engagement* (pp. 48–68). IGI Global. DOI: 10.4018/978-1-5225-8082-9.ch003

Holder, E., Tilevich, E., & Gillick, A. (2015). Musiplectics: Computational assessment of the complexity of music scores. *2015 ACM International Symposium on New Ideas, New Paradigms, and Reflections on Programming and Software (Onward!)*, 107–120. https://doi.org/10.1145/2814228.2814243

Husserl, E. (1982). *Ideas pertaining to a pure phenomenology and to a phenomenological philosophy: Second book studies in the phenomenology of constitution* (Vol. 3). Springer Science & Business Media.

Institute of Education Science (IES). (2021). *Learning before going to scale: An introduction to conducting pilot studies*. REL Appalachia at SRI International. https://ies.ed.gov/ncee/edlabs/regions/appalachia/resources/pdfs/Pilot-Study-Resource_acc.pdf [Accessed 23 September 2024].

Juntunen, M-L. (2016). 'The Dalcrose Approach: Experiencing and knowing music through embodied exploration', In C. R. Abril, & B.M. Gault (Eds.), *Teaching general music: Approaches, issues, and viewpoints*. Oxford University Press.

Käufer, S., & Chemero, A. (2021). *Phenomenology: An introduction*. John Wiley & Sons.

Kohli, M., Giuliano, M. E., & Minker, J. (1987). An overview of the PRISM project. *ACM SIGARCH Computer Architecture News*, 15(1), 35–42.

Kolb, D. A. (2014). *Experiential learning: Experience as the source of learning and development*. FT press.

Krishnan, K. (2020). *Our education system is losing relevance. Here's how to unleash its potential*. World Economic Forum, Geneva, Switzerland, https://www.weforum.org/stories/2020/04/our-education-system-is-losing-relevance-heres-how-to-update-it/

Lähdeoja, O., & De Oca, A. M. (2021). Co-Sounding: Fostering intersubjectivity in electronic music improvisation. *Organised Sound*, 26(1), 5–18.

Locke, J., & Daniel, E. (1913). *Some thoughts concerning education*.

Masethe, M. A., Masethe, H. D., & Odunaike, S. A. (2017). Scoping review of learning theories in the 21st century. *Proceedings of the World Congress on Engineering and Computer Science*, 1. https://www.iaeng.org/publication/WCECS2017/WCECS2017_pp227-231.pdf

Maurer, A. (2023). Medieval Philosophy. In *Encyclopaedia Britannica*. https://www.britannica.com/topic/medieval-philosophy

Merleau-Ponty, M. (1996). *Phenomenology of Perception*. Delhi: Motilal Banarsidass

McKay, T. (2021). *A semiotic approach to open notations: Ambiguity as opportunity*. Cambridge University Press.

Morris, S. L., Wagner, E. F., & Wales, E. (2018). Music education as a path to positive youth development: An El sistema-inspired program. *Journal of Youth Development*, 13(4), 149–163.

Muhamba, D., & Francis, B. S. (2023). Deconstructing Reality: A Postmodern Analysis of the Concept of Truth. *Journal of African Politics*, 3(2), 31–42. DOI: https://doi.org/10.58548/2023jap32.3142

Nichols, L., Berry, J., & Kalogrides, D. (2004). Hop on the Bus: Driving Stratification Concepts Home. *Teaching Sociology*, 32(2), 213–221. https://doi.org/10.1177/0092055X0403200207

Nijs, L., & Bremmer, M. (2019). Embodiment in early childhood music education. In S. Young & B. Ilari (Eds.), *Music in early childhood: Multi-disciplinary perspectives and interdisciplinary exchanges* (Vol. 27, pp. 87–102). Springer International Publishing. https://doi.org/10.1007/978-3-030-17791-1_6

Olivier, A. (2023). African phenomenology: Introductory perspectives. In E. Imafidon, M. Tshivashe, & B. Freter (Eds.), *Handbook of African philosophy* (pp. 1–27). Springer International Publishing. https://doi.org/10.1007/978-3-030-77898-9_37-1

Omoeva, C., Menezes Cunha, N., & Moussa, W. (2021). Measuring equity of education resource allocation: An output-based approach. *International Journal of Educational Development*, 87, 102492. https://doi.org/10.1016/j.ijedudev.2021.102492

Rose, J., & Paisley, K. (2012). White privilege in experiential education: A critical reflection. *Leisure Sciences*, 34(2), 136–154. https://doi.org/10.1080/01490400.2012.652505

Rousseau, J.-J. (1912). *Rousseau on education*. E. Arnold.

Roy, M. (2022). Relevance of Plato in modern education and curriculum. *International Journal of Multidisciplinary Educational Research*, 11(2), 38–43.

Rubin, D., & Kazanjian, C. (2011). "Just another brick in the wall": Standardization and the devaluing of education. *Journal of Curriculum and Instruction*, 5(2), 94–108.

Saevi, T. (2014). *Phenomenology in educational research* (pp. 9780199756810–0042) [Dataset]. https://doi.org/10.1093/obo/9780199756810-0042

Sanger, C. S. (2020). Inclusive pedagogy and universal design approaches for diverse learning environments. In *Diversity and inclusion in global higher education: Lessons from across Asia* (pp. 31–71).

Schiavio, A., Nijs, L., Van der Schyff, D., & Juntunen, M.-L. (2023). Community series: Towards a meaningful instrumental music education. Methods, perspectives, and challenges, volume II. *Frontiers in Psychology*, 14, 1303796.

Schutz, M., & Lipscomb, S. (2007). Hearing gestures, seeing music: Vision influences perceived tone duration. *Perception*, 36(6), 888–897.

Sedley, D. (2016). An introduction to Plato's theory of forms. *Royal Institute of Philosophy Supplements*, 78, 3–22.

Şentürk, C. & Baş, G. (2020). An Overview of Learning and Teaching From the Past to the Present: New Learning and Teaching Paradigms in the 21st Century. In Ş. Orakcı (Ed.), *Paradigm Shifts in 21st Century Teaching and Learning* (pp. 1–19). IGI Global Scientific Publishing. https://doi.org/10.4018/978-1-7998-3146-4.ch001

Silverman, M. (2020). Sense-making, meaningfulness, and instrumental music education. *Frontiers in Psychology, 11*, 837.

Smith, D. W. (2022). Phenomenology. In *The stanford encyclopedia of philosophy* (Summer 2018). September 21, 2024, from https://plato.stanford.edu/archives/sum2018/entries/phenomenology.

Smith, F. J. (1979). *The experiencing of musical sound: Prelude to a phenomenology of music.* Gordon and Breach.

Sokolowski, R. (2000). *Introduction to Phenomenology.* Cambridge UK: Cambridge University Press.

Stark, J. (2020). Dewey's theory of experience: A theoretical tool for researching music teacher learning. *Action, Criticism, and Theory for Music Education, 19*(1), 118–152. https://doi.org/10.22176/act19.1.118

Valentine, K. D., Kopcha, T. J., & Vagle, M. D. (2018). Phenomenological methodologies in the field of educational communications and technology. *TechTrends, 62*(5), 462–472. https://doi.org/10.1007/s11528-018-0317-2

Van Zijl, A. G., & Luck, G. (2013). Moved through music: The effect of experienced emotions on performers' movement characteristics. *Psychology of Music, 41*(2), 175–197.

Vass, E. (2018). Musical co-creativity and learning—the fluid body language of receptive-responsive dialogue. *Human Arenas, 1*, 56–78.

White, R. (2021). Authentic learning in senior secondary music pedagogy: An examination of teaching practice in high-achieving school music programmes. *British Journal of Music Education, 38*(2), 160–172. https://doi.org/10.1017/S0265051720000297

Williams, C. F. A. (1903). *The story of notation.* Walter Scott.

Xu, Y., & Liu, Y. (2024). Exploring the impact of music arts education on cognitive development in college students: A qualitative study at HD college in inner Mongolia, China. *Pacific International Journal, 7*(2), 126–130. https://doi.org/10.55014/pij.v7i2.584

Zahavi, D. (2008). Phenomenology. In *The routledge companion to twentieth century philosophy* (pp. 661–692). Routledge.

· 4 ·

TOWARDS RECLAIMING THE PRIMACY OF LIVED EXPERIENCE IN AN ARTIFICIAL INTELLIGENCE-CENTRED WORLD OF TEACHING AND LEARNING IN SOUTH AFRICA

Oscar Koopman & Karen Joy Koopman

Introduction: The Shifting Landscape of Education in the Age of Artificial Intelligence

As children, we grew up in a world vastly different from the one today's children experience. We, the authors of this chapter, vividly remember days filled with early mornings, running around the house, playing in parks, engaging in various sports activities, and meeting friends and family. To keep us occupied, our parents and older siblings encouraged us to develop hobbies, such as caring for a pet or taking up embroidery. For instance, the first author fondly recalls his fascination with pigeons, spending most of his childhood days in his "duiwehok" (pigeon loft), observing their movements and studying their flying patterns. Similarly, the second author proudly displays some of her embroidered cloths in her house, a testament to her childhood passion.

These examples highlight how our bodies were immersed in the physical world, and how our knowledge about these activities was not merely intellectual or cognitive, but rather a manifestation of lived through experiences that unfolded into habits, forming the foundation of meaning and understanding. Drawing on Merleau-Ponty's (1962) philosophy of the body's place in the world, our modes of knowing can be understood as perceiving bodies converging on an ontological exploration that acknowledges the ontological import and transformative capacities of a broad array of mediating actions and activities. These mediating action and activities range from bodily apparatus to artworks and language, and various other symbolic systems. Our subjective experiences and objective existence can be translated to acts of caring, whether in a pigeon loft, developing patience and attention to detail while crafting a skill in embroidery, or experiencing freedom, fun, and joy through unreflective movement. It has its basis in intercorporeality that "highlight the importance of embodied interactions between the self and the other in the process of social understanding" (Thorburn and Stolz, 2020, p. 99). Thus, from Merleau-Ponty we observe how our embodied experiences culminated in perceptions of how to care, how to develop patience, and how to be joyful via our unreflective movement and sense of aliveness, shape our understanding of the world. Thus, our embodied connections to the world open up spaces for rich, dynamic, and multi-dimensional perceptual fields that shape our continually evolving way of being and understanding ourselves and the world around us. In "Eye and Minds" Merleau-Ponty (1993) wrote:

> Visible and mobile, my body is a thing among things; it is one of them. It is caught in the fabric of the world, and its cohesion is that of a thing. But because it moves itself and sees, it holds things in a circle around itself. Things are an annex or prolongation of itself; they are incrusted in its flesh, they are part of its full definition; the world is made of the very stuff of the body. (1993, p. 124–125)

These primordial, first-order ways of knowing, whether it be climbing a tree or building castles in the sand, occurred during a time when the internet and social media did not yet exist in our world. These embodied experiences, among many others, informed the everyday knowledge with which we entered our classrooms and lecture theatres during our schooling and university years when we began our formal training. The continuous technological progress over the last three decades has ushered in a new virtual world or social order, where most children of the modern era, unlike our childhood, find themselves in a technologically textured world where they are not only exposed to the internet but are immersed in a technological ecosystem of advanced web-based applications, and an ever-expanding world of social media platforms. From WhatsApp and Facebook to Twitter, Instagram, and TikTok, the digital world has become an inescapable and concrete part of their lived experience, captivating their attention with an appeal that transcends the boundaries of physical space.

As academics—who are workers of knowledge—who prepare future teachers—future workers of knowledge—we also observe how the technological revolution has now infiltrated the very fabric of teaching and learning. Platforms such as Zoom, Microsoft Teams, and Google Meet, among many others, have become indispensable and pervasive tools for academics, facilitating synchronous and asynchronous teaching through live streaming, recorded lectures, and collaborative discussion forums. Learning management systems (LMS) such as Blackboard, Moodle, and Ikamva have, in some programmes, completely replaced the physical classroom space. These online platforms have emerged as costly teaching and learning environments that enable academics to disseminate course content, foster discussions, and cultivate collaborative teaching strategies that transcend the confines of traditional classrooms. However, the use of these systems can be conceived as a productive replacement for physical space as well as the body's capacity for relationality with both objects and subjects in the world. This lack of relationship or disconnect with students was particularly evident during the Covid-19 pandemic, where the focus was primarily on delivering the curriculum with limited engagement with the "flesh" of the teaching and learning space. Flesh—conceived as the "middle," "medium," or "environment" —is the middle ground between subject and object, the medium through which teacher and student interact, and the environment in which they are situated. In addition to these advancements, the emergence of more recent generative artificial intelligence tools such as ChatGPT, Perplexity, Anthropic, Gemini, Notebook LM, Bing, and Humata, among many others, has further revolutionised the use of technology and access to information. These large language models can answer almost any question across various disciplines, offering unprecedented support at the press of a button from virtually anywhere in the world. To solve mathematical, scientific, or problems in any other discipline at school or university, learners and students no longer require lived-through experience or the strenuous exercise of having to figure out mentally how to perform a calculation or craft an explanation. This development was unimaginable during our childhood, marking a significant shift in how we interact with technology and information today. The point we are trying to make here is not only how the world has changed in such a short period of time but also how teaching and learning have evolved over this brief period. In other words, human existence and modes of being have taken on new forms and structures, which have directly influenced different modes of teaching and learning.

The primary question that arises here, and the main aim of this chapter, is: How do we balance a technologically-driven, AI-centred, super-complex world of teaching and learning with the primacy of lived experience as the essence of teaching and learning? An AI-centred approach risks reducing the educational experience to a series of predetermined, measurable outcomes, potentially overlooking the nuanced, embodied nature of human learning. Drawing on postphenomenological insights, the chapter highlights the importance of students' embodied experiences in the classroom. It proposes a reconceptualisation of the body not as an instrumental technological object, but as a vital component of the learning process. This perspective opens up possibilities for authentic educational experiences where teachers and students coexist within the classroom environment, allowing teaching and learning to unfold as an ontological phenomenon. The chapter concludes by emphasising the importance of balancing technological advancements with human-centred pedagogical approaches. It suggests that by acknowledging the irreplaceable value of lived experiences in the classroom, we can foster a more holistic, engaging, and effective learning environment that honours the complexity of human cognition and interaction as a form of deeper learning. This research contributes to the ongoing dialogue about the role of technology in education, offering a critical perspective on the implications of AI-centred approaches and advocating for a renewed focus on the embodied, experiential aspects of teaching and learning.

The Danger in Marginalising Lived Experience

The continuously expanding role of AI, as argued by various scholars (such as Emeljulu & McGregor, 2016; Harari, 2023; Mitchell, 2019; McQuillan, 2022), has led to its evolution from an object to a subject. As an object, AI was once viewed as a passive tool or instrument with limited human capabilities, primarily used to perform specific tasks. For example, AI had no agency or autonomy. However, as a subject today, we observe how AI exhibits behaviours typically associated with human subjects. Modern AI can (1) make decisions for humans, (2) demonstrate deep learning and adaptive capabilities, and (3) interact with humans in complex and creative ways.

Mitchell (2009) asserts that this evolution occurred due to constant AI research. Over the last few years, we have observed significant strides in new AI tools, such as Notebook LM, due to increased computational power and vast amounts of data, resulting in more advanced learning algorithms. Nilsson (2019) highlights how AI will continue to evolve due to interest from governments and multinational corporations seeking to optimise efficiency and productivity. Governments, in particular, have shaped the future direction and use of AI through "so called" regulatory and ethical frameworks, promoting specific algorithmic architectures. Nilsson (2019) and Suleyman & Bhaskar (2022) suggest that AI will soon be viewed as smarter than its human inventors. These authors further point out that society evolves in concert with every technological leap in AI development. Each advancement in AI technology has led to its glorification, potentially diminishing the value of lived human experience. Governments, corporations, and societies increasingly view AI as the ultimate embodiment of progress. It is from this grandiosity that Mamlok (2024) highlights the glorification of AI, noting that technology is often presented as the solution to nearly every complex problem, including those requiring deep human interaction, such as teaching. This perspective may relegate lived experience to a lower level in teaching and learning while positioning AI as a superior solution to human endeavours. This raises a fundamental question: what are the philosophical dimensions of AI as a subject behind this technological evolution?

AI as Primary Quasi Cyber-Somatic Subject

Connecting these ideological visions of AI to the philosophical, Don Ihde (2002) in "Bodies in Technologies" differentiates between how AI technology as a subject can be viewed from two dimensions. These are the "here-body" and the "image-body." The "here-body", according to Ihde is articulated as a quasi-primary, fully sensory body using sensors and actuators directing and guiding their physical experiences in the world. In contrast, the image-body is referred as to the quasi-other body, alluding to a virtual presents or representations of AI such as images or avatars in digital environments. These descriptions of AI as a subject exhibits a cyber-somatic presence in the real world, compared to the human notions of embodiment. A cyber-somatic presents can be described as a form of quasi-primary virtual embodiment of AI systems, manifesting as a perceived physical presence within digital environments, capable of interacting and engaging in a manner that mimics corporeal existence. A good example of this virtual subjective capabilities of the "here" and "image" bodies of AI is the latest version of Googles Gemini LM, that exhibit a strong cyber-somatic presence, allowing students to interact with it in ways that feel nearly as engaging and responsive as interactions with human teachers, via its conversational podcast. Making students feel that they are part of the discussion.

While CSP attempts to bridge the gap between AI and embodied experience in virtual spaces, it falls short of Merleau-Ponty's profound conception of embodiment. For Merleau-Ponty, the "here-body" is not just primary but fundamental to our being-in-the-world, serving as the very medium through which we perceive and engage with reality through the flesh of the body. This stark contrast highlights the challenge of truly replicating or transferring the richness of human embodied experience to AI systems, raising questions about the limits of virtual presence in educational contexts. Central to this understanding of the "here body" is the concept of transcendental subjectivities, explaining that our being-in-the-world precedes conscious thought and pre-reflective experiences. Thus, the eye and mind reinterpret bodily awareness through an intertwining manifesting in language and speech (Merleau-Ponty, 1962). Embodiment, therefore, is integral to our culture and learning, not a separate activity.

Merleau-Ponty's phenomenology emphasises that our bodies are not mere objects in space but the very medium through which we perceive and interact with the world. This corporeal "here body" is imbued with tacit knowledge, a pre-reflective grasp of our environment that forms the bedrock of our conscious experiences. In contrast, CSP, no matter how sophisticated, remains tethered to algorithmic processes, lacking the rich, sensory-motor engagement that characterises human embodiment. This fundamental disparity limits real learning in several critical ways. First, it impairs the development of intuitive understanding. Learners, through their embodied experiences, develop a "feel" for subjects that transcends explicit knowledge. This intuition, born from countless bodily interactions with the world, allows for creative problem-solving and deep comprehension that AI, confined to its disembodied state, struggles to replicate or foster in learners. Secondly, the absence of true embodiment in AI systems hinders the cultivation of empathy and emotional intelligence in educational settings. Merleau-Ponty's (1962) concept of intercorporeality—the idea that we understand others through our bodily existence—underlies much of human social learning. AI's lack of genuine embodied presence limits its ability to engage in this crucial aspect of education, potentially stunting learners' social-emotional development.

Therefore, as teachers increasingly rely mainly on AI-generated content and predetermined learning outcomes, students may be exposed to a narrower range of perspectives and experiences of complex phenomena in the real world. This Secomandi (2015) argues, could lead to the creation of artificial minds or mindsets in our students. Meaning, an artificial mind has a conceptual or theoretical understanding of the world, and marks a turn to a reductionist form of Tylerism, that view and measure success in learning, primarily by instrumentality rather than the richness and complexity of human experience. This happens because human beings in the West, Lee (2023) underscore, has since the enlightenment era in the 18th century, believed that there is a universal framework to be applied to everyone in understanding who we are and establishing the relationship between ourselves and the world. The framework is understood as going beyond the particularity of a specific person, time, and place. This universality in the academe is now possible via an AI-centred teaching and learning approach. Levinas calls this nudging towards cognitive universality as the promotion of similar thought as "the return to the same" (Levinas, 2016). Within this view the world is regarded as an object of knowledge demanding rational understanding, and this brings with it an ideal of transparency, as if everything could be brought to light and be open to view. Furthermore, with regard to knowledge of human beings, we have also dealt with ourselves as understandable objects. This view by Levinas raises another significant concern, that is, the potential diminishment of the role of teachers in the learning process.

Furthermore, the growing prominence of AI in education can contribute to the deskilling and disenfranchisement of teachers. Instead of utilising their expertise and creativity to design meaningful learning experiences based on their deep understanding of students' interests and needs, teachers may be reduced to a managerial role, merely overseeing the delivery of AI-generated content. This shift can undermine the professional autonomy and agency of teachers, reducing them to "educational technicians" rather than authentic teachers. To mitigate these concerns, it is important to recognise the limitations of AI and to prioritise the value of lived experience in teaching and learning. While AI can be a useful tool in enhancing certain aspects of education, it should not be the central focus. Instead, teachers must strive to create a balance between the use of AI and the incorporation of their own knowledge, experiences, and pedagogical approaches to ensure that students receive a well-rounded inspirited education that values their individuality and fosters their growth as unique, thinking individuals.

This involves creating spaces where students can share and reflect on their lived experiences and where these experiences are valued as legitimate sources of knowledge. Teachers should encourage activities such as storytelling, dialogical argumentation, and experiential learning projects that allow students to connect their personal lives to the subject matter. By embracing diverse forms of knowledge and expression, such as art, music, and embodied practices, teachers can provide alternative ways of understanding and communicating lived experience.

Moreover, the development and use of AI in education should be guided by a commitment to human-centred values and ethics. This means ensuring that AI is used to support and enhance, rather than replace, human interaction, and decision-making. It also involves being transparent about the limitations and potential biases of AI systems and engaging in ongoing critical reflection about their impact on students and society. By prioritising lived experience and recognising the limitations of AI, educators can create a more inclusive, meaningful, and transformative educational landscape that values the full complexity of human knowledge and experience. This approach is particularly crucial in the South African context, where the wounds of apartheid and social injustice still linger, and where the importance of personal and communal narratives cannot be overstated. By giving more credence to lived experience in the classroom, we can foster a deeper understanding of the world and ourselves, empowering students to become active agents in shaping their own lives and the world around them.

Postphenomenology: Examining the Discourse of AI-centred Teaching and Learning

Postphenomenology provides a valuable lens for examining the complex human-technology relationship in teaching and learning. Rosenberg and Verbeek (2015) argue that postphenomenology is not about the "absolute foundations of reality or knowledge" or the "essence" of an object of study, but rather centred on "embodied and situated perspectives" (p. 1). These perspectives, they contend, refer to practical, empirically oriented problems in both phenomenology and pragmatism, hence its focus on case studies of human-technology relations. Theoretically, postphenomenology, introduced by Ihde (1990), is situated in an inter-relational ontology that integrates Husserl's notion of intentionality and Heidegger's mode of "being-in-the-world" into a mediating role in material technologies. Thus, "Human-technology-World" became the formalism expressing this inter-relationality.

Ihde (2015) states, "humans actionally using technologies mediatingly relate to a world" (p. xiii). This became Ihde's "phenomenology of technics," which began with a descriptive analysis of *embodiment, hermeneutic, background* relations, and later *alterity* relations in technology as the primacy of the lifeworld were added (Ihde, 1990). With these four elements (*embodiment, hermeneutic, background, and alterity*), Ihde laid the foundational philosophy for postphenomenology, which Rosenberg and Verbeek (2015) echo, for others to expand upon and develop a better understanding of the epistemic dimensions of individuals trapped in a technology-dominated world. He writes:

> Those working in the school of postphenomenology refine and expand on Ihde's framework, and they apply these ideas to a wide range of philosophical issues, including technological agency, ethics, selfhood, anthropological methodology, politics, philosophy of design, and scientific practice. Just a few of the concrete topics addressed by case studies in this perspective include scientific and medical imaging, computer interface, virtual reality, traffic safety, robotics, educational technologies, sustainable design, wearable computing, and bodily implants. (p. 76)

As AI becomes increasingly integrated into teaching and learning practices, it is important to draw on Ihde's framework to develop a deeper understanding of how these technological developments and advances shape our interpretation of the world (and those of students) and how we mediate our experiences with these large language models such as ChatGPT, Humata, Perplexity, Anthropic, amongst others.

According to Ihde (1990) *embodiment*, is where technology becomes an inseparable part of our bodies and is seamlessly integrated with our sensory experiences. In the context of teaching and learning, this manifests in the use of virtual reality or augmented reality technologies that immerse academics and students in interactive learning environments. These technologies, and its further developments and advances three decades later, which lead to the creation of these modern day artificial intelligence large language models, can enhance understanding of complex concepts by providing them with embodied experiences that closely *mimic real-world scenarios*. Ihde schematises *embodiment* as (human-technology) → world (Mamlok, 2024). Let us put this (human-technology) → world in context. Consider a pilot in a high-fidelity flight simulator. When the pilot first enters the simulator, she is acutely aware of the technology around them—the screens, controls, and the artificial environment. As the pilot spends more time in the simulator, they begin to focus less on the technology itself and more on the simulated flying experience. Eventually, with enough practice, the simulator becomes transparent to the pilot. They no longer consciously think about using a simulator; instead, they feel as if they are directly interacting with the airspace and the aircraft. At this point, Ihde's schema of (human-technology) applies as the (pilot-simulator) become a unified entity. The controls, displays, and even the simulated physical sensations become extensions of the pilot's body and senses. This unified human-technology is directed towards the simulated world. The pilot experiences and interacts with this world as if it is real. The pilot does not think, that she is moving the control in a simulator. Instead, they think, they are physically inside the plane. This is when technology has become embodied in their experience.

Hermeneutic relations, on the other hand, is unique and distinct from *embodiment* relations, as it involve the interpretation and mediation of information or knowledge facilitated by technology Ihde (2012) schematises these relations as human → (technology-world). Firstly, the human is separate from and directed towards (technology-world). The parentheses here indicate that technology and world are coupled or unified in some way. In hermeneutic relations, technology does not become transparent or embodied as in embodiment relations. Instead, it provides a representation of the world that requires interpretation. The technology mediates our experience of the world by providing information that we must read or interpret to understand the world. In the hermeneutic relation our experience of the world is mediated by technology in a way that requires active interpretation. This means the individual is not experiencing the world directly through the technology (as in embodiment relations), but rather reading and interpreting the world as represented by the technology. AI-powered learning analytics platforms exemplify this dimension, as they collect and analyse vast amounts of data to provide insights into learning patterns, strengths, and weaknesses. These systems interpret the data and present it in a meaningful way, enabling academics and students to make data-driven decisions and personalise teaching and learning to meet individual student needs.

Alterity expands on this by describing the interaction between humans and technologies that mimic or simulate human-like qualities. Idhe schematises alterity relations as I → technology (-world). The "I" (representing the human) is directed towards or interacting with something (technology). The technology is the direct object of the person's attention or interaction (-world). The world in parentheses, indicates it's in the background or context of this interaction. In *alterity* relations, the technology is experienced as a quasi-other or as having a kind of "otherness." The human interacts with the technology as an object in itself, rather than as a transparent tool (as in embodiment relations) or as a representation to be interpreted (as in hermeneutic relations). In teaching, this can be seen in the use of AI-powered chatbots that engage with students in natural language conversations, providing a more personalised and interactive learning experience.

Background, the last of the four relation in Idhe's framework refers to the presence of technological devices that operate in the background, shaping our experiences without being actively engaged with the tool or device. Ihde (2012) schematises these relations as I → technology (world-). The "I" (representing the person) is directed towards or engaged with something. Although the technology is present it is not the direct focus of attention to the teacher or the student. The world [expressed as (world-)] in parentheses with the technology, with the hyphen after "world" indicates that the world is the primary focus or context. In background relations, technology shapes our experience of the world but does so from the background, often without our direct conscious awareness. The technology is present and influential, but it's not the focus of our attention, nor is it something we directly interpret or interact with. The LMS and other educational platforms that handle administrative tasks, such as grading and attendance tracking, fall under this category. These systems automate routine processes, allowing academics and teachers to focus on more meaningful aspects of teaching and learning. However, it is crucial to ensure that these background technologies do not dominate the entire learning experience and that academics retain the autonomy to make pedagogical decisions based on their professional judgment.

By applying Ihde's postphenomenological framework to the integration of AI in education, we can gain a more nuanced understanding of how these technologies shape our lived experiences and mediate our interactions with the world. It is essential to critically examine the implications of these technological advancements and ensure that they are used in a manner that enhances, rather than diminishes, the quality of teaching and learning. However, each of these elements underscores an *object-centred pedagogy of learning,* which is inconsistent with Oakeshott's (1989) understanding of the university as an autonomous intellectual space for deep personal growth and development of the student.

The overreliance on AI can lead to the modularisation of the curriculum into isolated *silos of learning,* where students become customers or consumers who purchase access to knowledge without understanding, as digital pools, such as AI-driven large language models like ChatGPT and Anthropic, become potential sources for assessment answers. Instead of the student becoming a co-constructor of knowledge who co-dwells with the lecturer in the classroom, as underpinned by the constructivist student-centred teaching and learning philosophy, we observe what Scott (1993) refers to as the objectification of the student as a customer. Therefore, it is important to recognise the limitations of these AI-driven systems and ensure that they do not replace the value of human interaction and empathy in the learning process.

While postphenomenology offers a valuable framework for understanding human-technology relations in education, it also highlights the hidden limitations and potential drawbacks of an AI-driven approach that prioritises rationality over lived experience. As Feenberg (2020) argues, postphenomenology often overlooks the socio-political dimensions in the construction of technology. In the context of the classroom, this means that AI-driven approaches may perpetuate existing inequalities and power structures, as they are designed and implemented by those in positions of power, driving a neoliberal-political agenda. The growing reliance on AI driven by governments and multinational corporations can be seen as an example of the constant nudging towards alterity relations, where technology is treated as a quasi-other, mimicking human interaction and decision-making processes. While AI-driven systems may offer certain benefits, such as personalised learning experiences and efficient data analysis, they also risk marginalising the importance of human lived experience and the role of subjective, contextual knowledge in the learning process. An overemphasis on rationality and AI in education can lead to a reductionist view of learning, with strong leanings towards Tylerism, where students are treated as mere data points and their success is measured by quantifiable metrics. This approach fails to account for the richness and complexity of human experience, which is essential for fostering empathy, critical thinking, and a deeper understanding of the world. To counteract these limitations, educators must adopt a more critical and reflexive approach to the integration of AI in teaching and learning. This involves recognising the value of lived experience and embodied knowledge, fostering dialogic and collaborative learning environments, and ensuring that AI technologies are used in a manner that supports, rather than replaces, human interaction and empathy. By striking a balance between the benefits of AI and the importance of human experience, teachers can create a more inclusive, meaningful, and transformative educational landscape that values the full complexity of human knowledge and understanding. By embracing a phenomenological approach, one that prioritises lived experience and recognises the socio-political dimensions of technology, we can create a more inclusive, meaningful, and transformative educational landscape. This approach is particularly crucial in the South African context, where the legacy of apartheid and social injustice demands a deep understanding of personal and communal narratives in order to foster genuine social transformation and healing.

The Importance of Lived Experience in the South African Classroom

The concept of lived experience is fundamental to phenomenological inquiry, particularly in the South African context, where people have endured the profound impacts of colonialism and apartheid for over 350 years. These experiences have shaped the collective consciousness and individual realities of South Africans, creating a unique milieu that affects and is affected by the people within it. As Deleuze & Guattari (1987) argue—although they are not referring to the South African context—experience is not rendered meaningful by grounding empirical particulars in abstract universals, but rather through active experimentation on ourselves, which is especially relevant in a nation that has undergone such significant upheaval and transformation. But let us first concretise and contextualise what we mean with the "profound impact of colonialism and apartheid for over 350 years", and its direct relation to the current educational space.

At the time of writing this chapter, South Africa is described as the most unequal society globally, both by income and wealth, with unemployment at a record high and these socio-economic maladies disproportionately affecting the majority of the population. Koopman & Koopman (2024) report that 55% (30.4 million people) of South Africans live in abject poverty, with 61% of poor households relying on the child support grant, currently R500 per month per child, which changes annually, making it difficult for grant-reliant South Africans to make ends meet. To illustrate these statistics, let's closely examine the experiences of Sipho during a typical day, as his experiences resonate with those of millions like him.

Sipho lives and attends school in an informal settlement township community, where dwellings, known as shacks, are built in close proximity, forming severely congested settlements often associated with serious health and social problems due to rapid urbanisation and large-scale migration to cities in search of better economic opportunities. His mother, a domestic worker, leaves home early to travel to her job, while his father works as a labourer on a construction site. By the time Sipho wakes up, his parents already left home, leaving the responsibility to him to care for his younger siblings, ensuring they eat and safely arrive at school before making his own way, often arriving late and missing work due to his responsibilities. Lacking access to a cell phone, MacBook, iPad, or any affordable technological tools and Wi-Fi, Sipho's school is ill-equipped with the technological tools and infrastructure needed to align with the government's AI-centred approach to teaching and learning. Moreover, Sipho struggles with reading and writing due to his parents' lack of education.

Sipho does not fit the student profile for which the South African Curriculum and Assessment Policy Statement (Knowledge Promotion) is streamlined, nor is he a learning-willing student. Academically weak, his results in most subjects are low compared to students in affluent neighbourhoods. Sipho shows little interest in anything but football, his only visible ambition being to perfect his skills to minimise his school day. He avoids learning situations and, despite receiving academic support through a special education programme, manages to hide from learning and escape prescribed tasks. Sipho never completes homework, lacking access to a well-resourced library or necessary technological tools to connect to the internet. His teacher, feeling overwhelmed by the many students facing similar challenges, sometimes turns a blind eye to Sipho's struggles, rendering him invisible but providing him with a brief respite from pressure. This snapshot captures the lived experiences of Sipho and many other learners like him.

The lived experiences of the masses in South Africa are deeply intertwined with the social, cultural, political, economic, and historical conditions that have defined the country's past and continue to influence its present (Koopman & Koopman, 2024). These experiences are not merely properties of individuals, but are part of a collective and contextual phenomenon that constitutes subjects through their relations within the experience itself. This is particularly evident in the lives of South Africans, whose actions, thoughts, and behaviours are often prompted by the unique demands and appeals of the objects and phenomena around them, shaped by the legacy of the country's complex history (Koopman & Koopman, 2024). It is in such complex situations that Deleuze (1995) notes, experience is qualitative, multidimensional, and inclusive, encompassing a wide range of phenomena. The English word "experience" finds its roots in the Latin "experientia," denoting "trial, proof, and experiment." However, the German word *Erlebnis*, which inherently embodies the concept of "living" or "life," more aptly captures the essence of "living through" something. Therefore, Husserl (1970) proclaimed, "All knowledge as a form of awareness begins in experience, but it does not arise from experience" (p. 109), underscoring that awareness itself is a form of experience. Thus, the South African lived body represents a dynamic relationality between human spontaneity and receptivity, where the world itself is not merely a passive canvas for human whims, but an active, primordial force that serves as the bedrock for all human knowledge, development and becoming. Waldenfels (1999, p. 233) eloquently states, "Man is also dependent on a world beyond himself," a sentiment that resonates with the experiences of all living beings. This notion is particularly evident in the lives of children, whose actions and explorations are often prompted by the appeal of objects and phenomena around them. For example, watching a colourful butterfly flitting through the garden, a stack of building blocks inviting them to construct and create. The character of these "demands" corresponds to the inherent nature of the objects themselves, revealing their true meaning within the context of the situation. While experienced as lived might be raw and unstructured, it is through reflection that a deeper connection and understanding of phenomena emerges, weaving knowledge, feeling, and perception into a cohesive embodied awareness of the world. The living and breathing body is regarded as the fundamental axis around which all orientations and movements originate (Hua IV, p. 158). Thinkers like Husserl (1970) and Merleau-Ponty (1962/2005) have embraced the notion of "lived experience" as a means to explore the consciousness and actions that define human existence directly.

From this perspective, Deleuze (2000) argues experience is always already public, constituted by the relations between different schemes or systems of meaning. To make sense of our experiences, we must understand these relations in practice, rather than seeking to subsume them under abstract, universal principles. As experiences unfold in the fluid continuum of time and space, the body-mind initially processes them as raw, imperceptive phenomena. However, through the act of reflection, our sensory faculties begin to interpret and ascribe meaning to these phenomena. Therefore, Van Manen asserts that the ultimate goal of phenomenology is to transform lived experience into visceral, embodied encounters into a textual expression that captures their essence. For instance, when one encounters a car or a tree, it is at this juncture that the subjective "I" begins to establish a connection with the objects of experience. This connection occurs through the interconnection of three fundamental elements, namely, knowing, feeling, and perceiving, which together culminate in an embodied awareness of the world. In essence, experience and awareness are deeply connected, resulting in a synthesis where thoughts, emotions, sensations, and perceptions intertwine like motifs in the andante movement of a symphony.

Therefore, seeing that phenomenology is an experience-oriented philosophy (Husserl, 1967), its main aim is to understand the nature of a person's awareness. By peeling away the layers that obscure the deeper meanings within consciousness which provide valuable insights into the motivations, thoughts, and behaviours of learners this understanding is essential for creating educational experiences that are responsive to the unique needs and challenges of the South African context, rather than relying solely on the abstract universals generated by artificial intelligence models. Ultimately, while large language models and other AI technologies can be useful tools in education, they must not be allowed to dominate the teaching and learning process in South Africa given the richness of the historicity of its people. Instead, teachers must prioritise the lived experiences of their students, engaging with the social, cultural, political, economic, and historical conditions that have shaped their realities. By doing so, they can create educational experiences that are truly transformative, empowering students to understand and engage with the world around them in meaningful ways.

Towards Reclaiming the Primacy of Lived Experience

In this section, I want to return to our embodied experiences as children to highlight how our bodies can be conceived as non-instrumental technological objects. As children, when we spent our days watching our pigeons or doing embroidery, our bodies were not merely passive observers but active participants in the development of meaning and understanding. Through our embodied interactions with the world, we developed habits, skills, and ways of being that shaped our perceptions and relationships in a non-screen way/world that were stable and consistent.

However, one of the drawbacks of technology, as Ihde (2012) points out, is its multistability, which is characterised by variational methods that often lead to various understandings of the same phenomena and therefore lacks consistency. Multistability, Secomandi (2015) explains, refers to the idea that technologies can be interpreted and used in multiple ways, depending on the context and the user's perspective. For example, a smartphone can be used for communication, entertainment, or productivity, each of which involves different bodily comportments and habits. When individuals are submerged in technology and experience a breakdown, it makes the user aware of "her embodied interaction with the keyboard, mouse, screen icons … users may also adopt a different relational strategy towards slowly loading webpages, implicating a different set of bodily comportments and habits that are more adequate for the situation" (Secomandi, 2015, p. 117). This breakdown becomes a way of disciplining the body as a way of adapting to the challenges posed by AI. For instance, when AI-powered language models provide false information, it creates suspicion and self-doubt in the user, leading them to adopt a more critical and cautious approach to engaging with the technology.

In contrast, our childhood experiences relied on sight, touch, feelings, gestures, communication, and so forth, making our perceptions non-instrumental. When things broke down, like hurting a finger while doing embroidery or creating skew lines, we developed a deeper understanding by becoming more skilful as we learned from our failures, as opposed to experiencing multistability and adopting variational methods based on relational strategies. Merleau-Ponty's (1962) concept of flesh applies here, as it emphasises the ontological significance of this mediation, suggesting that it is not a connection between pre-existing entities but rather a generative and formative process that interrelates and constitutes the very nature of our existence. Thus, our childhood experiences with pigeons and embroidery were not simply encounters with external objects but transformative moments in which our being and the world were mutually shaped and defined through the mediation of our flesh. In other words, our bodies, as an expansive and expressive dynamic of flesh, do not stop at embodied perception but extend into and comprise intellectual life (Saint Aubert, 2008). This expansive and dynamic notion of flesh presents a very different notion of mediation, not in its representational sense, where the medium is conceived as a vehicle for a pre-given meaning. The point we want to make here is how the body mediates our experiences by filtering, interpreting, and translating sensory information, as well as by enabling or limiting our actions and interactions. This mediation extends to our relationships with other people, as our bodies influence how we communicate, empathise, and form social bonds. In this sense, our lived experiences are not just subjective impressions but technological artifacts that mediate our existence and give form to our relationships with others and the world around us.

Bringing this discussion closer to teaching and learning the pedagogical focus for teachers should be on engaging with students' experiences and reflections, and understanding holistically how students are progressing and interacting with their learning environments. This means that something greater than passive instrumental engagement with subject disciplines occurs, and teachers must take steps to engage with these enhanced expectations of their practice. To achieve this, it is crucial to prioritise lived experience as the primary focus while relegating AI to a lower level. This approach allows for a more authentic and meaningful educational experience that recognises the complexity and richness of human interaction and understanding. Thorburn & Stolz (2020) argue that, in philosophical terms, these types of developments highlight the nature of intersubjective and intercorporeal experiences necessary in educational contexts.

In the same vein, Seaman (2008) argues that the constructivist-informed sequential or cyclical approaches to experiential learning, which are based on the assumed coherence between experience, reflection, and learning, can oversimplify the highly interactive and bodily qualities of experiences. By reducing these qualities to secondary elements in an individual's learning experience, we risk adopting an ideology of experiential learning rather than a true philosophy or theory. Moreover, the selective use of educational theory by proponents of experiential learning has led to the conflation and underrepresentation of two opposing ideas: the championing of the autonomous learner and the collective benefits of shared educational experiences. This inconsistency highlights the need for a more nuanced and comprehensive approach to teaching and learning that recognises the importance of both individual and collective experiences.

By returning to lived experience as the main form of teaching and learning, we can foster a deeper understanding of the world and ourselves. This approach acknowledges the inherent complexity and subjectivity of human experience, allowing students to engage with their surroundings and each other in a more meaningful way (Koopman and Koopman, 2018; Mamlok, 2024). Through direct interaction with the world and others, students can develop critical thinking skills, empathy, and a sense of social responsibility that extends beyond the confines of the classroom. While AI can be a valuable tool in education, it should not be the central focus. Instead, AI should be used to support and enhance the learning experience, providing students with access to information and resources that can enrich their understanding of the world. However, it is essential to recognise the limitations of AI, particularly in terms of its ability to capture the nuances and complexities of human experience. By relegating AI to a lower level and prioritising lived experience, we can create a more holistic and engaging educational environment that fosters personal growth, critical social awareness, and a deep appreciation for the richness and diversity of the human experience. This approach recognises the importance of both individual and collective experiences, allowing students to develop a sense of autonomy while also benefiting from the shared insights and perspectives of their peers. Ultimately, by emphasising lived experience as the primary focus of teaching and learning, educators can cultivate a more authentic, meaningful, and transformative educational landscape that prepares students for the complexities of the world beyond the classroom.

In closing, as we navigate the ever-evolving landscape of education in the age of AI, it is critical to remain grounded in the fundamental importance of lived experience. By embracing a phenomenological approach that values subjective, contextual knowledge and fosters genuine human connection, we can create an educational environment that truly serves the needs of students, particularly in the South African context. In doing so, we not only prepare them for the challenges of the future but also empower them to become active agents in shaping their own lives and the world around them.

References

Deleuze, G. (1995). *Negotiations, 1972–1990*. Columbia University Press.

Deleuze, G., & Guattari, F. (1987). *A thousand plateaus: Capitalism and schizophrenia*. University of Minnesota Press.

Deleuze, G. (2000). *Proust and signs: The complete text* (R. Howard, Trans.). *Theory out of Bounds* (Vol. 17). Minneapolis: University of Minneapolis Press.

Emejulu, A., & McGregor, C. (2016). Towards a radical digital citizenship in digital education. Critical Studies in Education, 60(2), 131-147.

Feenberg, A. (2020). Postphenomenology and critical theory of technology. In *Postphenomenology and media: Essays on human-media-world relations* (pp. 85–99).

Harari, Y. N. (2023). *Nexus: A brief history of information networks from the Stone Age to AI*. New York, NY: HarperCollins.

Husserl, E. (1967). *Ideas: General introduction to pure phenomenology*. Collier Books.

Husserl, E. (1970). *The crisis of European sciences and transcendental phenomenology: An introduction to phenomenological philosophy*. Northwestern University Press.

Ihde, D. (1990). *Postphenomenology: Essays in the postmodern context*. Northwestern University Press.

Ihde, D. (2002). *Bodies in technology*. Minneapolis: University of Minnesota Press.

Ihde, D. (2009). *Postphenomenology and technoscience: The Peking University lectures*. SUNY Press.

Ihde, D. (2012). *Experimental phenomenology: Multistabilities* (2nd ed.). Albany: State University of New York Press.

Ihde, D. (2015). Positioning postphenomenology. In R. Rosenberger & P. Verbreek (Eds.), *Postphenomenological investigations: Essays on human-technology relations*. New York: Lexington Books.

Koopmnan, O. (2018). *Science education and pedagogy in South Africa*. New York: Peter Lang

Koopman, O., & Koopman, K. (2018). The body as blind spot: Towards lived experience and a body-specific pedagogy. *South African Journal of Education*, 38(1), 1–9.

Koopman, O., & Koopman, K. (2024). Towards a phenomenology of the broken [South] African body as a site for education research. *Journal of Education*, 94, 127–145.

Levinas, E. (2016). *Totality and infinity: An essay on exteriority*. Pennsylvania: Duquesne University Press.

Lee, K. (2023). Becoming Humanist: Worldview Formation and the Emergence of Non-Belief in Britain. Sociology of Religion, 85(4), 454–472.

Mamlok, D. (2024). Landscapes of sociotechnical imaginaries in education: A theoretical examination of integrating artificial intelligence in education. *Foundations of Science*, 1–12

McQuillan, D. (2022). *Resisting AI: An anti-fascist approach to artificial intelligence*. Bristol, UK: Bristol University Press.

Merleau-Ponty, M. (1962/2005). *Phenomenology of perception*. New York: Routledge.

Merleau-Ponty, M. (1993/1961]. Eye and mind. In G. A. Johnson (Ed.), *The Merleau-Ponty aesthetics reader: Philosophy and painting* (pp. 121–149). Evanston, IL: Northwestern University Press.

Mitchelle, M. (2019). *Artificial intelligence: A guide for thinking humans*. NY: Fararr, Strauss and Giroux.

Mohamed, S., Png, M., & Issacs, W. (2020). Decolonial AI: Theory of socio-technical foresight in artificial intelligence. *Philosophy of Technology*, 33, 659–684.

Nilsson, N. J. (2019). *The quest for artificial intelligence: A history of ideas and achievements*. Cambridge University Press.

Oakeshott's, M. (1989). The idea of the university. In T. Fuller (Ed.), *The voice of liberal learning: Michael Oakeshott on education*. London: Yale University Press.

Rosenberg, R., & Verbreek, P. (2015). Introduction. In R. Rosenberger & P. Verbreek (Eds.), *Postphenomenological investigations: Essays on human-technology relations*. New York: Lexington Books.

Saint Aubert, E. de. (2008). From consciousness and behaviour to perceptive consciousness: Critiques and issues. Revue Internationale de Philosophie, 62(2), 127–147.

Scott, P. (1993). The idea of the university in the 21st century: A British perspective. *British Journal of Educational Studies*, 41(1), 4–25.

Seaman, J. (2008). Experience, reflect, critique: The end of the "learning cycles" era. *Journal of Experiential Education*, 31(1), 3–18.

Secomandi, F. (2015). Bodies as technology: How can postphenomenologists deal with the matter of human technique. In R. Rosenberger & P. Verbreek. *Postphenomenological investigations: Essays on human-technology relations*. New York: Lexington Books.

Suleyman, M., & Bhaskar, R. (2022). *The coming wave: Technology, power and the 21 century greatest dilemma.* New York: Crown Publishing Group

Thorburn, M., & Stolz, S. A. (2020). Embodied learning and school-based physical culture: Implications for professionalism and practice in physical education. *Sport, Education and Society, 25*(7), 721–733.

Waldenfels, B. (2011). The Phenomenology of the Alien. Northwestern University Press.

· 5 ·

CRITICAL PHENOMENOLOGICAL PERSPECTIVES OF REFLECTIVE ENTREPRENEURIAL LEARNING THROUGH MINI-ENTERPRISE PROJECTS

Gosaitse E. Solomon & Suriamurthee M. Maistry

Introduction

Mini companies are used globally to introduce and teach learners of different ages about entrepreneurship. In some cases, they are part of student organisations that augment classroom teaching (as in the mould of Junior Achievement-Young Enterprise) or as part of the examined public school curriculum. The latter is a common approach in Botswana's Junior Secondary School curriculum, where mini-enterprise projects form part of the examinable aspects of Business Studies (Sithole, 2010). Although there have been calls to teach entrepreneurs through approaches that closely simulate the entrepreneurial journey in how entrepreneurs learn, think and act (Jones & English, 2004; Mitchell et al., 2007), the learning process in this type of experience-based projects has not been thoroughly investigated. Coinciding with this call is the urgency to develop reflective entrepreneurs who can learn from their experiences (Cope, 2003; Higgins et al., 2013; Hunter Lindqvist, 2017; Kassean et al., 2015; Pepin, 2012; Pittaway & Cope, 2007; Yeoh, 2017). Despite this call, Hägg & Kurczewska (2016) decry the uncertainty regarding the effective implementation of reflection and justify its importance from a theoretical standpoint. They further lament its low incorporation into teaching and learning, and entrepreneurship education still struggles with teaching learners how to reflect and operationalise it in experience-based entrepreneurial activities.

Entrepreneurship is founded on a process world ontology that can be described as fluid and dynamic events in an unstable environment characterised by uncertainty, chaos, instability, ambiguity, discontinuities, risks, loss and success (Hjorth et al., 2015; Selden & Fletcher 2020). Therefore, entrepreneurial learning involves the whole person in the experience, dynamically affecting corporeality, cognition, affection, and temporality in social contexts. This is because to simulate the authentic and real-world of entrepreneurs, entrepreneurial activities are designed to possess certain factors that are believed to influence entrepreneurial learning such as being experience-based, hands-on, action-oriented, and learning by doing (Arpiainen et al., 2013; Pittaway et al., 2011); involving ambiguity and uncertainty from wicked or ill-structured, complex, and vaguely understood problems (Higgins et al., 2013); personal emotional exposure or risk from critical incidents (Arpiainen et al., 2013; Cope, 2003; Cope & Watts, 2000; Pittaway & Thorpe, 2012); mistakes, crisis, failures, interaction with the real world, social interactions, and context dimensions that require problem-solving through collective reflective dialogue and action (Arpiainen et al., 2013; Pittaway & Cope, 2007; Pittaway et al., 2011).

The main research question guiding this study is: how do learners experience entrepreneurial and reflective learning in mini-enterprise projects? Considering the chaotic, ambiguous, and crisis-laden nature of the entrepreneurial process (Selden & Fletcher), this study deliberately takes a critical stance to examine learners' lived experiences in the mini enterprise project as they engage in reflective learning. Therefore, the issues of embodiment, affectivity, intersubjectivity and group dynamics become of interest to understand how learners cope with critical incidents while pursuing reflective entrepreneurial learning. It helps us with a vested interest in entrepreneurial education understand what works about certain pedagogical approaches and why it works in learners' entrepreneurial knowledge, skills and attitudes development. Critical phenomenological perspectives are important, especially for a field whose growth is driven mainly through policy rather than scientific research (Ellborg, 2023), to critically explore the taken-for-granted experiences of learners in this pedagogical vehicle. Therefore, this study aims to examine learners' taken-for-granted reflective learning experiences and also find out why reflection remains elusive in entrepreneurial activities such as the mini-enterprise experience.

Literature Review

Recent research in entrepreneurship education has shifted towards more subjective entrepreneurial learning experiences. This follows the evolution of entrepreneurship impact studies from thought-based studies to action-based studies and, more recently, to emotion-based approaches (Lackéus, 2014; Lackéus & Sävetun, 2019). The emotion-based approach to researching entrepreneurship are of interest to the current study. This approach builds on the desire of entrepreneurship researchers and educators to understand how entrepreneurship knowledge is developed. It is predicated on the assumption that emotional events or critical incidents explain how entrepreneurial knowledge and skills are developed from entrepreneurial activities (Lackéus, 2019; Lackéus & Sävetun, 2019). Thus, emotion-based studies have tended to lean more towards qualitative approaches and sometimes mixed methods to research subjective experiences of entrepreneurs and students of entrepreneurship in higher education and secondary education (Lackéus, 2014; Lackéus & Sävetun, 2019; Pittaway et al., 2011). Jason Cope is among the pioneers of researching entrepreneurial learning from practising entrepreneurs using phenomenology (Cope, 2003; Cope & Watts, 2000; Pittaway & Thorpe, 2012). Related studies were undertaken in higher education, researching the link between emotional exposures and entrepreneurial competencies (Lackéus, 2014), sources of emotions (Arpiainen et al., 2013), development of reflective learning through making mistakes and solving problems (Pittaway et al., 2011; Pittaway et al., 2015). Following the same trend, Lackéus and Sävetun (2019) extended this research to secondary education. Their findings emphasised the value of peer collaboration, interaction with stakeholders outside the school, feedback from different stakeholders and a sense of ownership to have a crucial role in entrepreneurial learning. Although many of these studies helped develop our understanding of entrepreneurial learning, they mostly used a general qualitative approach, neglecting phenomenology, which has the potential to gain access to understanding subjective human experiences (Hägg & Kurczewska, 2021) from a holistic and critical perspective to understanding entrepreneurial learning experiences.

Hermeneutic Phenomenological Theoretical Inspirations

Following a recommendation by Larsen & Adu (2021), the theoretical framework of this study was developed following a scoping review of the literature, which sought to answer the question: "What theories could potentially explain how students experience entrepreneurial learning in experience-based contexts that emphasise reflective learning and meaning or sense-making of experiences?" This process led to settling on a pragmatism-oriented hermeneutic phenomenology theoretical framework described below. Although a phenomenological study should be grounded on the theory of phenomenology, Peoples (2021) submits that under certain circumstances, another theory outside of phenomenology may be added, especially if it enhances phenomenology in investigating the phenomenon of interest. In this instance, given that entrepreneurial experiences, a pragmatic project of learning was the focus of interest, Dewey's pragmatism and the potency of Hermeneutic phenomenology was harnessed to explore the multiple and contingent nature of the historical, cultural, and social context that affected the participants' experiences.

Heideggerian phenomenological inspiration was important in this study because it helps describe how an individual who is deeply engaged in the flow of events with objects masterfully and unconsciously copes with objects in the lived world (Koopman & Koopman, 2020). *Dasein* or being in the world far transcends physical location in the world, but what it "means to be embedded in it within a complex web of relations, to be familiar with it, and to be open to it in a way that matters to us" (Elpidorou & Freeman, 2015, p. 662). Koopman & Koopman (2020) further expand their thought, arguing that *Dasein* is not necessarily only concerned about how people think or believe but that their thoughts manifest in their actions. Epistemologically, Heideggerian phenomenology focuses on the hermeneutic interpretation and understanding people draw from everyday experiences they encounter through their "acting" in the lived world. This was particularly salient for this study as we undertook to interpret the profound significance of participants' entrepreneurial learning experiences.

Merleau-Ponty's emphasis on the embodied nature of our interaction with the world and how that interaction shapes our context-bound view of the world offers a germane conceptual heuristic for the study of embodied entrepreneurial experiences—experiences that are premised on the inseparability of the entrepreneurial mind and body. Bodily perceptions in this perspective become a means through which mental processes trigger the capability of consciousness to reveal representations of the world (Larsen & Adu, 2021). Merleau-Ponty's phenomenology thus helps to interrogate and illuminate the value of embodied interactions between an individual and others in the learning process. Merleau-Ponty viewed learning as a sedimentation process (Magrì & McQueen, 2022) in which the body accumulates layers of past experiences together with their unique characteristics and associated feelings and emotions, which are re-activated in similar current situations and serve as a latent background for making sense of emergent experiences. In essence, the entrepreneurial experiences under study happen through what Merleau-Ponty describes as the lived body.

Although Merleau-Ponty's philosophy helped investigate embodied experiences, it seemed to fall short of fully understanding reflective learning because it primarily focuses on the habit formation of body schema without reflection on experience. He believed that reflection had the potential to modify thoughts or perceptions, thereby distorting their conception of the world (Koopman & Koopman, 2020). For this reason, Dewey's soft pragmatism became a viable option to augment phenomenology. This is because Dewey's philosophy emphasises the embodied nature of cognition and perceives learning as a transactive interaction between an acting agent and their continuously changing environment in which they reflect on their experiences and make adaptive changes through action (Biesta & Burbules, 2003; Kyrö, 2008). This process-world ontology and epistemology dovetails with the fluidity and constantly changing nature of entrepreneurship as practiced in terms of its unstable environment characterised by uncertainty, chaos, instability, ambiguity, discontinuities, risks, loss and success (Hjorth et al., 2015; Selden & Fletcher, 2020). Reflection on experience allows learners to revisit, challenge and revise their current knowledge claims when faced with problematic situations and insights developed thereby are integrated into their repertoire of habits of action to solve future problems (Pepin, 2012; Hägg & Kurczewska, 2021) in experience-based activities such as the mini enterprise project.

Overall, phenomenological research makes it possible investigate "the impact of conditions of existence" and the "enabling conditions" lay bare how the environment within which learners operate shapes their thinking and perspectives (Koopman & Koopman, 2020). In an era where entrepreneurship is driven by a global proliferation of neoliberal educational policies and not empirical data (Ellborg, 2023; Komulainen et al., 2013) and oversold appearing almost as propaganda in textbooks of secondary school learners (Maistry & David, 2017), hermeneutic phenomenology allows for these embodied experiences and "conditions of existence" to disrupt and question narratives and things are assumed to be true without critical examination (Moules et al., 2014).

Method

This qualitative study adopted a hermeneutic phenomenological methodology because it resonated with the aim of this study, which is to investigate students' subjective experiences of reflective learning in experience-based platforms of the mini enterprise project. This study contributes to a growing body of research in entrepreneurship education that is seeing value in a qualitative approach, especially in studying the process of entrepreneurial learning (Cope, 2003; Hägg & Kurczewska, 2021; Kyrö, 2008). This is a stark contrast with positivist approaches that dominated early entrepreneurship research, which focused studying mostly on identifying psychological traits presumed entrepreneurial and measuring the impact of entrepreneurship programmes of entrepreneurial intentions, attitudes and self-efficacy beliefs (do Paço et al., 2015; Kassean et al., 2015; Oosterbeek et al., 2010; Testa & Frascheri, 2015). Apart from churning out mixed findings (Kassean et al., 2015), they could not tell what works about entrepreneurship programmes, how it work and why it works (Maritz & Brown, 2013; Politis, 2008). Thus they contributed very little to our understanding of entrepreneurial learning and how best to facilitate it (Maritz & Brown, 2013).

On the contrary, hermeneutic phenomenology has the potential to delve into the subjective experiences of learners, either as individuals or groups in a given environment through their stories (Kafle, 2013). Therefore, it is appropriate for researching collaborative learning that happens in the mini enterprise experience. As a philosophy of the embodied consciousness operating from the assumption that people's relations to objects and other things are always mediated by the body's sensory capacities (Larsen & Adu, 2021), it is best positioned to help unearth rich descriptions of learners' the embodied, enactive, affective, cognitive experiences as embedded in the contexts within which the mini enterprise experience is situated. By uncovering the meanings and interpretations of their lived experiences (Dibley et al., 2020, p. 19) with reflective learning, critical insights were garnered in the process of entrepreneurial learning in the mini enterprise experience.

Sample and Sampling Strategies

The study participants were thirteen former students of Business Studies who had participated in mini enterprise projects over the past five years. This consisted of nine males and four females, whose ages ranged between 19 and 22 years old. Past students were selected because data was generated during the Covid 19 pandemic in the year 2022, and the health protocols such as social distancing and risks of infection and spreading of the virus were high because the mini enterprise projects are collaborative, and students often prepare and sell food items. Purposive sampling was used to select potentially "information rich" (Creswell, 2012, p. 206) participants due to their mini-enterprise experience and willingness to participate in the study. Snowball sampling was used to identify and recruit these type of participants through other respondents' referrals to their former classmates whom they worked with or participated in the mini enterprise projects at the same school around the same time. The sample size is appropriate since a hermeneutic phenomenological study does not aim at the generalisability of results, which would have required fulfilling the criterion of representativeness. Our interest was in obtaining a detailed description and interpretation of the findings (Dibley et al., 2020; Hommel et al., 2023).

Data Generation

Students were contacted through referrals from their peers and contacted through a cell phone call, where they would be asked to participate in the study. After the initial contact, an appointment was made with each participant where they were formally introduced to the study and made aware of their rights and obligations, including the freedom to quit the study if they felt the need to discontinue for any reason. After that, they were given the opportunity to sign informed consent forms. Data was collected through online interviews, lasting about an hour each, through the Zoom platform. Before the interview, participants were reminded of their rights again and assured anonymity and truthfulness in the reporting of the data. The interview was conducted in a conversational style whereby the interviewer asked short questions and allowed the interviewee to be as detailed as possible in their answer. They were also allowed to code-switch languages between Setswana and English to their comfort. This, together with the aforementioned conditions ensured that interviewees spoke more comfortably and freely. The interviewer would ask questions of clarity and confirmation so that the participants' thoughts were captured correctly and accurately.

Data Analysis

Data was analysed manually according to emerging themes using Creswell & Poth's (2018) data analysis spiral, augmented with insights from the hermeneutic phenomenological research literature (Beck, 2023; Dibley et al., 2020; Love et al., 2020; Smith et al., 2009). This process involved immersion into the data through organising and reading transcripts. Following data the data generation process, the audio recordings were transcribed and cleaned to remove mistakes and portions of the transcription where respondents used Setswana were translated to English for consistency and ease of analysis. Also, each respondent was assigned a code to ensure anonymity. Secondly, reading and coding emerging ideas followed. To develop familiarity with the data significant lived experiences and relationships of phenomenological relevance to respondents were noted and coded in subcategories of themes (Love et al., 2020). Thirdly, codes were described and classified into themes using a deductive process guided by aspects developed through literature review and theoretical and conceptual framework. In the fourth major step, interpretations were developed through fragmentation and reorganisation of data (Beck, 2023). Employing the hermeneutic circle, where parts of each transcript were compared with the whole in a back and forth process to arrive at interpretations that are true to the narrative of the respondents (Dibley et al., 2020; Moules et al., 2014). This non-linear and iterative process involved a "fusion of horizons" where insights from the phenomenological literature were incorporated into the data to develop new and defensible interpretations and insights (Creswell & Poth, 2018; Dibley et al., 2020). Phenomenology not only seeks convergence of ideas as every individual is different but also gives those with an unusual subjective experience a voice. In this way, new and unexpected insights can surface from a deconstructive process of questioning taken-for-granted assumptions and beliefs (Dibley et al., 2020) through the uncommon data findings.

Findings

The research study aimed to understand how learners in the mini enterprise projects experience reflective learning from a holistic perspective that does not privilege the mind above other modalities. Therefore, several themes emerged from the data analysis, and these include conation and corporeality, critical incidents as triggers of reflection, the epistemic role of emotions, and the influence of referential total in reflective learning. These are presented in more detail below.

Critical Incidents, The Self, The Others and Reflection

Participants were asked to identify and describe the discontinuities or crises as well as other events that may have been either positive or negative or stood out to them as impactful on their experiences and how these impacted their reflective thinking and acting. For the majority of respondents, the incidents reported were mostly negative with only a few reporting positive events. The negative critical incidents they include reported incidents of theft of their stock, theft of funds by team members, low sales that forced them to sell perishable stock on credit or risk loss, clients getting their products on credit and failing to pay, conflicts with peers. These formed the basis for reflective thinking and acting in the mini enterprise projects and shaped learners' experiences as a whole.

The self and the others: The findings reveal that critical incidents the complex interaction between individual learners and other stakeholders in the mini enterprise and how self-reflection may give direction at such emotive and challenging situations.

> I was anxious and disappointed . . . because . . . we came to our community and promised them a product. If we don't deliver. They [the community] will look at my team. My team will look at me. Right? Because it will mean that me as a leader I have failed them and they as a team have failed my community. [. . .] Which is why I really had to say, 'JMS, you promised these people this and that. Now you have to deliver no matter what. No matter what hiccups arise, [or if the] service provider did not come to the event, it doesn't mean that production has to stop.' [JMS]

The excerpt above shows the intricate interaction between *the self* and the *others* during occurrences of episodic disruptions and the self-reflections learners may go through in the mini enterprise project. It represents a dynamic interaction the authentic self and their care structure the mounts pressure for reflective thinking and action during such moments. The team leader goes through a tumult of different emotions and pressure as he feels his personal integrity and that of the team mates is at stake due to the failure of their supplier. This demonstrates how crisis may force learners to reflect on their core values and resolve and whether they want to be true to their true. In fact one respondent confirms that these episodic discontinuities caused them to be "under pressure" to engage in "problem solving" [TMS] which contributed the most to their learning, while another reported that "the levels of stress that we encountered, I don't really want to experience that again" [PSS]. Thus making entrepreneurship as a career choice unattractive.

Strained Relationships: The findings revealed that experiences of reflective meetings and the mini enterprise project in general brought about very hostile situations to learners as they related with one another

> Like I said, we held weekly meetings where even though mostly it was fights ... We fought because we were selling to people on credit that we don't even know. [PSS] We were ... just these using harsh words against each other verbally. [MKS]

The respondents' voices above illustrate how learners struggled to manage reflective meeting to deal with arising problems. For some students, the meetings escalated into fights involving cross accusations and unpalatable words directed at one another instead productive reflective thinking and problem solving characterised by mutual respect. The "others" here also extended beyond team members as a trigger of the fights. The sentence "selling to people on credit that we don't even know" does not seem to imply lack of knowledge only, but people the not be able to recognise even facially. The following statement illustrates, after PSS sold a product to someone on credit and went to look for him at a class the client claimed he belonged to:

> I asked to see that person in class ... and they said, "This person doesn't exist!" So, it means that person told me different name, and I couldn't even remember his face, for crying out loud![PSS]

Issues of corporeality here may at face value have to do with the inability to recognise faces, but also at a deeper level, the ability to read intentions of a potential swindler or trickster. This vicious circle of selling to dishonest people who would not pay proved difficult because some students sold perishable products they were always forced to sell on credit or risk incurring a loss.

The conflicts also erupted as a non-cooperation of team members that formed the subject of reflection for different teams to come up with solutions.

> A group member ... wasn't really active with the whole project. Being absent is **not good to them as well as to us**. The team felt jeopardized in the sense that now they have to compromise their duties or leave what they were assigned to do only to go fill that person's spot because they were not being active. [TMS]
> Team members were upset. They were annoyed. They didn't like it. They felt like there is no progress when people don't cooperate. [OMS]

The phenomenon of non-cooperation by team members was not isolated to only the excerpts above, but many more. The above serve only the purpose of exemplars. In their reflection, students demonstrate awareness of the effects of non-participation of their team member. The phenomenon of the self-absconding team member described above is causing friction between the absentee and the whole team, as shown by emotions of being "upset," "annoyed" and "dislike" [OMS]. Being absent is noted as not good to the *absconding self* and the *present others*. The absconding self misses opportunities to learn by doing in their assigned roles but also jeopardises the whole team by overburdening them with more duties in a project that is already demanding physically and also affecting the progress of the whole team.

Emotions and Feelings and Reflection

Participants were asked to share about the role that emotions played in the mini enterprise in general and in the reflective process, especially in relation to critical incidents that occurred during operation. Questions on emotions also attempted to investigate emotions of individual participants as well as those of their peers with whom they worked and engaged in collaborative reflection.

The burden of unpleasant emotions: The data revealed that emotions could either be positive or negative, possess intentionality, and are evaluative in nature giving them an epistemic function in reflection. This is demonstrated in the presentation of findings below.

> We found out some money was missing. It kind of **demoralized us** about venturing into partnerships and when it came to businesses .... I just **gave up hope** on the running of the business. [BLS].
> It was just so **devastating** because ... [when as a debtor you] just tell lies that you are going to pay, yet you're not going to pay. [PSS]

Negative emotions such as anger, annoyance, anxiety, discouragement, frustration, disappointment, devastation, fear, disillusionment, demoralisation, and embarrassment seemed to dominate students' reflections on critical incidents. Phenomenologically, all emotions seem to have intentionality, as they are directed to events that have occurred. For example, the demoralisation is directed to the incident of a treasurer embezzling funds, discouragement to the failure or giving "up hope" of the business, while devastation is directed towards incidents of dishonesty and lack of servicing debts by clients as they had promised. Emotions in the direct quotes above also seem to represent evaluative judgement in that they assess incidents or actions as good or bad and acceptable or unacceptable. Hence they form an essential aspect of reflection.

Emotions and learners' developmental maturity: The findings below revealed that emotions during critical incidents by bringing to the fore learners' care structure can reveal a lot about the maturity of learners through their attitude towards situations they faced:

> The other problem that we encountered was that sometimes the bakery would not deliver the doughnuts to us. [...] The team wasn't impressed at all .... [but] some would be rejoicing ... Saying, "today we don't need to walk around the school looking for customers or selling doughnuts." [PTS]
> They were happy with it is because they wanted to consume some of the fat cakes and we were always refusing. [OSS]

Some learners seemed to lack the development maturity to appreciate the educational purpose of the mini enterprise experience. They were just excited to engage in selling and the value of engaging in reflection was not apparent to them. Some over reacted emotionally when met with what they perceived to be problems which deep engage, demonstrating that they "were not ... mentally mature to deal" [TMS] with situations with the sober attitude they required. The mixed emotions when crisis event occurred, as demonstrated by others being "*unimpressed,*" while others were "*rejoicing*" and "*happy*" because misfortunes would allow them to feast on their products, instead of worrying about the impact on their projects or educational goals.

Corporeality, Contextual Factors and Reflective Learning

Participants were also asked questions on social, environmental, and temporal factors that might have had a bearing in the reflective learning process in the mini enterprise experience. Learners reported experiencing challenges include time demands, too much workload and exhaustion, conflict with other practical subjects, and conflict with teachers of other subjects. Some of them do of course overlap with critical incidents and act as impediments to quality reflection, and there is no denying that they could trigger reflection.

Workload demands and Competition with other practical subjects: When asked about the workload of the project demands of the project taking into account other subjects, and whether that affected their ability to engage in effective reflection, students revealed that they faced challenges. The interview extract below illustrates the conundrum students faced.

> It was tiring to ... come from running the business to having a meeting, then walking home. For some of us, school is like five kilometers away. So it was tiring. [SGS]
> So others [students] had Design and Technology, it had its own practical, others had Art. So ... all these other projects are demanding. [PSS]
> So there is always a lot of work to do because you also have the Agriculture project ... and the marks were higher than that of the business project. [MKS]

As shown above, some students taking part in the mini enterprise project reported experiencing tiredness from business activities which were tiring which were then followed by meetings on the already strained body. The situation was compounded by the fact that some learners were, in addition, doing other practical subjects such as Design and Technology, Art, Home Economics, Physical Education, and Agriculture, which added to the weight of exhaustion. These subjects have projects or portfolios which competed with the mini enterprise projects for both time and effort on the part of learners. This is evident in the statements such as, "*it was very hectic ...*" [KW], "*it was a lot of work ...*" [SG] and "*all these other projects are demanding*" [PSS]. Another learner decried that the Business Studies project required more time, yet the weight of marks of subjects like Agriculture project "*were higher than that of the business project*" [MK]. The combination became stressful for learners because the projects for all the practical subjects are done at around the same time of the year, and all hold high stakes for learners. The practical nature of the subjects means that there is an increased workload for learners to the extent that the time available for reflection was limited.

Time-related challenges: Many students reported experiencing a myriad of time-related challenges that made engaging in meaningful reflection a challenge.

> The big challenge we had was limited time. We had to attend to our studies and also do business. [OMS]
> We just like consumed time from teachers and they were not happy about it. Because they thought we were like being selfish, focusing on one subject. [SGS]
> You won't even have time to study during the study time, because you are busy counting money and the money is refusing to balance. [PSS]

The time challenge motif runs through almost all participants' responses. This explains why both respondents reported "*limited time*" even to do other academic duties. Moreover, during break time, they must make time for selling and eating within the allocated time. The time constraint problem spiralled to both practical and general education subjects, resulting in conflicts with teachers of other subjects as students struggled to complete assigned work on time as noted above. Another learner reported that they *"asked teachers of different subjects to release us early to go and prepare ourselves for selling"* [SG] and this *"consumed time from those teachers' lessons, and they were not happy about it"* [SG]. Some teachers would be available for consultation during break time or lunchtime, but it was the time students had to commit to selling as well. It is, therefore, understandable why some respondents reported that they *"never sat down and reflected on the failures or the achievements"* or that it was *"honestly all about to have work done and not to reflect, or to look back"* [MK] and draw lessons from experiences because they *"did not have time,"* except when forced by circumstances. This challenges seem to occur because schools also do not adjust their schedules or make school-wide accommodations for learners so that they can have time for production and selling, as well as regular school time.

Discussion

Taking a pragmatism-oriented hermeneutical approach to researching students' experiences of reflective learning brings new insights into the dynamical interactions between the learner as a whole person (mind, body and emotions), their relation relationships with others and their broader educational contexts. Like the real entrepreneurial process, the mini enterprise has been shown to be replete with a plethora of critical incidents or crisis events that force learners to engage in a process of coping through reflective thinking to come up with solutions to keep their businesses afloat and drawing lessons for the future in the process (Lindh & Thorgren, 2016). Critical incidents or discontinuities and reflection are often valorised for their potential educational value in terms of engender deeper learning by forcing learners to meticulously combine their previous experiences and new ideas from their present experiences while also evaluating their thoughts and actions at the same time (Cope & Watts, 2000; Lindh & Thorgren, 2016). However, the impact of these incidents on learners' embodied, emotional, and their social wellbeing seem to be equally important and deserving the attention of educators, researchers and policy makers. These experiences impose a toll on the body, on the emotions and strain relations of learners among themselves, with their clientele and with their teachers of various subjects, consequently forcing them to develop coping mechanisms through intuitive reflection akin to problem directed coping done by real world entrepreneurs (Singh et al., 2007).

Like in the case of real entrepreneurs the experiences have been shown to be challenging and at times traumatic, forcing learners to learn expensive and painful lessons through personal emotional exposure consciously through reflection (Cope & Watts, 2000; Cope, 2003) or unconsciously draw on to function and interpret their experiences in their environment (Koopman & Koopman, 2020). In this way, the negative emotional experiences, for other learners, may trigger their motivation, effort, resilience, and resolve follow through with their goals, objectives, values and core beliefs (Cacciotti et al., 2016). However, the opposite is also true, and seemed more prevalent in learners' experiences. That is, for many, these episodic problematic situations evoked feelings of disappointment, hopelessness and disillusionment to the extent that they disengage, experience a paradigm shift about aspects of entrepreneurship or even become totally disoriented about the possibility of becoming entrepreneurs. In this way emotions, and attitudes would have gone through a process of sedimentation in to new ways of feeling about entrepreneurship as a whole or certain aspects of it. This perhaps explains why some students who have participated in entrepreneurial programmes may have lower entrepreneurial intentions compared to those who have not (do Paço et al.,2015; Testa & Frascheri, 2015).

On the bright side, negative emotions, through their phenomenological intentiality, have been shown to wield potential to propel learners to engage in reflection and making concerted efforts to either to solve current problems or proactively devise strategies to prevent potential disruptions or problems and their accompanying unpleasant emotions (Brady, 2013; Goldie, 2002; Thompson et al., 2020). Notwithstanding, through their revelation of acting agents care structure, they also revealed that some learners lack the maturity and emotional intelligence to understand the educational purpose of the mini enterprise and thus compromising their ability to respond to critical incidents appropriately. Thus emotions of learners of entrepreneurship do not just reveal how traumatic and emotionally unhealthy the mini enterprise project could be, they also reveal that some students lack the emotional maturity to handle the pressures and disruptions arising from the different crisis in the mini enterprise project.

The transactive interaction between the learners and contextual factor in the environment wherein learners experience the mini enterprise project further reveal how unhealthy and toxic this project could be. The workload seems too much to bear and exhausting for learners, and the situation is not helped by the fact that some students are doing two practical subjects which are both taxing and require lots of time individually. Schools do not make adjustments to accommodate complexities, labour, and time demands of the project. This puts learners in a predicament of having to fight with teachers of other subjects at a very sensitive time when they are doing their final year and preparing for high stakes external examinations which would determine their transition to senior secondary school. Worse still, the demanding nature of the project, together with the associated time constraint factors compromise the ability of learners to engage in reflective learning because they are either too tired to do it or they honestly do not have the time to do it. It calls for more thoughtfulness and understanding the embodied experiences and "conditions of existence" of learners in an era of neoliberal educational governance that is only pursuing turning entrepreneurial citizens (Komulainen et al., 2013; Tabulawa, 2023) without being sensitive to their lived experiences where critical voices are few.

Conclusion

This study explored lived experiences of learners engaged in the mini enterprise and examined how their conditions of existence are challenged, even affecting reflective learning. The phenomenological approach helped in highlighting some of these shortcomings that also hamper reflective learning and an overall meaningful experience in the mini enterprise experience, thus shedding some light on what it means to be a student of entrepreneurship. The findings reveal that although the mini enterprise project as implemented in the Botswana junior secondary school curriculum may be useful teaching entrepreneurship, it is quite problematic and may need to be re-examined.

References

Arpiainen, R. L., Lackéus, M., Täks, M., & Tynjälä, P. (2013). The sources and dynamics of emotions in entrepreneurship education learning process. *Trames, 17*(4). https://doi.org/10.3176/tr.2013.4.02

Beck, C. T. (2023). Introduction to Phenomenology: Focus on Methodology. Sage. https://doi.org/10.4135/9781071909669

Biesta, G., & Burbules, N. (2003). Pragmatism and educational research. In *Educational Research*.

Biesta, G., & Burbules, N. (2003). Pragmatism and educational research. Rowman & Littlefield.

Brady, M. S. (2013). *Emotional insight: The epistemic role of emotional experience*. OUP Oxford.

Cacciotti, G., Hayton, J. C., Mitchell, J. R., & Giazitzoglu, A. (2016). A reconceptualization of fear of failure in entrepreneurship. *Journal of Business Venturing*, 31(3), 302–325.

Cope, J. (2003). Entrepreneurial learning and critical reflection: Discontinuous events as triggers for "Higher-level" learning. *Management Learning*, 34(4). https://doi.org/10.1177/1350507603039067

Cope, J., & Watts, G. (2000). Learning by doing–an exploration of experience, critical incidents and reflection in entrepreneurial learning. *International Journal of Entrepreneurial Behavior & Research*, 6(3), 104–124. https://doi.org/10.1108/13552550010346208

Creswell, J. W. (2012). Educational research: Planning, conducting, and evaluating quantitative and qualitative research (4th ed.). Pearson.

Creswell, W. (2012). *Educational research fourth edition* (4th ed.). Pearson Education. *Qualitative inquiry and research design: Choosing among five approaches*. Sage Publications.

Creswell, J. W., & Poth, C. N. (2018). *Qualitative inquiry and research design: choosing among five approaches* (4th ed.). Thousand Oaks: Sage

Dibley, L., Dickerson, S., Duffy, M., & Vandermause, R. (2020). *Doing hermeneutic phenomenological research: A practical guide*. Sage.

do Paço, A., Ferreira, J. M., Raposo, M., Rodrigues, R. G., & Dinis, A. (2015). Entrepreneurial intentions: is education enough? *International Entrepreneurship and Management Journal*, 11, 57–75. https://doi.org/10.1007/s11365-013-0280-5

Ellborg, K. (2023). Scientifically based or policy driven?: Using a didaktik approach to encompass transformative and critical entrepreneurship education. In *The age of entrepreneurship education research: Evolution and future* (pp. 33–50). Emerald Publishing Limited.

Elpidorou, A., & Freeman, L. (2015). Affectivity in Heidegger I: Moods and emotions in being and time. *Philosophy Compass*, 10(10), 661–671.

Goldie, P. (2002). Emotions, feelings and intentionality. *Phenomenology and the Cognitive Sciences*, 1(3), 235–254. https://doi.org/10.1023/A:1021306500055

Hägg, G., & Kurczewska, A. (2016). Connecting the dots: A discussion on key concepts in contemporary entrepreneurship education. *Education and Training*, 58(7–8). https://doi.org/10.1108/ET-12-2015-0115

Hägg, G., & Kurczewska, A. (2021). Toward a learning philosophy based on experience in entrepreneurship education. *Entrepreneurship Education and Pedagogy*, 4(1), 4–29. https://doi.org/10.1177/2515127419840607

Higgins, D., Smith, K., & Mirza, M. (2013). Entrepreneurial education: Reflexive approaches to entrepreneurial learning in practice. *Journal of Entrepreneurship*, 22(2). https://doi.org/10.1177/0971355713490619

Hjorth, D., Holt, R., & Steyaert, C. (2015). Entrepreneurship and process studies. *International Small Business Journal*, 33(6), 599–611.

Hommel, M., Fürstenau, B., & Mulder, R. H. (2023). Reflection at work–A conceptual model and the meaning of its components in the domain of VET teachers. *Frontiers in Psychology*, 13, 923888.

Hunter Lindqvist, S. (2017). *What and how students perceive they learn when doing mini- companies in upper secondary school (Doctoral dissertation)*. Karlstads universitet.

Kafle, N. P. (2013). Hermeneutic phenomenological research method simplified. *Bodhi: An Interdisciplinary Journal, 5*(1). https://doi.org/10.3126/bodhi.v5i1.8053

Kassean, H., Vanevenhoven, J., Liguori, E., & Winkel, D. E. (2015). Entrepreneurship education: a need for reflection, real-world experience and action. *International Entrepreneurial Behaviour and Research, 21*(5). https://doi.org/10.1108/IJEBR-07-2014-0123

Komulainen, K. J., Korhonen, M., & Räty, H. (2013). On entrepreneurship, in a different voice? Finnish entrepreneurship education and pupils' critical narratives of the entrepreneur. *International Journal of Qualitative Studies in Education, 26*(8), 1079–1095.

Koopman, K. J., & Koopman, O. (2020). *Phenomenology and educational research: Theory and practice*. Whale Coast Academic Press.

Kyrö, P. (2008). A theoretical framework for teaching and learning entrepreneurship. *International Journal of Business and Globalisation, 2*(1), 39–55. https://doi.org/10.1504/IJBG.2008.016133

Jones, C., & English, J. (2004). A contemporary approach to entrepreneurship education. *Education+Training, 46*. https://doi.org/10.1108/00400910410569533

Lackéus, M. (2014). An emotion based approach to assessing entrepreneurial education. *The International Journal of Management Education, 12*(3), 374-396. https://doi.org/10.1016/j.ijme.2014.06.005

Lackéus, M., & Sävetun, C. (2019). Assessing the Impact of Enterprise Education in Three Leading Swedish Compulsory Schools. *Journal of Small Business Management, 57*(S1)33-59. https://doi.org/10.1111/jsbm.12497

Larsen, H. G., & Adu, P. (2021). The theoretical framework in phenomenological research: Development and application. In *The theoretical framework in phenomenological research: Development and application*. https://doi.org/10.4324/9781003084259

Lindh, I., & Thorgren, S. (2016). Critical event recognition: An extended view of reflective learning. *Management Learning, 47*(5), 525–542. https://doi.org/10.1177/1350507615618600

Love, B., Vetere, A., & Davis, P. (2020). Should interpretative phenomenological analysis (IPA) be used with focus groups? Navigating the bumpy road of "iterative loops," idiographic journeys, and "phenomenological bridges." *International Journal of Qualitative Methods, 19*. https://doi.org/10.1177/1609406920921600

Maistry, S. M., & David, R. (2017). Phantasmagoria: communicating an illusion of entrepreneurship in South African school textbooks. *Educational Research for Social Change, 6*(2), 101–114. https://doi.org/10.17159/2221-4070/2017/v6i2a7

Magrì, E., & McQueen, P. (2022). *Critical phenomenology: An introduction*. John Wiley & Sons.

Maritz, A., & Brown, C. R. (2013). Illuminating the black box of entrepreneurship education programs. *Education + Training, 55*(3), 234–252.

Mitchell, R. K., Busenitz, L. W., Bird, B., Marie Gaglio, C., McMullen, J. S., Morse, E. A., & Smith, J. B. (2007). The central question in entrepreneurial cognition research. *Entrepreneurship Theory and Practice, 31*(1), 1–27. https://doi.org/10.1111/j.1540-6520.2007.00161.x

Moules, N. J., Field, J. C., Mccaffrey, G. P., & Laing, C. M. (2014). *Conducting Hermeneutic Research:* Journal of Applied Hermeneutics, p1-7. *The address of the topic*. https://doi.org/10.11575/jah.v0i0.53242

Oosterbeek, H., van Praag, M., & Ijsselstein, A. (2010). The impact of entrepreneurship education on entrepreneurship skills and motivation. *European Economic Review, 54*(3). https://doi.org/10.1016/j.euroecorev.2009.08.002

Peoples, K. (2021). *How to write a phenomenological dissertation: a step-by-step guide.* SAGE. https://cir.nii.ac.jp/crid/1130285378485341824.bib?lang=en

Pepin, M. (2012). Enterprise education: A Deweyan perspective. *Education + Training, 54*(8/9), 801–812.

Pittaway, L., & Cope, J. (2007). Simulating entrepreneurial learning: Integrating experiential and collaborative approaches to learning. *Management Learning, 38*(2). https://doi.org/10.1177/1350507607075776

Pittaway, L., Rodriguez-Falcon, E., Aiyegbayo, O., & King, A. (2011). The role of entrepreneurship clubs and societies in entrepreneurial learning. *International Small Business Journal, 29*(1). https://doi.org/10.1177/0266242610369876

Pittaway, L., & Thorpe, R. (2012). A framework for entrepreneurial learning: A tribute to Jason Cope. *Entrepreneurship and Regional Development, 24*(9–10). https://doi.org/10.1080/08985626.2012.694268

Pittaway, L. A., Gazzard, J., Shore, A., & Williamson, T. (2015). Student clubs: experiences inentrepreneurial learning. Entrepreneurship & Regional Development, 27(3-4), 127-153. https://doi.org/10.1080/08985626.2015.1014865

Politis, D. (2008). Does prior start-up experience matter for entrepreneurs' learning? A comparison between novice and habitual entrepreneurs. *Journal of small business and Enterprise Development, 15*(3), 472–489.

Selden, P., & Fletcher, D. E. (2020). Temporality and embodied practice: Theorizing the relationality of entrepreneurial events. *Research handbook on entrepreneurial behavior, practice and process,* 263–282.

Singh S, Corner P, Pavlovich K. (2007). Coping with entrepreneurial failure. *Journal of Management & Organization. 13*(4), 331–344. https://doi.org/10.5172/jmo.2007.13.4.331

Sithole, B. M. (2010). Pedagogical practices of business studies teachers in Botswana Junior Secondary Schools: Are teachers and curriculum planners singing from the same hymnbook? *International Journal of Scientific Research in Education, 3*(1), 21–28.

Smith, J. A., Flowers, P., & Larkin, M. (2009). Interpretative phenomenological analysis: theory, method and research. Sage.

Tabulawa, R. (2023). *Globalisation and education policy reform in Botswana.* Routledge.

Testa, S., & Frascheri, S. (2015). Learning by failing: What we can learn from un-successful entrepreneurship education. *International Journal of Management Education, 13*(1), 11–22. https://doi.org/10.1016/j.ijme.2014.11.001

Thompson, N. A., Van Gelderen, M., & Keppler, L. (2020). No need to worry? Anxiety and coping in the entrepreneurship process. *Frontiers in Psychology, 11,* 398. https://doi.org/10.3389/fpsyg.2020.00398

Yeoh, K. K. (2017). Entrepreneurship students distilled their learning experience through reflective learning log. *Journal of Research in Innovative Teaching & Learning, 10*(2). https://doi.org/10.1108/jrit-06-2017-0012

· 6 ·

INSIGHTS INTO THE LIVED EXPERIENCES OF A SOUTH AFRICAN BLACK HIGH SCHOOL PRINCIPAL IN LEADING THE SCHOOL TOWARDS A LEARNING ORGANISATION

Karen J. Koopman, Juliana M. Smith & Keith Long

Introduction

The concept of schools as "learning organisations" has gained significant traction among scholars, researchers, and policymakers worldwide (Kools & Stoll, 2016). The success of such organisations depends mainly on the quality of leadership, particularly the role of school principals in fostering environments conducive to continuous learning and adaptation (Long, 2024). Kools & Stoll (2016) argue that transforming a school into a learning organisation, is a complex process that requires substantial change and effort. It demands a reimagining of the teacher in the classroom and school leader professionalism, viewing both as high-quality knowledge workers, driving the same agenda and necessitates modifications to organisational structures and processes to create adaptive institutions capable of thriving in a continuously changing external environment (Kools & Stoll, 2016).

At the heart of this transformation lies the concept of strategic leadership. As Quong & Walker (2010) assert, strategic leadership in education goes beyond mere vision-setting; it involves acknowledging the complex and unpredictable nature of the future and developing strategies to "prepare for the unexpected" rather than simply "planning for the known" (p. 23). This approach is particularly crucial in the South African context, where principals are expected to fulfil multiple tasks and navigate complex educational landscapes.

The South African education system presents unique challenges and opportunities for school leaders. As outlined in the Personnel Administrative Measures (PAM), principals are tasked with ensuring satisfactory school management in compliance with applicable legislation, regulations, and personnel administration measures (Department of Education, 2016). They are responsible for implementing educational policies, managing personnel, overseeing academic performance, and facilitating extra-curricular activities, all while maintaining effective communication with various stakeholders.

Given these multifaceted responsibilities, the concept of shared leadership becomes crucial. High schools, in particular, require a distributed approach to leadership if they are to function effectively and meet the expectations defined in their vision and mission statements. This also means that the school management team (SMT) will have to play a vital role in this process, working alongside principals in supporting them to develop the school into a robust learning organisation (Senge et al., 2012).

However, while there exist a myriad of theories on management, teaching, and learning as well as policy documents that provide guidance to principals, they often do not take into consideration the context in which principals work. Often these studies fall short in capturing the lived experiences of principals in how to navigate the complexities of transforming their schools into learning organisations. This gap in the literature, namely to provide an understanding of how South African principals provide leadership on a day-to-day basis in leading their school as a learning organisation, has inspired this study. The lack of in-depth research into the lived experiences of principals as they attempt to lead their schools towards becoming learning organisations creates a significant gap in the educational leadership literature. Most studies in this area focus on broad policy implementations or theoretical discussions, while the personal, subjective experiences of principals—the very actors responsible for driving this transformation—are often overlooked. Understanding how principals interpret and enact strategic leadership is crucial because their ability to foster learning organisations depends heavily on their capacity to navigate the complexities of daily leadership. Their decisions, values, and experiences influence not only their own leadership but also the culture of the school, the professional development of teachers, and ultimately, student achievement. This study addresses this gap by investigating the following main research question: What are the lived experiences of a black South African principal in leading his school towards a learning organisation. The aim is to provide fresh insights into the strategic leadership responsibilities of this principal focussing on the school as a learning organisation. By drawing on both Husserl's descriptive phenomenology and Heidegger's interpretive phenomenology, this study aims to provide a holistic understanding of the principal's leadership practices, by blending the descriptive accounts of his experiences with deeper interpretive insights of Senge's (2006) structured framework for understanding how the principal's experiences align with the core elements of a learning organisation.

The rationale for this research lies in its potential to provide new insights into the intersection of strategic leadership and leading the school towards a learning organisation. Principals are at the forefront of educational transformation, yet in the broader discourse, their voices and experiences are often marginalised regarding educational reform. By foregrounding the lived experiences of a principal, this study integrated with Senge's practical framework, will offer both theoretical and practical contributions, in so doing, it sheds light on the challenges and opportunities of one principal on leading his school towards a learning organisation.

Theoretical Framework

This theoretical framework is grounded in Peter Senge's (2006) concept of the learning organisation, that has revolutionised our understanding of organisational development and leadership. Originally developed in the corporate sector but later adapted for educational contexts, Senge's framework provides a comprehensive approach to transforming schools into dynamic learning environments. The framework is particularly valuable for understanding how principals can systematically lead their schools toward becoming true learning organisations.

Senge et al. (2012) present five fundamental disciplines as essential tools for creating schools that learn. These disciplines offer more than mere theoretical constructs—they provide practical pathways for educational leaders such as principals to transform their schools into adaptive, responsive systems capable of continuous growth and innovation. The framework's strength lies in its holistic approach, recognising the interconnected nature of personal development, collective learning, and systemic change in educational settings.

Personal Mastery

For principals, personal mastery involves continually clarifying and deepening their own vision for their school while maintaining a clear view of current reality. This discipline is crucial for educational leaders who must navigate complex challenges while inspiring others. Principals can cultivate personal mastery by articulating a clear personal vision for their school's future, regularly assessing the current reality of their school, and maintaining the creative tension between vision and reality (Kools & Stoll, 2016).

By embodying personal mastery, principals can inspire teachers and students who often struggle with motivation and purpose. Many schools in South Africa face situations where learners lack clear goals and discipline and see education as merely a means to please teachers or achieve grades, while teachers may abandon their aspirations, simply complying with systemic demands (Senge et al., 2012). Principals can counteract this by modelling and encouraging the articulation of personal visions and the understanding of current realities. As Retna (2011) notes, "it is not the vision itself but what the vision does that matters" (p. 454–455).

Shared Vision

While personal mastery focuses on the principal's individual vision, shared vision involves aligning the aspirations of all stakeholders into a collective future for the school. Principals play a crucial role in facilitating this process, which involves collaborative reflection on future goals, values, and guiding practices (Senge et al., 2012). To develop a shared vision, principals can facilitate processes of telling, selling, testing, consulting, and co-creating (Senge et al., 2012). This approach builds leadership capacity at all levels and ensures that the vision has "staying power and an evolving life force that lasts for years, propelling people through a continuous cycle of action, learning and reflection" (Senge et al., 2012, p. 87).

Effective principals recognise that a truly shared vision serves as motivation for sustained action. It is crucial for transforming a school into a learning organisation that does not resist change but has "enough capabilities to learn, to adapt and to change" (Fanikhayavi et al., 2014, p. 79). By involving all stakeholders in the visioning process, principals can ensure that the shared vision shapes the organisation (Stoll & Kools, 2017).

Mental Models

Mental models are the "images, assumptions and stories that we carry in our minds of ourselves, other people, institutions, and every aspect of the world" (Senge et al., 2012, p. 99). For principals, understanding and working with mental models is essential in leading a learning organisation. They must recognise that these models shape behaviour and attitudes, influencing how staff, students, and the community interpret and respond to the school environment.

Principals can lead in this area by encouraging the examination and evolution of mental models within their school community. This involves creating opportunities for reflection and inquiry, facilitating open conversations, and encouraging the sharing of diverse viewpoints. By doing so, principals can foster "a significant cultural shift, a change of mind-sets and a school-wide commitment to self-reflection and evaluation" (Harris & Jones, 2018, p. 352). This process is crucial for creating an environment where unexamined assumptions do not limit the school's ability to change and adapt.

Team Learning

In the context of school leadership, team learning emphasises the principal's role in fostering collaborative learning environments. Principals must ensure that various teams within the school—including teaching staff, administrative teams, and leadership groups—can "act in concert even if they do not think alike" (Senge et al., 2012). This requires regular practice and the promotion of both team and individual learning (Stoll & Kools, 2017).

Effective principals organise retreats, staff workshops, and other team-building activities to improve communication skills and foster collaboration. However, they also recognise that true team learning goes beyond these events, transforming day-to-day communication, staff meetings, and classroom interactions. Principals should encourage "the collective learning of minds coming together" (Kools & Stoll, 2016, p. 40), creating an environment where respectful dialogue and deliberation about key issues become the norm.

Systems Thinking

Systems thinking, often described as the main element of Senge's framework, is particularly crucial for principals. It involves understanding the school as a complex system where various elements "hang together" and continually affect each other over time (Senge et al., 2012). For principals, adopting a systems thinking approach means viewing leadership as "a world view" (Shaked & Schechter, 2020, p. 107) that considers the intricate interactions within the school ecosystem.

In practice, principals applying systems thinking avoid focusing solely on isolated parts of the school system. Instead, they consider the complex interactions among various components, enabling them to better face "the contemporary growing complexity, change and diversity characterising school organisations" (Shaked & Schechter, 2020, p. 112). This approach helps principals navigate the often fragmented nature of educational issues, bringing together diverse perspectives from teachers, parents, students, and other community members.

By embracing systems thinking, principals can create a supportive culture that invests time and resources in quality professional learning opportunities for all staff (Stoll & Kools, 2017). They recognise that quality education depends on "a whole suite of life choices" (Senge et al., 2012, p. 125) and work to create an environment where these choices can be made and learned.

Foundational Ideas of Husserl and Heidegger in Enhancing

Understanding of the Principal's Lived Experiences

Building upon Senge's five disciplines this theoretical framework is further rooted in both Husserl's (1970) transcendental phenomenology and Heidegger's (1967) hermeneutic phenomenology, combining descriptive and interpretive elements to gain a comprehensive understanding of the principal's leadership practices. Husserl's (1970) descriptive phenomenology provides a foundation for examining the "consciousness" of the principal as he engages with Senge's five disciplines. Lopez & Willis (2004) note that Husserl believed "experience as perceived by human consciousness has value and should be an object of scientific study" (p. 727). This perspective allows us to explore how the principal in this study perceives and internalises concepts such as personal mastery, shared vision, mental models, team learning, and systems thinking in his daily leadership practices. The concept of "intentionality" in Husserl's work is particularly relevant to understanding how the principal directs his consciousness towards specific aspects of his leadership role. Gorner (2001) explains that "Perceiving, desiring, imagining, fearing, hoping are all examples of intentional experiences" (p. 547). By examining these intentional experiences, we gain insight into how the principal consciously approached the challenges of leading a learning organisation.

Husserl's notion of "universal or eidetic structures" suggests that certain features of lived experiences are common to all who have the experience. As Lopez & Willis (2004) write, "For the description of the lived experience to be considered a science, commonalities in the experience of the participants must be identified, so that a generalised description is possible" (p. 728). This concept allows us to identify shared elements in the principal's experiences of implementing Senge's disciplines.

However, recognising the limitations of a purely descriptive approach, this study also incorporates Heidegger's hermeneutic phenomenology. Heidegger's concept of "being-in-the-world" or "*Dasein*" acknowledges that individuals cannot be abstracted from their context. This is crucial when considering how the principal implemented Senge's disciplines within the specific context of his school and community.

Heidegger's approach allows us to move beyond description to interpretation, looking for "meanings embedded in common life practices" (Lopez & Willis, 2004, p. 728). This is particularly valuable when examining how the principal integrated the five disciplines into his leadership styles, as these meanings may not always be apparent to the principal himself but can be gleaned from his narrative.

The concept of "lifeworld" in Heidegger's work is especially relevant to understanding the principal's leadership experiences. As Neubauer et al. (2019) explain, "The realities of a person are invariably influenced by the world they live in" (p. 95). This perspective allows us to consider how factors such as school culture, community expectations, and educational policies influence this principal's implementation of Senge's disciplines.

Furthermore, Heidegger's notion of "situated freedom" provides a lens through which to examine the constraints and opportunities the principal faces in leading his school as a learning organisation. While leaders have the freedom to make choices in their leadership approach, "their freedom is not absolute ... it is circumscribed by the specific conditions of their daily lives" (Lopez & Willis, 2004, p. 729). This concept helps us understand how this principal navigated the tensions between his vision for the school and the practical realities he faces.

The integration of both Husserl's and Heidegger's approaches allows for a deeper examination of the principal's experiences. Husserl's focus on the "essence" of experiences helps identify common themes across the principal's narrative, while Heidegger's interpretive approach acknowledges the unique contexts and meanings he (the principal) brings to his leadership role.

In applying this phenomenological framework to the study of this principal leading a learning organisation, we recognise that the researchers' own understandings and experiences play a role in the interpretation process. As Heidegger (1967) argues, researchers cannot entirely free themselves from their background understandings. This acknowledgment aligns with the concept of "constitutionality," where the meanings derived from the research are "a blend of the meanings of both the participant and the researcher" (Lopez & Willis, 2004, p. 729).

The phenomenological part of the theoretical framework enhances our understanding of how the principal engaged with Senge's five disciplines by allowing us to explore his conscious experiences, intentionality, and the contextual factors that influence his leadership.

Research Methodology

This study employs a qualitative approach rooted in the phenomenological traditions of Husserl and Heidegger. The research strategy combines both descriptive (Husserlian) and interpretive (Heideggerian) phenomenological methodologies, providing a comprehensive framework for exploring the lived experiences of one high school principal.

The choice of a phenomenological research design aligns with the objectives of this study, which is to uncover new knowledge about this high school principal's lived experiences. This approach allows for an in-depth exploration of the participant's views, enhancing existing knowledge in the field (Akanle & Shittu, 2020). The research strategy was carefully matched with the desired outcomes, focusing on revealing the essence of the principal's experiences in leading his school towards a learning organisation.

Research Instruments and Sampling

The primary research instrument consisted of a semi-structured interview, supplemented by the researchers' field notes. This combination allowed for a rich collection of data reflecting the lived experiences of the participant. The study employed purposive or non-probability sampling. This sampling technique is particularly suited to phenomenological research, which seeks to uncover the invariant structures or essence of lived experiences.

This study focuses on only one high school principal in the Western Cape, South Africa. By focussing on only one research participant, we hope this study attempts to examine real-life phenomena in depth. The selection of the participant took into account, especially the socioeconomic context of the school this principal is leading. The school at which this principal works, is situated in a poor community. Important to note is that this interview was conducted during 2022. A brief summary of who the principal (or participant that was selected for this study) is, follows below.

Description of the Participant and School in Which He Works

The research participant, Lwando (pseudonym), is a 54-year-old black African male who teaches in a township school. Important to note is that English is not Lwando's first language. For the purposes of this study the school will be referred to as Harbour High School. Lwando has twenty-four years of experience as a teacher and has been leading the same school for the past thirteen years. He holds a Secondary Education Diploma in Natural Science, an Advanced Certificate in Education in Mathematics, a Bachelor's in Education Honours degree, and a Postgraduate Certificate in Leadership and Management.

Harbour High School is located in a coastal town in the Overstrand District in the Western Cape. A huge disparity exists between the wealth of the inhabitants in this town as a whole and those in the township in which the school is situated. Contrary to those residents living in the more scenic areas in this town, considerable poverty exits in the community in which the school is situated. Although the township consists of formal brick houses a substantial portion of the housing consists of shacks (a sink house). The brick houses are Government Subsidised Housing, formerly referred to as the Reconstruction and Development Programme (RDP) housing, provided free to the occupants due to their level of poverty. There is a high level of unemployment in the area, therefore many people roam aimlessly in the streets near the school, which is secured by a high fence.

There is a substantial amount of informal business activity in the community with many informal traders running their business activities in the vicinity of the school. The school is close to a busy main road, which runs through the township. Harbour High School experiences a fair amount of disturbance from noise because of the number of people in the streets, the taxis and other nearby activities. The school property is treated with respect by the community and the gates are open to allow easy access for learners, teachers, visitors, and others who need to be at the school.

Description of the Context Within Which the School Functions

The school has an enrolment of almost 2,200 learners with a Western Cape Education Department (WCED) educator complement of fifty-seven, which includes the principal. There is an average of fifty learners per class. Almost all the learners are isiXhosa speaking with a few foreign black students. Two of the educators are so-called Coloured whilst the remaining are black African isiXhosa speaking teachers of which two are isiZulu speaking. Harbour High School enjoys support from the parent community. The School Governing Body (SGB) parent component consists entirely of women and the school struggles to retain parent governing body members for the full term of three years.

In South Africa public schools are categorised in quintiles, that is, from quintile 5 to quintile 1; 5 being the best resourced schools and 1 being the least. This particular school is placed in quintile 1, hence it falls in the poorest category. In the best resourced schools the school fees are much higher than that of the least resourced schools. This particular schools is considered a no-fee school, meaning that parents do not need to pay school fees. Most of the learners live in the township in which the school is situated whilst about ten percent travel from other neighbouring towns as these schools do not offer the schooling required by the learners, that is, a no-fee school. The school is situated in a new building, but it only caters for half of the number of learners enrolled. The school has many prefabricated classrooms to accommodate all learners and enable teaching and learning to take place. Despite the challenge of space, learners were mostly in their classes when we interviewed the principal.

Data Explication

In this phenomenological study the data-explication process was conducted in two complementary phases, aligning with the philosophical underpinnings of both Husserl's (1970) descriptive phenomenology and Heidegger's (1967) interpretive phenomenology. This dual approach allowed for a rich and nuanced analysis of the participant's lived experiences.

Initially, following Husserl's descriptive phenomenology, the researcher engaged in bracketing, setting aside preconceptions to focus on the participant's direct experiences. Units of meaning were identified from the transcripts, encompassing both verbal and non-verbal communication.

These units were carefully examined to discern emerging themes, with the researcher maintaining a stance of phenomenological reduction to capture the essence of the participant's experiences.

Subsequently, the analysis transitioned to Heidegger's interpretive phenomenology. This phase involved a hermeneutic circle of understanding, where the researchers moved between parts (individual units of meaning) and the whole (the entire context of the participant's experiences). This iterative process allowed for a deeper exploration of meanings, considering the contextual factors that shape the principal's lived experiences.

Throughout both phases, conceptual analysis was employed to unpack the nuanced meanings of words and phrases used by the participant. This linguistic focus helped to reveal underlying assumptions and worldviews that might not be immediately apparent.

To further enrich the interpretive process, Senge's (2006) five disciplines of a learning organisation were applied as an analytical lens. This framework provided a structured approach to understanding how the principal's experiences relate to the concepts of personal mastery, shared vision, mental models, team learning, and systems thinking within his school context.

The entire data-explication process was characterised by continuous reflection and refinement.

The researcher repeatedly returned to the original data, ensuring that interpretations remained grounded in the participant's actual experiences. This cyclical approach allowed for the emergence of increasingly refined themes and insights, culminating in a comprehensive understanding of the principal's lived experiences in leading his school as a learning organisation.

Findings and Discussion

The main aim of this section is to answer the following main research question, that is: What does the lived experience of a high school principal tell us about him leading his school towards becoming a learning organisation?

Husserlian Descriptive Narrative of Lwando at Harbour High

Whilst enquiring what it means to be the principal of Harbour High, we asked Lwando what the school community expects of him as principal. He spoke about the expectations and told us that upon his arrival he ... "had to develop a turnaround strategy because the results in grade twelve were at twenty-nine percent." He started in October of a particular year, and was unaware of which teachers would be best allocated to teach grade twelve the following year. He said that for the first year the results were still down and that he was demotivated when his superiors averred that he had not done anything to improve the situation of the grade twelve results. He told us that he responded to his superiors by saying: "You must give me at least five years to change things around because I don't even know the staff that I'm working with." He also told us that his biggest challenge was the expectations of the community. He said: "They were looking up to me to make drastic changes."

We asked Lwando to describe what happened in his first year as principal and he told us that: "The first thing, in fact, within two weeks, I was informed by police intelligence here [at the school] that I am going to be assassinated." He said that the Minister of the Executive Council (MEC): Education visited the school during the same week, and when he arrived the District Safety Officer asked him to inquire from the principal what had happened that week. Lwando responded by saying: "I was staying here in the township, and I was told that my house would be burnt ... and that was coming from the intelligence." The MEC: Education arranged "... a meeting with the police to make sure that I am safe." The MEC: Education met with the police and asked them to ensure Lwando's safety. He (Lwando) stated that he was advised to leave this community and stay in the safe place.

Lwando then shifted the conversation to the expectations of the community and the absenteeism of staff. He told us that "... in 2011, when I was doing allocations, I decided to move all those educators that were not coming to school from teaching grade twelve". He allocated teachers that had been teaching grade twelve to teach grade eight and that was a fight because educators were thinking that they were being demoted. Lwando decided to use new educators who had just finished university to teach the grade twelve learners. He related that the results, and consequently the pass rate, improved "... moved from thirty-two percent to sixty-six percent that year."

When we asked Lwando which changes that he implemented he would highlight, he mentioned that it would be the "... increase in the number of learners enrolled at this school." He said that previously most parents would take their children to other schools rather than Harbour High "but once they had seen the number of learners passing and an increase in the number of Bachelors they started to bring their kids here". He emphasised that "when I arrived here, there were only four kids who were getting Bachelors, and the rest were getting the National Certificate." This led to many more learners enrolling at the school as the parents "... started to like the school and appreciate it ... also the department has supported me by giving me this new building."

We inquired whether he wanted to add anything else about the changes he had implemented. He mentioned working in partnership with Symphonia, a Non-Governmental Organisation, that paired the principals with managers in companies who "... assisted by getting sponsors for the school." He told us about the "... School of Excellence in Bellville, which we use, to assist us at the end of term ... with the materials to analyse the results." Lwando also spoke of a Swedish man who worked with them and who was assisting the school. This man located some Swedish sponsors who donated laptops to the top performing learners in grade 12. He also took "... learners to the university in Cape Town and paid registrations for them." These gestures motivated the children and "now each and every year we've got kids coming from our school, graduating at CPUT, UWC, and now to even have kids that are at UCT." (These are three of the institutions of higher learning in the Western Cape, namely, Cape Peninsula University of Technology, the University of the Western Cape, and the University of Cape Town.)

We asked Lwando whether the school had a vision and whether it is a shared vision. He told us that he constantly reminds the staff of the school's vision and added that: "We were once asked by someone who came here: What is the vision of the school? And they'll [staff] say that the vision was there. It has been taken by the kids. They [staff] do not know the vision". This being said, Lwando felt that the vision impacted the school. He continued to say that:

If they can have that vision and make it their own then we won't have the situation that we are experiencing now [namely] of kids that are always arriving late. Every time the bell rings here we need to stand outside to make sure that the kids go to the classes. If we can just succeed here. The principal has to be visible and also be seen by them. That impacts them because they also do not go to the classes if I haven't gone to tell them that the period has started. Go to classes.

We spoke about what Lwando thought would get the staff to buy into the vision. He told us that it needs to be revisited despite having been reviewed three years ago seeing that since then more than twenty educators were employed. He questioned whether the vision was relevant and whether they should start looking at a new one. He said that "all the new educators do not even know what the vision is. I think they do not even know ... because we are not producing the symbols, and they are also not part of it."

Lwando told us that the school was experiencing a problem regarding the mentoring of new educators. He told us that they are being mentored, but that there is no formal mentoring system in place and that he is struggling to design one. He said that classroom management was also a problem as "... some of our educators cannot manage their classes." He told us that they got someone in to do "... a workshop on classroom management, but it didn't assist." We asked him who does the staff development and he stated that "We do have the committee that looks at that ... the committee starts with the IQMS or QMS of the staff from which they identify the development they need .... we look at their growth plans ... we check ... and we say, ... this is what will be required this year." (IQMS meaning Integrated Quality Management System; and QMS meaning Quality Management System.) He added that "... they contact the district, CTLI [Cape Teaching and Leadership Institute] and other providers sent by the district to assist with training." He also told us that "This year, we had one of the judges ... who was expelled from being a judge, and then went to a prison, and then came back to be a motivational speaker. And he came to motivate our teachers."

We asked Lwando how he would describe the attitude and the relationship between him and the staff. He spoke of people not wanting to say things but that it was easy to find out what "... they do not like. You get it from other educators." He told us that once a problem comes to his attention, he wants to address it and look at "how we can solve these things so that we can all be on the same path ... others will come to my office ..." and tell him that what he did that week "did not go down well with some educators." Some staff members would say that they do not want to tell him what to do but that they are rather advising him. He said that "... I always say ... it is better to say something to me." We asked about relationships amongst the members of the SMT. He mentioned that the SMT met every fortnight. He added that: "We give people a chance to say whatever. If they want to blame me, they must blame me in front of me and say [for example] this is how we think we should do it." He stated that he also would check whether what staff says coincides with policies of the Education Department. He believes that the relationship between the (ordinary) staff members and the SMT is positive. When it came to addressing matters with the staff Lwando informed us that "I'm not always one that is addressing them all the time. I always say, today it's me, the next day you, as the deputy principal, need to speak with the staff. The director also came to speak with them, motivating the educators." He said that this assures the staff that the district is "behind us and aware of the problems that we're experiencing ... It has motivated some of our educators, in fact most of them." He spoke of staff members arriving late at school. He said that this has been a problem for many years "but after these developments and also the talk from the circuit manager, we started to see that our educators' attitudes have changed."

The focus of the interview moved to systems thinking and we asked Lwando about the systems the school used. We also reminded him of his comments regarding new ideas that some of the teachers brought to the table. He said that:

> You see, we have had a problem when it comes to discipline, in such a way that we have been warned several times, because we didn't want to move away from corporal punishment. But now we decided to have the turnaround strategy by including the RCL [Representative Council of Learners] when we're doing the code of conduct.

We asked him whether there were any other worthwhile systems. He told us that on a particular day in each term "... there is what we call the curriculum monitoring framework." During this process the Head of Department (HOD) compares the curriculum documents and teaching resources of a teacher with the books of the learners to verify whether the teacher has indeed covered the curriculum. He said that "... the HOD will choose some of the books and take them to the deputy principal ... and the principal will also check and give the feedback to the HoDs." He spoke of the deputy principal reporting to the principal who checks whether what has been done is recorded in the register. He told us that this "... is how I'm monitoring the curriculum and doing book control." We probed Lwando on how well the interventions were working, and he responded by telling us that they were working well, and that they were also having extra classes. These "... extra classes were mostly in Grade twelve and were being used to revise." He spoke of the use of question papers and the telematics programme, which the learners can access with their cell phones, "... and the teachers can also just recap to say this topic was taught and then just play (telematics) in the class." He told me that the school has "... two internet services. There's one that is from WCED, and we also have our own that is being paid for by the school."

Heidegger's Interpretive Narrative

Being Principal: Thrownness and Personal Mastery

Lwando's initiation into principalship exemplifies Heidegger's concept of thrownness (Geworfenheit). Confronted with poor National Senior Certificate (NSC) results and a death threat within weeks of his appointment, Lwando found himself thrust into a world that demanded immediate action and personal transformation also referred to as a re-constitution of his world. This existential crisis aligns with Senge's discipline of personal mastery, as Lwando had to rapidly develop his leadership capabilities while maintaining a clear vision for the school's improvement.

The principal's decision to consult educators on teaching assignments in his first year, resulting in no improvement, reflects the challenges of navigating pre-existing mental models within the school. Lwando's subsequent strategic reassignment of teachers demonstrates a shift towards systems thinking, recognising the interconnectedness of staff allocation and learner outcomes.

Positive Outcomes: Shared Vision and Being-in-the-World

As the NSC results improved, Lwando's being-in-the-world (*Dasein*), as a principal, evolved. The increased parental support and student enrolments signify a change in the school's relationship with its community, echoing Heidegger's notion of care (from the German, *Sorge*). Lwando's partnership with Symphonia exemplifies Senge's shared vision, as external collaboration aligned with the principal's aspirations for improvement.

Strategic Management: Authenticity and Team Learning

Lwando's approach to staff absenteeism through rigorous record-keeping and progressive discipline demonstrates Heideggerian authenticity. By confronting this issue directly, Lwando chose to engage with the reality of his situation rather than succumb to inauthentic modes of being. His focus on hiring and grooming new staff aligns with Senge's team learning discipline, creating an environment where collective learning could flourish.

Vision: *Dasein* and Shared Vision

The school's lack of a shared vision highlights a disconnect in the collective *Dasein* of the school community. Lwando's recognition of the need for a new, relevant vision demonstrates an understanding of Senge's shared vision discipline and its importance in shaping the school's lived experience. The absence of personal visions among staff underscores the challenge of fostering personal mastery within the organisation.

Team Learning: Care and Collective Growth

Lwando's efforts to mentor new staff and arrange workshops embody Heidegger's concept of care (*Sorge*) in leadership. For Heidegger, *Sorge* represents more than simple concern—it is a fundamental structure of human existence, reflecting our essential nature as beings who are inherently involved with and responsible for others' growth and development. This philosophical understanding of care manifests in Lwando's leadership through two distinct but interrelated forms that Heidegger identifies. These are *Besorgen* (concern for tasks and objects) and *Fürsorge* (solicitude or care for others).

Through his mentoring initiatives, Lwando demonstrates what Heidegger terms "authentic care" where leadership is not about doing things for others or taking over their challenges, but rather about helping them realise their own potential and authenticity. His workshop arrangements reflect an understanding that professional development must go beyond mere skill acquisition to foster genuine understanding and personal growth. These practices, aligned with Senge's team learning discipline, reflect Lwando's deep comprehension that the school's transformation depends on the collective growth of its members.

Mental Models: Discourse and Authenticity

The reluctance of staff to speak openly in meetings reveals the entrenched mental models within the school culture. Lwando's encouragement of open communication in SMT meetings demonstrates an attempt to create an authentic space for dialogue, aligning with both Heidegger's concept of discourse and Senge's mental models discipline. For Heidegger, genuine discourse isn't merely the exchange of information, but rather a way of "being-with-others" (Mitsein) that allows for the disclosure of shared meanings and truths. This aligns powerfully with Lwando's efforts to transform traditional hierarchical meeting structures into spaces of authentic engagement where staff can show up as their genuine selves, sharing their concerns and insights openly.

The intersection between Heidegger's phenomenological understanding of discourse and Senge's emphasis on challenging mental models becomes evident in how Lwando attempts to surface and examine the tacit assumptions that govern school interactions. This approach recognises that meaningful organisational change requires not just structural adjustments, but a fundamental shift in how people relate to and communicate with each other in their everyday professional lives.

Systems Thinking: World-Building and Holistic Perspective

Lwando's revised school discipline system and implementation of a curriculum management framework exemplify both Heidegger's concept of world-building and Senge's systems thinking. These initiatives demonstrate Lwando's understanding of the school as an interconnected system, where changes in one area automatically affects others.

Throughout his journey, Lwando's leadership embodies the tension between thrownness and projection, key elements of Heidegger's notion of *Dasein*. He continually projects possibilities for the school's future while grappling with the situatedness of his role. This interplay between present challenges and future aspirations aligns closely with Senge's vision of a learning organisation, where continuous adaptation and growth are paramount.

Lwando's experience reveals the complex, lived reality of transforming a school into a learning organisation. His actions demonstrate that such transformation is not merely a matter of implementing new systems or policies, but of fundamentally altering the way the school community understands and engages with its world. The challenges he faces – from staff resistance to external threats—highlight the profound difficulty of leading authentic change in education.

Conclusion

This study set out to explore the lived experiences of a black African high school principal, who teaches in a township school in South Africa and his efforts in leading the school towards becoming a learning organisation. The study employed a phenomenological approach grounded in both Husserl's descriptive and Heidegger's interpretive traditions, framed by Senge's five disciplines of learning organisations. This study we have gained profound insights into the challenges and opportunities of transformative educational leadership.

The primary aim was to understand if and how Lwando could lead his school to become a learning organisation. Through the lens of Heideggerian phenomenology, we observed Lwando's "being-in-the-world" as a principal, his thrownness into challenging situations, and his authentic responses to these challenges. Concurrently, Senge's framework provided a structure to analyse Lwando's actions in terms of personal mastery, shared vision, mental models, team learning, and systems thinking.

Lwando's journey reveals a leader grappling with the complexities of transforming a struggling school. His initial experiences, marked by poor NSC results and personal threats, exemplify Heidegger's concept of thrownness. Yet, Lwando's response to these challenges demonstrates a commitment to personal mastery, as he rapidly adapted his leadership approach and vision for the school.

The data indicates significant progress in several areas aligned with Senge's disciplines. Lwando's strategic management of staff absenteeism and his focus on hiring and developing new teachers show an evolving understanding of systems thinking and team learning. His partnership with Symphonia and efforts to improve NSC results reflect a growing shared vision within the school community.

However, the study also reveals ongoing challenges. The lack of a well-established shared vision among staff and the difficulties in fostering open communication highlight areas where the school falls short of fully embodying a learning organisation. These challenges align with Senge's emphasis on the importance of mental models and shared vision in organisational learning.

Lwando's efforts to implement a curriculum management framework and revise the school's discipline system demonstrate an understanding of systems thinking. These initiatives show promise in creating structures that support ongoing learning and adaptation within the school.

From a Heideggerian perspective, Lwando's leadership journey illustrates the dynamic interplay between authenticity and inauthenticity in facing the demands of principalship. His willingness to confront difficult issues head-on, such as staff absenteeism and poor academic performance, reflects an authentic engagement with his role. At the same time, his struggles with fostering open communication and a shared vision among staff reveal the ongoing tension between different modes of being in leadership.

In answering whether Lwando could lead the school to become a learning organisation, the data suggests a nuanced response. While significant strides have been made, particularly in areas of systems thinking and personal mastery, the full realisation of a learning organisation remains a work in progress. The school shows elements of transformation, but challenges persist in fully embodying all five of Senge's disciplines.

Lwando's leadership demonstrates the complex, non-linear nature of organisational change in education. His experiences underscore that becoming a learning organisation is not a destination but an ongoing journey of growth and adaptation. The phenomenological approach of this study reveals the deeply personal and contextual nature of this journey, highlighting how theoretical concepts of organisational learning are lived and negotiated in the day-to-day realities of school leadership.

Lastly, while Harbour High School, under Lwando's leadership, has made significant progress towards becoming a learning organisation, the transformation is incomplete. The study reveals both the potential and the challenges of applying learning organisation principles in a high school setting. Lwando's journey illustrates that leading a school towards becoming a learning organisation is a complex, ongoing process that requires persistence, reflexivity, and a willingness to confront and reshape deep-seated mental models and organisational structures.

This study contributes to our understanding of educational leadership by illuminating the lived experience of a principal striving to create a learning organisation. It highlights the value of combining phenomenological inquiry with organisational learning theory to gain a rich, nuanced understanding of school transformation. Future research could build on these insights to explore how principals can more effectively navigate the challenges of fostering shared vision and open communication in their journey towards creating true learning organisations in education.

References

Akanle, O. & Shittu, O. S., 2020. Study justification in social research. In A. S. Jegede & U. C Isiugo-Abanihe (Eds.), *Contemporary Issues in Social Research* (pp. 93–104). Ibadan: Iban University Press.

Department of Education. (2016). *Personnel administrative measures*. Government Gazette No. 39684, 12 February 2016. Pretoria: Government Printer.

Fanikhayavi, R., Mardani, N., & Mardani, S. (2014). Analysis of Peter Senge's five commandments learning in organizations and adherence to the Islamic Azad University staff of its components. *CES Working Papers*, 6(1), 77–86.

Gorner, P. (2001). Reid, Husserl and phenomenology. *British Journal for the History of Philosophy*, 9(3), 545–555.

Harris, A. & Jones, M., (2018). Leading schools as learning organisations.

Heidegger, M. (1967). *Being and time* (J. Macquarrie & E. Robinson, Trans.). New York: Harper and Row.

Husserl, E. (1936/1970). *The crisis of European sciences and transcendental phenomenology: An introduction to phenomenological philosophy*. Northwestern University Press. for the phenomenological analysis of interview data. *Human studies*, 8(3), pp. 279–303.

Kools, M. & Stoll, L. (2016). A guide for policy makers, school leaders and teachers (OECD (OECD Education Working Papers No. 137). Paris: OECD Publishing.

Long, K. W. (2024). A phenomenological investigation into the lived experiences of selected high school principals focussing on the school as a learning organisation (Unpublished thesis). University of the Western Cape, South Africa.

Lopez, K. A. & Willis, D. G. (2004). Descriptive versus interpretive phenomenology: Their contributions to nursing knowledge. *Qualitative Health Research*, 14(5), 726–735.

Neubauer, B. E., Witkop, C. T. & Varpio, L. (2019). How phenomenology can help us learn from the experiences of others. *Perspectives on Medical Education*, 8(2), 90.

Quong, T. & Walker, A. (2010). Seven principles of strategic leadership. *International Studies in Educational Administration (Commonwealth Council for Educational Administration & Management (CCEAM))*, 38(1).

Retna, K. S. (2011). The relevance of 'personal mastery' to leadership: the case of school principals in Singapore. *School Leadership & Management*, 31(5), 451–470.

Senge, P. M. (2006). *The fifth discipline: The art and practice of the learning organisation*. New York: Currency. (Original work published in 1990).

Senge, P. M., Cambron-McCabe, N., Lucas, T., Smith, B., & Dutton, J. (2012). *Schools that learn (updated and revised): A fifth discipline fieldbook for educators, parents, and everyone who cares about education*. New York: Currency.

Shaked, H., & Schechter, C. (2020). Systems thinking leadership: New explorations for school improvement. *Management in Education*, 34(3), pp. 107–114.

Stoll, L., & Kools, M. (2017). The school as a learning organisation: a review revisiting and extending a timely concept. *Journal of Professional Capital and Community, 2*(1), 2–17.

Thomasson, A. L. (2007). 15 Conceptual analysis in phenomenology and ordinary language philosophy. *The Analytic Turn,* 270.

· 7 ·

UNVEILING POWER DYNAMICS IN SOUTH AFRICAN CLASSROOMS: A CRITICAL PHENOMENOLOGICAL EXPLORATION INTO STUDENT TEACHERS' TEACHING PRACTICUM SCHOOLING PLACEMENTS

Clive Jimmy William Brown & Sarasvathie Reddy

Introduction

Phenomenology in education focuses on understanding the lived experiences of individuals within educational contexts, emphasising the subjective and interpretive nature of these experiences (Gallagher & Zahavi, 2020). It seeks to uncover the meanings that students and teachers (or any other research participant) ascribe to their educational encounters, highlighting the importance of personal perspectives in shaping educational realities. This approach is grounded in the belief that individuals are not isolated entities but are deeply connected to the social systems they inhabit, which influence their educational experiences (Samuel, Reddy & Brown, 2022). By examining the interplay between personal identity and social context, phenomenology provides insights into how students navigate diverse educational environments. It emphasises the need to consider the dialogical relationship between individual experiences and structural, systemic elements, acknowledging the role of power dynamics in educational settings. Phenomenology in education also explores the complexities of crossing socio-economic and racial divides as individuals bring their unique backgrounds and perspectives into diverse schooling contexts (Vagle, 2018). This approach highlights the challenges and opportunities that arise when individuals encounter different cultural and social environments during their educational journeys. Williams (2021) asserts that by focusing on the lived experiences of students and teachers, phenomenology offers a nuanced understanding of the educational process, moving beyond quantitative measures to capture the richness of human experience. It encourages educators to reflect on their own experiences and assumptions, fostering a more empathetic and inclusive approach to teaching and learning. Phenomenology also underscores the importance of agency and empowerment in education as individuals navigate their educational paths and make sense of their experiences (Chiramba & Maringe, 2022). This perspective challenges traditional notions of education as a one-size-fits-all process, advocating for a more personalised and context-sensitive approach. By examining the persistence of historical legacies, such as apartheid in South Africa, phenomenology reveals the enduring impact of systemic inequalities on educational experiences. It calls for critical reflection on the power dynamics within educational settings, urging educators to address these issues to create more equitable opportunities for all students. Phenomenology in education ultimately seeks to illuminate the diverse and complex realities of educational experiences, providing a framework for understanding and addressing the challenges students and teachers face in a rapidly changing world. Through its focus on lived experiences, phenomenology offers valuable insights into how individuals make meaning of their educational journeys, contributing to a deeper understanding of the educational process (Van Manen, 2023).

Significance of Studying Lived Experiences in the South African Context

Studying lived experiences in the South African context is significant because it provides insights into the complex realities shaped by the country's historical and socio-political landscape (Samuel et al., 2022). This approach helps to uncover the enduring impact of apartheid legacies on education, highlighting the persistent racial and socio-economic divides that influence students' and teachers' experiences. By focusing on lived experiences, researchers can better understand how individuals navigate these divides and the challenges they face in diverse educational settings. This understanding is crucial for developing strategies to address systemic inequalities and promote equitable educational opportunities (Ainscow, 2020). Additionally, examining lived experiences allows for a deeper appreciation of the personal and social dimensions that shape educational journeys, emphasising the importance of context-sensitive educational approaches (Fomunyam & Teferra, 2017). In the South African context, where diversity and multiculturalism are central themes, studying lived experiences can inform more inclusive and empathetic educational practices (Davids & Waghid, 2016; Le Grange, 2016; Soudien, 2012). This perspective also highlights the agency and resilience of individuals as they adapt to and transform their educational environments, offering valuable lessons for fostering positive change. By capturing the voices and stories of students and teachers, researchers can contribute to a more nuanced understanding of the educational landscape, ultimately supporting efforts to create a more just and equitable society (Morrow, 2007).

Context: Brief Overview of the South African Educational Landscape

Historical Background of Apartheid and its Impact on Education

Apartheid, a system of institutionalised racial segregation and discrimination, significantly shaped South Africa's education system for decades, fostering inequities that still persist today (Christie, 2020; Soudien, 2012). Under apartheid, education was deeply segregated along racial lines, with Black South Africans subjected to a substandard curriculum designed to limit their opportunities for socio-economic advancement. The notorious Bantu Education Act of 1953, for example, restricted the quality of education for non-white students, denying them access to the same resources, opportunities, and career pathways available to white students. Schools for Black South Africans were severely under-resourced, overcrowded, and intentionally structured to produce a labour force fit only for low-skill jobs in an economy dominated by white employers (Christie, 2020).

The legacy of apartheid education extended far beyond the content taught; it embedded a structural inequality into South Africa's education system that systematically disenfranchised generations of learners (Jansen, 2009). The impact of this racially tiered education system is still evident today. Many historically marginalised schools remain under-resourced, with insufficient infrastructure, inadequate learning materials, and overburdened teaching staff (Mouton et al., 2013; Taylor, 2008). This historical background is crucial for understanding the enduring disparities that student-teachers, especially those from historically disadvantaged groups, must navigate during their training and professional development.

Current Challenges in Post-Apartheid South African Schools

More than three decades after the end of apartheid, the South African education system still grapples with deep-rooted challenges, many of which are legacies of its divisive past. Spaull & Jansen (2019) assert that the education system has evolved into a two-tiered structure where a divide exists between well-resourced schools, often catering to the financially privileged and under-resourced schools that continue to serve marginalised communities. This inequality manifests in access to basic facilities, teacher-to-student ratios, and the availability of learning materials, which are often skewed in favour of affluent schools.

Despite numerous policy efforts, including the South African Schools Act of 1996 and ongoing reforms under the Department of Basic Education, underfunded township and rural schools face structural limitations that hinder educational outcomes (Msila, 2005). The Minimum Requirements for Teacher Education Qualifications (DHET, 2015) emphasises that student-teachers need exposure to a diverse range of schools. Yet, disparities in placement opportunities exacerbate challenges for developing professionals who must adapt to radically different teaching environments. Many student-teachers report feeling inadequately prepared to handle overcrowded classrooms, varying sociocultural dynamics, and lacking basic resources such as textbooks or proper classroom infrastructure (Pillay & Gopal, 2019).

Moreover, the persistence of socio-economic inequities continues to shape educational experiences. Township and rural schools struggle with high dropout rates, a lack of access to technology, and, in some cases, unsafe learning environments, all of which contribute to a broader systemic failure in achieving educational equity. These post-apartheid challenges create an increasingly complex landscape for both student-teachers and policymakers, who must find new ways to bridge the gap between policy aspirations and classroom realities (Soudien, 2018).

The Role of Student-Teachers in this Transitioning Landscape

In this shifting educational environment, student-teachers play a critical role in bridging the gap between historical inequities and the aspirations of a more equitable post-apartheid education system. As future educators, they are uniquely positioned to confront and transform the enduring disparities in schools. Their teaching practice (TP), a key component of initial teacher education (ITE) programmes, places them at the heart of this challenge. Teaching practice serves as the practical application of pedagogical theories learned in university and as an immersive experience where student-teachers engage with the socio-economic realities of the classroom (Fuller & Brown, 1975a).

During their placements, student-teachers are exposed to the diversity of South African schools, from well-resourced urban institutions to underfunded township and rural schools. This immersion forces them to reconcile their academic training with the often-harsh realities of the classroom (Zyster, 2023). Their challenges—ranging from large class sizes and inadequate learning materials to language barriers and varying levels of learner discipline—are integral to their professional growth and development (Zyster, 2023). The emotional labour involved in managing these diverse contexts is substantial, yet it provides critical insights into the country's broader systemic issues affecting education.

As South Africa continues its transition toward a more inclusive and equitable education system, student-teachers act as both learners and change agents (Novelli & Sayed, 2016). They must navigate the complexities of unequal schooling environments while also playing an active role in reshaping these spaces. Their experiences during teaching practice influence their development as educators and contribute to the larger project of educational transformation. By embracing critical reflection and engaging with the socio-cultural dynamics of their placements, student-teachers are equipped to foster inclusive, learner-centred classrooms that challenge the inequalities inherited from apartheid (Groenewald & Mpisi, 2022).

In this transitioning landscape, student-teachers must be prepared to teach and advocate for the needs of all learners, particularly those in marginalised communities. They are at the forefront of transforming a system still shaped by the legacies of the past into one that holds promise for a more equitable future (Ramrathan, 2024).

Theoretical Framework: Critical Phenomenology

Overview of Phenomenology and its Evolution

As a philosophical tradition, phenomenology originated with Edmund Husserl in the early 20th century and focused on studying consciousness and the structures of experience. Husserl proposed that by bracketing our preconceptions and assumptions, we could return *"to the things themselves"* and gain insights into how individuals experience the world through subjective perception. Zahavi (2018) highlights that Husserl (2012) emphasised that phenomenology sought to uncover the essence of experiences by understanding how things present themselves to consciousness (Husserl 1913).

As phenomenology evolved, students of Husserl, such as Martin Heidegger, expanded upon his ideas, introducing ontological dimensions to the study of human existence. Heidegger's seminal work Being and Time (1927/1967) shifted the focus from a purely descriptive approach of lived experiences to a deeper inquiry into the nature of "being" itself. Heidegger argued that human beings, referring to their Dasein, are always already embedded in a world of relationships, structures, and meanings that shape their experiences (Moran, 2015). This ontological turn in phenomenology brought a more existential and contextual perspective, suggesting that our engagement with the world is not passive but an active interpretation of being in the world (Heidegger, 1962).

Over time, phenomenology has influenced various fields, including education, psychology, and sociology, offering a framework for understanding lived experiences. In the context of student-teacher teaching practicum (TP) placements, phenomenology provides a powerful tool to explore how individuals navigate complex learning environments, allowing for a deeper understanding of their personal, emotional, and professional development (Brown, 2024). This framework helps unpack the intricate processes through which student-teachers interpret their roles within the classroom, engage with diverse learners, and confront the challenges posed by real-world teaching contexts (Brown, 2024).

Critical Phenomenology: Integrating Individual Experience with Social Context.

Critical phenomenology extends traditional phenomenology by incorporating a focus on the social, political, and cultural dimensions of lived experiences.

This approach, drawing on scholars such as Maurice Merleau-Ponty and contemporary thinkers like Lisa Guenther (2019), seeks to reveal the ways in which power dynamics, oppression, and social inequalities shape individual experiences. While classical phenomenology centres on personal perception, critical phenomenology emphasises the importance of the external world in influencing and constraining individual agency (Samuel et al., 2022).

In the context of student-teacher TP placements, critical phenomenology provides a robust framework for exploring the intersection of personal experience and the broader societal structures that govern education. It offers a metaphorical window through which the tensions between theoretical knowledge gained in university settings and practical challenges encountered in diverse schooling environments can be examined. Issues such as race, class, and gender, which shape both teaching environments and student teachers' perceptions of their professional identity, are key focus areas in this critical inquiry (Soudien, 2020; Jansen, 2019).

The notion of power dynamics is central to this critical approach, particularly in the context of South African classrooms where the legacies of apartheid continue to impact educational opportunities and resources (Carnoy et al., 2015). By applying critical phenomenology, this chapter highlights student-teachers' challenges in navigating these complexities, highlighting the often-hidden structures that influence their development as professional educators. This approach deepens our understanding of individual experiences and calls for a broader reflection on how educational systems perpetuate or challenge existing inequities (Jansen, 2019).

Relevance of Heidegger and Husserl to the Study

Both Martin Heidegger and Edmund Husserl provide foundational philosophical frameworks for understanding the lived experiences of student-teachers during their teaching practicum. Husserl's transcendental phenomenology, emphasising how consciousness shapes experiences, serves as the initial steppingstone for exploring how student-teachers interpret their roles and the challenges they encounter in diverse classrooms. His notion of epoché—the suspension of preconceived beliefs—encourages student-teachers to approach their practicum placements with fresh perspectives, open to the complexities of the teaching environment (Husserl, 1970; Heidegger, 1962).

Heidegger's ontological focus on *Dasein* (being in the world) further enhances this exploration by situating student-teachers within the specific sociocultural contexts of South African schools. Heidegger's philosophy, which emphasises the entanglement of individuals with their environments, allows for a deeper interrogation of how student-teachers learn and "exist" within the classroom setting. His assertion that "we are ourselves the entities to be analysed" resonates strongly with the phenomenological approach taken in this chapter, as it seeks to understand the essence of student-teachers experiences through their first-hand narratives.

Moreover, Heidegger's concept of "thrownness" (Geworfenheit), the idea that individuals are "thrown" into a pre-existing world with its own structures and limitations, is particularly relevant to the South African education system. Student-teachers are thrown into a schooling landscape, still grappling with the legacies of apartheid, navigating under-resourced environments, racial tensions, and socio-economic disparities (Welch, 2002). Drawing on both Heidegger's and Husserl's philosophies, this chapter provides a theoretical foundation that allows for a rich exploration of the existential and experiential dimensions of teaching in such a complex and evolving educational landscape (Brown & Samuel, 2022).

These philosophical perspectives, grounded in the lived experiences of individuals, provide the necessary tools for interpreting the multifaceted challenges and opportunities that student-teachers face, offering valuable insights into their journey toward becoming professional educators.

Methodology

Description of Arts-Based Data Production Strategies

Arts-based research methods have gained traction within qualitative inquiry, offering a creative and often transformative way to capture participants' lived experiences (Howlett et al., 2016; Merryfield, 1993). In this study, arts-based data production strategies are employed to enrich the understanding of student teachers' TP experiences, particularly when traditional verbal methods may not fully capture the emotional and embodied dimensions of their journeys. Through the creation of visual sketches better known as the *Tree of Life* and other artistic expressions, student teachers are given an alternative medium to represent their encounters with power dynamics, identity struggles, and pedagogical challenges in South African classrooms.

Arts-based methods align with the critical phenomenological stance of this research by offering students a space to express experiences that may be difficult to articulate through language alone. These sketches, as visual metaphors, allow participants to symbolically communicate feelings of marginalisation, disempowerment, or professional growth during TP placements. The use of arts-based strategies fosters a deeper engagement with the research process. It encourages student teachers to reflect on their roles in shaping and being shaped by the educational environment (Morris & Paris, 2022). By integrating these visual narratives with other qualitative data, the research creates a multidimensional understanding of the subtle power dynamics that permeate teaching and learning spaces (Leavy, 2020).

Interactive Semi-Structured and Focus-Group Interviews

Interactive semi-structured and focus-group interviews form the backbone of the data collection process in this study. Semi-structured interviews allow for open-ended, flexible conversations that explore the nuanced experiences of student teachers as they navigate their teaching practicums. These one-on-one dialogues provide an intimate setting for participants to share their personal stories, reflect on their challenges, and discuss the complexities of power relations within South African classrooms (Creswell & Poth, 2016).

In addition to semi-structured interviews, focus groups serve as a dynamic platform for collective reflection and peer interaction. In these settings, student teachers engage in dialogue with one another, comparing experiences and offering different perspectives on the shared challenges they face. The focus-group format fosters a collaborative atmosphere, encouraging participants to build on each other's insights and deepening the collective understanding of power dynamics in the practicum setting (Krueger & Casey, 2015). This interactive approach ensures that the research not only privileges individual voices but also captures the shared, communal aspects of teaching practicum experiences.

Both interview formats are designed to be interactive, allowing for iterative exploration of key themes as they emerge during the conversation. By blending individual and group-based interviews, the research creates a comprehensive picture of how student teachers experience and interpret power, identity, and pedagogical practice in their TP placements (Brinkmann & Kvale, 2015). These methods align with the critical phenomenological approach, uncovering individual and collective narratives of marginalisation, resistance, and empowerment in educational spaces. This study aligns with the stance of Guenther's (2019, pg. 2) position of "critical phenomenology":

> Critical phenomenology goes beyond classical phenomenology by reflecting on the quasi-transcendental social structures that make our world experience possible and meaningful and engaging in a material practice of "restructuring the world" to generate new and liberatory possibilities for meaningful experience and existence.

Ethical Considerations and Reflexivity

Ethical considerations are paramount in any research involving human participants, particularly in studies that explore sensitive topics such as power dynamics, marginalisation, and identity (Orb et al., 2001). This study adheres to strict ethical guidelines, ensuring that the voices of student teachers are represented with respect, care, and integrity. Consent forms are obtained from all participants, emphasising their right to withdraw from the study at any time, and confidentiality is maintained throughout the research process. Pseudonyms are used to protect participants' identities, and the data collected through interviews, journals, and arts-based methods are handled with sensitivity (Arifin, 2018).

Reflexivity is crucial in the researcher's engagement with the data and the participants (Finlay, 2002). As a postgraduate researcher deeply embedded in the South African educational context, I am aware of my own positionality and the potential influence it may have on the interpretation of data. My previous experiences as a student and researcher shape how I understand student teachers' challenges during TP placements. Through ongoing reflexive practices, I critically examine how my own biases, assumptions, and power dynamics may influence the research process and outcomes (Olmos-Vega et al., 2023).

By adopting a critical phenomenological stance, I strive to remain attuned to how power operates within the research setting and in my interactions with participants. This reflexive awareness is crucial for ensuring that the research does not reinforce existing power imbalances but instead seeks to uncover and challenge them. In doing so, the research remains committed to ethical rigor, fostering a respectful and collaborative relationship with student teachers as co-creators of knowledge. The reflexive approach enhances the depth and integrity of the research, ensuring that the findings are grounded in a critically aware, ethically sound methodology (Darawsheh, 2014).

Case Studies: Lived Experiences of Student-Teachers

Participant Backgrounds and Biographical Heritage

Natasha, a 23-year-old self-identified Coloured female, grew up in the suburb of Steenberg, a community primarily consisting of lower-to middle-class households. English is her home language, and her upbringing was shaped by her working-class family, where both her parents were employed—her mother worked as a cleaning lady, a source of pride for the family. Natasha's educational journey began in 2018 when she enrolled in the BEd Intermediate Phase degree programme. Her strong leadership skills were evident early on as she served as an elected class representative throughout her years of study. Natasha's background in a close-knit coloured community, where resources were limited but valued, significantly shaped her worldview and approach to teaching. Her biographical heritage, combined with her ambitious and hard-working nature, has influenced how she navigated both personal and professional spaces within the South African education system.

Dumo, a vibrant 22-year-old female from the Nguni ethnic group, specifically identifying as Zulu, grew up in Germiston, a small city in the East Rand of Gauteng, South Africa. Upon being accepted into the ITE programme in 2019, she relocated to Mowbray, Cape Town, marking a significant personal and academic transition. Her decision to pursue a teaching career led her to diverse school environments, fostering a deep understanding of South Africa's complex educational landscape. As a Black African female, Dumo's biographical heritage is pivotal in navigating both the classroom and the broader socio-political dimensions of South African education. Her experiences reflect an intersection between her identity and the evolving educational spaces she engages with, particularly in post-apartheid South Africa, where historical legacies still have an impact.

Transitioning into Diverse School Environments

When Natasha and Dumo embarked on their teaching practicum, their transitions into diverse school environments presented contrasting challenges influenced by their biographical heritage.

Natasha's TP experiences placed her in various school contexts, each offering its unique set of challenges and opportunities. In her first year, she selected Zeal Academy, a Quintile 5 primary school in Retreat, Cape Town, which, despite its history as a former Whites-only school, had become racially and socio-economically diverse. This placement mirrored Natasha's own primary school experience, which involved working-class learners and limited resources. In her second year, she faced the global pandemic, which disrupted her physical TP experience, pushing her to adapt to an alternative online teaching model. By her third year, Natasha was placed at St. Jackson R.C. Primary School, a no-fee Quintile 1 Catholic school serving primarily Coloured and Black learners from impoverished communities. The contrast between this school and her previous placements offered her a new perspective on teaching in under-resourced environments. Her final placement at the well-resourced Elizabeth House Constantia Private School in an affluent area provided an entirely different setting, allowing her to experience the vast disparities between schools in South Africa.

Dumo's teaching practicum placements exposed her to a range of multicultural, socio-economic, and racially diverse school environments. Her first placement was at Sunflower Boys Primary School, a Quintile 5 public school with a historical legacy as a whites-only institution. Despite its transformation into a mixed-race school, Dumo noted the persistent socio-economic privilege within the predominantly middle-to upper-class student population. In her second-year placement, she moved to Bethel Street Primary, a more multicultural school with learners from varied racial, linguistic, and religious backgrounds. This placement offered her a unique opportunity to learn how to engage with a diverse learner cohort, adapting her teaching style to suit different cultural and socio-economic needs. Her experience at Cliftonville Adventist Primary, an independent, faith-based school, added a religious dimension to her exposure, broadening her understanding of how educational contexts vary across different school settings.

Navigating Changing Power Dynamics and Social Contexts

The participants' experiences in transitioning into these environments brought into focus the changing power dynamics and social contexts of South African classrooms.

Throughout her TP placements, **Natasha** encountered various power dynamics that required her to adjust her teaching approaches. At Zeal Academy, the socio-economic diversity of the learners meant that she had to navigate between different cultural and financial backgrounds, which reminded her of her own schooling experience. The stark contrast between the learners at St Jackson R.C. Primary School, many of whom came from gang-infested and impoverished areas, required Natasha to adopt a more empathetic and resourceful approach to teaching. She learned to navigate the power dynamics between teachers and learners, particularly when learners face significant socio-economic challenges. Her final placement at the prestigious Elizabeth House Constantia Private School revealed the disparities in power and resources between schools serving wealthy communities and those serving underprivileged areas. Natasha's adaptability in these diverse settings highlighted her belief in the importance of being able to teach under any circumstances, whether in a well-resourced private school or an underprivileged state school and her commitment to developing innovative teaching methodologies that address the needs of all learners.

Throughout her placements, **Dumo** encountered shifting power dynamics that shaped her teaching practice and understanding of the learner-teacher relationship. In her reflection, she noted the shift from authoritarian teaching methods to more learner-centred approaches that fostered mutual respect and comfort between learners and teachers. The historical context of the schools she worked in, and their present-day realities highlighted how power relations still influence educational experiences. Dumo's classroom observations of race, culture, and socio-economic status allowed her to develop a more critical awareness of how these factors intersect with power structures. As a student-teacher, she had to navigate her own position within these power dynamics, particularly in relation to her identity and background, while learning to adapt her teaching to the diverse needs of her learners.

In both Dumo's and Natasha's cases, their experiences underscored the profound impact of social contexts and power dynamics on their teaching practicum journeys. Dumo, transitioning from her hometown in Gauteng to diverse school environments in Cape Town, grappled with varying cultural, racial, and socio-economic realities. She learned to adapt her teaching strategies to meet the needs of learners from different backgrounds, gaining insights into how resources and social status influence the learning experience. Natasha, coming from a Coloured working-class community, navigated similarly contrasting school environments—from under-resourced state schools to affluent private institutions—highlighting the disparities in educational access and opportunity. Her experience reinforced the importance of adaptability and creativity in resource-rich and resource-constrained settings.

Their journeys illustrate how student teachers in South Africa must engage not only with the pedagogical aspects of teaching but also with the nuanced social realities that define the country's educational landscape. These experiences contribute to the broader discourse on how power, privilege, and identity intersect in South African classrooms, offering critical insights into the ongoing evolution of teaching and learning in diverse and often unequal contexts.

Analysis: Intersecting Personal and Social Dimensions

The Interplay Between Personal Identity and Social Context

The data underscores the significant role of personal identity and social context in shaping students' experiences during their TP. It illustrates that individuals are deeply connected to the social systems they inhabit, influencing their expectations and interactions. For instance, Natasha reflects on her TP experience, stating:

> **Natasha:** So, I chose picture number one. I think picture number one depicts me, the type of teacher I love. I feel that there's interaction, raising hands, eager to learn, and that is what I see as myself. I think this would be learner-centered. They are not just sitting there and listening to you; you are asking them questions and interacting. The learners and I are involved in the learning because this is where I get to develop my professionalism in the sense of what methodologies or teaching strategies, I am equipping myself to be and, um ... and then yeah. And I think the learners are learning here, and as a teacher, I am learning here. You are learning what you, as a teacher, want and understand the learners' needs. You can also reflect on yourself as an individual. I feel the raising of the hands means there's a sense of they understand, there's interaction, they are willing to learn, there's an eagerness to learn, and when you teach a topic after your lesson, and now you are asking questions, everybody is raising their hands, it means that now they understand, and they are eager to answer. I think it's a sense of security and comfort.

Dumo's experiences during her TP illustrate the significant role of personal identity and social context. Her journey from Johannesburg to Cape Town for her studies marked a transition from a familiar environment to an unfamiliar one, which she described as moving from a "*zone of comfort to a zone of fear*". This shift highlights how her personal identity as a developing teacher was influenced by the new social context she encountered, prompting her to adapt and grow in response to these changes.

Challenges of Crossing Socio-Economic and Racial Divides

The data discusses the challenges faced by participants as they navigate socio-economic and racial divides during their TP placements. Natasha's experience in a diverse private school illustrates these challenges:

> **Natasha:** The second picture, I feel that it looks very much like my last teaching practice. It looked like the school I was at. And here, firstly, why I chose this picture; as I said, it brings back memories of my final teaching practice, and it was a good thing. I was at a very diverse school. It was a private school, and I learnt so much, and it contributed so much to my knowledge in the sense that, um . . . the kind of teacher I needed to be in the private school and the things you need to go through and the things you need to develop on. You really think you are doing it by yourself, but in actual fact, you're not and then, um, the people involved in this image were definitely the staff for me at the school and the learners. For me, at the school, the learners were so different. I was in a very diverse school, a very diverse classroom, and they made me feel a certain way. They made me question meetings. Um, so . . . I think I had to learn how to deal with this kind of learner. That was the challenge for me. How to work with them. How to think like them, and what I need to do to make them comfortable in my classroom. This made me doubt myself as a teacher.

Dumo's TP experiences in different school settings exposed her to the challenges of crossing socio-economic and racial divides. She noted the stark differences between private and government-funded schools, stating, "She had a wake-up call. She quickly learned that the private school setting was vastly different from government-funded institutions". This experience underscored the complexities of navigating diverse educational environments and the impact of socio-economic disparities on teaching and learning.

Reflections on the Persistence of Apartheid Legacies

The data reflects on the enduring legacies of apartheid, particularly in education. The socio-economic and racial divides encountered by participants during their TP placements are remnants of apartheid's systemic inequalities. **Natasha's** experience in a rural school, described as "a classroom in a rural school (Quintile 1, since there is a chalkboard, and the class is made up of all Black students)", underscores the persistence of these legacies. These historical disparities continue to shape educational environments, highlighting the ongoing challenges in achieving equitable opportunities and the need for critical reflection on power dynamics within educational settings.

Dumo's reflections on her TP placements reveal the persistence of apartheid legacies in South African education. Her experiences in a rural school, characterised by a classroom with "*All Black students and a Black female teacher*", highlight the ongoing racial and socio-economic divides that continue to shape educational contexts. These experiences reflect the enduring impact of historical inequalities and the challenges of fostering equitable educational opportunities in a post-apartheid era.

Discussion: Implications for a Socially-Just Education

This chapter explores the broader implications of the findings from the critical phenomenological inquiry into student teachers' teaching practicum placements, with a particular focus on fostering a socially just education system in South Africa. By critically examining the power dynamics that persist in educational spaces, the chapter contends that addressing these challenges is crucial for achieving equity, inclusivity, and transformation in post-apartheid South African classrooms. It emphasises that education can become a powerful tool for dismantling the deep-rooted inequalities embedded in historical legacies and contemporary structures when aligned with social justice principles (Leibowitz, 2016).

The Role of Critical Phenomenology in Understanding Educational Challenges

Critical phenomenology has been a vital theoretical and methodological lens in this research, offering a nuanced framework for interpreting the lived experiences of student teachers (Qutoshi, 2018). It enables an in-depth exploration of the intersection between individual experiences and the larger socio-political context. By foregrounding the personal narratives of student teachers, critical phenomenology helps unveil the ways in which power, identity, and agency manifest in educational settings. These narratives highlight how historical inequalities continue to shape students' experiences despite efforts to democratise education (Jansen, 2019).

The application of critical phenomenology in this study reveals the challenges student teachers face in negotiating the gap between theoretical knowledge acquired at the university and the practical realities of teaching placements in diverse and unequal South African classrooms. Through this lens, the research not only captures individual struggles but also contextualises these within the broader societal structures, offering a deeper understanding of the educational challenges that persist. As a result, critical phenomenology provides a means to confront and critique the enduring disparities related to race, class, and geography that are evident in student teachers' experiences.

Insights for Fostering a More Equitable and Inclusive Education System

The findings from this inquiry underscore the need for a transformative approach to education that acknowledges and actively addresses the inequalities that student teachers encounter during their practicum placements. The narratives reveal that student teachers often find themselves positioned within a system that perpetuates the very inequities it seeks to challenge. For education to become a catalyst for social transformation, it is essential to centre inclusivity, equity, and empowerment at the heart of pedagogical practices.

One of the key insights from this research is the importance of creating spaces for critical dialogue and reflection in teacher education programmes. By encouraging student teachers to critically engage with their own experiences of power dynamics, educators can foster a deeper understanding of the social injustices that affect teachers and learners. Additionally, practicum placements should be intentionally structured to expose student teachers to diverse educational environments, providing opportunities to work in both under-resourced and well-resourced schools. This exposure is critical for breaking down the barriers of race and class that continue to limit professional development and perpetuate inequality in the teaching profession.

Recommendations for Future Research and Practice

The complexities uncovered in this critical phenomenological inquiry suggest several avenues for future research and practice. First, there is a need for further exploration into how institutional policies and practices within teacher education programmes can be reformed to better support student teachers, particularly those from historically marginalised backgrounds. Research should focus on developing strategies that enhance the preparation of student teachers for the challenges they will face in the classroom, emphasising not only pedagogical skills but also social awareness and advocacy for justice.

Future research could also benefit from comparative studies that examine how different educational contexts, both within South Africa and globally, address issues of equity and inclusion in teacher education. Such studies would provide valuable insights into how other systems navigate similar challenges and what practices might be adapted to the South African context.

Teacher education programmes should integrate more opportunities for reflective practice and critical engagement with power, privilege, and oppression issues. Creating collaborative networks between universities, schools, and communities could enhance the professional development of student teachers while fostering a shared commitment to social justice. Furthermore, continuous support for novice teacher's post-practicum is essential to ensuring that the lessons learned during their placements translate into sustained efforts towards equitable and inclusive teaching practices in their future careers.

By advancing these recommendations, future research and practice can contribute to the ongoing work of transforming the South African education system into one that truly reflects the democratic values it aspires to uphold.

Conclusion

Summary of Key Findings

This chapter has provided a critical phenomenological examination of student teachers' experiences during their teaching practicum placements, particularly focusing on power dynamics in South African classrooms. The key findings reveal that student teachers navigate a complex web of sociopolitical and historical legacies and institutional practices that often perpetuate inequality. By foregrounding the voices of student teachers, the research uncovers the subtle and overt power relations that shape their experiences, from the choice of placement schools to the daily realities of teaching and learning in diverse, post-apartheid classrooms. The narratives gathered highlight the ongoing influence of race, class, and geographical disparities despite efforts to democratise the education system.

Contributions to Phenomenology and Educational Research

This work contributes significantly to both phenomenology and educational research by advancing the application of critical phenomenology in the South African context. As discussed, phenomenology, particularly its critical variant, offers an invaluable lens for exploring individuals' subjective, lived experiences and the broader societal structures that shape these experiences (Qutoshi, 2018). Critical phenomenology goes beyond surface-level interpretations, providing deeper insights into power dynamics and the contextual realities of educational practices (Guenther, 2021).

The study also addresses a gap in South African educational research, where a need exists for more explicit guidance on how emerging scholars can effectively apply phenomenological frameworks. By incorporating critical phenomenology, this research adds complexity to the understanding of student-teacher development, urging future scholars and educators to adopt more reflective, interdisciplinary approaches in their investigations.

Furthermore, this research emphasises the importance of creating spaces within higher education where seasoned phenomenologists can mentor emerging scholars, particularly in understanding the intricacies of phenomenological theory and method. Such mentorship is crucial to broadening the field and enhancing its contribution to transforming educational practices in South Africa.

Final Reflections on the Potential for Transformative Education in South Africa

The findings of this study underscore the transformative potential of education in South Africa, particularly when approached through a critical, socially conscious lens. By embracing critical phenomenology, this research advocates for a deeper understanding of the power dynamics inherent in the educational system, pushing for practices that not only recognise these inequities but actively work to dismantle them. The transformative goals of critical research align closely with the broader aspirations of social justice, equity, and inclusion in education.

The potential for education as a force for social change lies in the commitment of educators, policymakers, and scholars to critically engage with the historical and social contexts that continue to influence the education system. Reflexivity, power analysis, and participatory methods are essential tools for fostering a more equitable and inclusive system that prepares student teachers for their professional roles and equips them to be agents of social change.

In closing, this chapter calls for sustained efforts to integrate critical phenomenological insights into research and practice. By doing so, we move closer to an educational landscape in South Africa that not only reflects democratic ideals but also embodies the transformative power of education in addressing the legacies of apartheid and creating a more just society for future generations.

References

Ainscow, M. (2020). Promoting inclusion and equity in education: lessons from international experiences. *Nordic Journal of Studies in Educational Policy*, 6(1), 7–16.

Arifin, S. R. M. (2018). Ethical considerations in qualitative study. *International journal of care scholars*, 1(2), 30–33.

Brinkmann, S., & Kvale, S. (2015). *Interviews: Learning the craft of qualitative research interviewing*. Sage Publications.

Brown, C. J. W., & Samuel, M. A. (2022). Sustaining evolving teaching practicum models in higher education: A conversational ethnodrama between South African teacher educators. *Perspectives in Education*, 40(3), 163–180.

Brown, C. J. W. (2024). *Student-teachers' lived experiences in diverse teaching practicum contexts* (Unpublished doctoral thesis)—University of KwaZulu-Natal.

Carnoy, M., Ngware, M., & Oketch, M. (2015). The role of classroom resources and national educational context in student learning gains: Comparing Botswana, Kenya, and South Africa. *Comparative Education Review*, 59(2), 199–233.

Chiramba, O., & Maringe, F. (2022). State-less, Identity-less and miseducated: The experience of refugee students in higher education in South Africa. In *Pedagogical responsiveness in complex contexts: Issues of transformation, inclusion and equity* (pp. 37–54). Cham: Springer International Publishing.

Christie, P. (2020). *The right to learn: The struggle for education in South Africa* (Revised ed.). Pan Macmillan South Africa.

Creswell, J. W., & Poth, C. N. (2016). *Qualitative inquiry and research design: Choosing among five approaches*. Sage Publications.

Darawsheh, W. (2014). Reflexivity in research: Promoting rigor, reliability and validity in qualitative research. *International Journal of Therapy and Rehabilitation*, 21(12), 560–568.

Davids, N., & Waghid, Y. (2016). Educational leadership reconsidered: On being inclusive, democratic, and ethical in troubled times. *South African Journal of Higher Education*, 30(1), 97–111. https://doi.org/10.20853/30-1-558

Department of Higher Education and Training. (2015). *Minimum requirements for qualification in teacher education*. South African Government. https://www.dhet.gov.za/Teacher%20Education/National%20Qualifications%20Framework%20Act%2067_2008%20Revised%20Policy%20for%20Teacher%20Education%20Quilifications.pdf

Finlay, L. (2002). "Outing" the researcher: The provenance, process, and practice of reflexivity. *Qualitative Health Research*, 12(4), 531–545.

Fomunyam, K. G. (2017). Curriculum responsiveness within the context of decolonisation in South African higher education. Perspectives in Education, 35(2), 196–207. https://doi.org/10.38140/pie.v35i2.3403

Fuller, B., & Brown, R. (1975a). *Exploring the role of teaching practice in the preparation of student-teachers*. Journal of Education for Teaching, *1*(2), 173–185. https://doi.org/10.1080/02607 47750010209

Gallagher, S., & Zahavi, D. (2020). *The phenomenological mind*. Routledge.

Groenewald, E., & Mpisi, A. (2022). *Student teachers' perceptions and experiences of certain modules within a transformed curriculum to foster social justice*. South African Journal of Education, *42*(3), 1–12.

Guenther, L. (2019). Critical phenomenology. In G. Weiss, G. Salamon, & A. V. Murphy (Eds.), *50 Concepts for a Critical Phenomenology*, (pp. 11–16). https://muse.jhu.edu/book/67156

Guenther, L. (2021). *Six senses of critique for critical phenomenology*. Puncta: Journal of Critical Phenomenology, *4*(2), 5–23. https://doi.org/10.5399/PJCP.v4i2.2

Heidegger, M. (1927). *Being and time* (J. Macquarrie & E. Robinson, Trans., 1962). Harper & Row. (Original work published 1927)

Heidegger, M. (1962). *Being and time* (J. Macquarrie & E. Robinson, Trans.). Harper & Row. (Original work published 1927).

Howlett, C., Ferreira, J.A., & Blomfield, J. (2016). Teaching sustainable development in higher education: Building critical, reflective thinkers through an interdisciplinary approach. *International Journal of Sustainability in Higher Education*, *17*(3), 305–321. https://doi.org/10.1108/IJSHE-07-2014-0102

Husserl, E. (1970). *The crisis of European sciences and transcendental phenomenology* (D. Carr, Trans.). Northwestern University Press. (Original work published 1936).

Husserl, E. (2012). *Introduction to the logical investigations: A draft of a preface to the logical investigations (1913)*. Springer Science & Business Media.

Jansen, J. D. (2009). *Knowledge in the blood: Confronting race and the apartheid past*. Stanford University Press.

Jansen, J. D. (2019a). *Decolonisation in universities: The politics of knowledge*. Wits University Press.

Jansen, J. D. (2019b). Inequality in education: What is to be done? *South African Schooling: The Enigma of Inequality: A Study of the Present Situation and Future Possibilities*, 355–371.

Krueger, R. A., & Casey, M. A. (2015). Focus group interviewing. *Handbook of practical program evaluation*, 506–534.

Le Grange, L. (2016). Decolonising the university curriculum. *South African Journal of Higher Education*, *30*(2), 1–12. https://doi.org/10.20853/30-2-709

Leavy, P. (2020). *Method meets art: Arts-based research practice*. Guilford publications.

Leibowitz, B. (2016). In pursuit of socially just pedagogies in differently positioned South African higher education institutions. *South African Journal of Higher Education*, *30*(3), 219–234.

Merryfield, M. M. (1993). Reflective practice in global education strategies for teacher educators. *Theory into Practice*, *32*(1), 27–32. https://doi.org/10.1080/00405849309543569

Moran, D. (2015). Dasein as transcendence in heidegger and the critique of Husserl. In P.J. Ennis & T. Georgakis (Eds.), *Heidegger in the twenty-first century* (pp. 23–45). Dordrecht: Springer Netherlands.

Morris, J. E., & Paris, L. F. (2022). Rethinking arts-based research methods in education: Enhanced participant engagement processes to increase research credibility and knowledge translation. *International Journal of Research & Method in Education*, 45(1), 99–112. https://doi.org/10.1080/1743727X.2021.1926971

Morrow, W. (2007). *Learning to teach in South Africa*. HSRC Press.

Mouton, N., Louw, G. P., & Strydom, G. (2013a). Critical challenges of the South African school system. *International Business & Economics Research Journal (IBER)*, 12(1), 31–44. https://clutejournals.com/index.php/IBER/article/view/7510/7576

Msila, V. (2005). *The education exodus: The flight from township schools*.

Msila, V. (2005). The education exodus: The flight from township schools. *Africa Education Review*, 2(2), 173–188. https://doi.org/10.1080/18146620508566299

Novelli, M., & Sayed, Y. (2016). Teachers as agents of sustainable peace, social cohesion and development: Theory, practice & evidence. *Education as Change*, 20(3), 15–37.

Olmos-Vega, F.M., Stalmeijer, R.E., Varpio, L., & Kahlke, R. (2023). A practical guide to reflexivity in qualitative research: AMEE Guide No. 149. *Medical teacher*, 45(3), 241–251.

Orb, A., Eisenhauer, L., & Wynaden, D. (2001). Ethics in qualitative research. *Journal of Nursing Scholarship*, 33(1), 93–96.

Pillay, A. (2017). How teachers of English in South African schools recognise their change agency. *South African Journal of Education*, 37(3), 1-11.

Qutoshi, S.B. (2018). Phenomenology: A philosophy and method of inquiry. *Journal of Education and Educational Development*, 5(1), 215–222.

Ramrathan, L. (2024). *Critical reflections on teacher education in South Africa*. Springer Nature.

Samuel, M.A., Reddy, S., & Brown, C.J.W. (2022). Critical reflections on researching lived and learning experiences: towards a critical phenomenology. *African Perspectives of Research in Teaching & Learning*, 5(1), 185–205. https://www.ul.ac.za/aportal/application/downloads/sp_2022_13_Samuels%20et%20al%20article.pdf

Soudien, C. (2012). *Realising the dream: Unlearning the logic of race in the South African school*. HSRC Press.

Soudien, C. (2018). The education of black South Africans: An overview of socio-economic inequities and policy challenges. *South African Journal of Education*, 38(2), 1–13. https://journals.ufs.ac.za/index.php/pie/article/view/3805

Soudien, C. (2020). *The struggle for university education in post-apartheid South Africa*. Routledge.

Spaull, N., & Jansen, J. D. (Eds.). (2019). *South African schooling: The enigma of inequality. A study of the present situation and future possibilities*. Springer.

Taylor, N. (2008, February). What's wrong with South African schools? In *What's Working in School Development Conference*, JET Education Services, Cape Town.

Vagle, M. D. (2018). *Crafting phenomenological research*. Routledge.

Van Manen, M. (2023). *Phenomenology of practice: Meaning-giving methods in phenomenological research and writing*. Routledge.

Welch, T. (2002). Teacher education in South Africa before, during and after apartheid: an overview. *Challenges of teacher development: An investigation of take-up in South Africa*, 17–35.

Williams, H. (2021). The meaning of "Phenomenology": Qualitative and philosophical phenomenological research methods. *The Qualitative Report*, 26(2), 366–385.

Zahavi, D. (2018). *Phenomenology: The basics*. Routledge.

Zyster, J. D. N. (2023). *The emotional experiences of Cape Peninsula University of Technology education students in navigating teaching practice*. [Doctoral thesis, University of Stellenbosch] University of Stellenbosch. https://scholar.sun.ac.za/handle/10019.1/127647

· 8 ·

CONCLUSION: TOWARDS EDUCATION AND EDUCATIONAL RESEARCH: AS AN "ACT OF CARING" FOR THE AFRICAN LEARNER

Oscar Koopman & Karen Koopman

Introduction: The Shadow Burdens of the African Child

As we conclude this book on phenomenological insights for the classroom, we are compelled to focus on two interrelated phenomena that deeply shape the educational landscape in [South] Africa. These are the "shadow burdens of the African child" and "caring as a virtue" for teachers. These phenomena, when examined through the lens of phenomenology, offer valuable insights into the challenges and possibilities for curriculum, in a post-colonial African context.

The "shadow burdens of the African child" encapsulate the persistent, often invisible forces and challenges that African learners face daily. These challenges are deeply rooted in the long-standing legacy of colonialism—spanning more than three-and-a-half millennia—including the nearly five decades of apartheid in South Africa. These historical traumas, resulting from colonialism and apartheid, have not only left deep scars on the psyches of multiple generations but have also shaped an education system and curriculum that often give precedence to outcomes that relegate understanding and needs of the local learner. The shadow of these burdens extends beyond historical trauma to encompass contemporary challenges such as systemic poverty, ongoing social inequalities, and the psychological impacts of rapid societal changes.

In response to these shadow burdens, we propose a renewed focus on caring as a fundamental virtue for teachers. This approach draws upon teachers' innate qualities of kindness and compassion towards African children, both as a learner and as a research participant. This invocation demands a radical change in our approach to education and educational research in African contexts, where learners are recognised as complete human beings deserving of full dignity and care.

To address these intertwined phenomena, we now turn to the intellectual guidance of two phenomenologists, namely Ted Aoki (2005) and Jan Patočka (1927/1996) to explore these inter-related phenomena and how they provide a philosophical foundation for reimagining education and curriculum in postcolonial societies burdened with the lingering effects of colonialism, racism, poverty, and various other invisible forces that weigh down both teachers and learners psychologically and intellectually.

Ted Aoki's profound insight that the being of a teacher should be infused with "caring as a virtue" gains deeper significance when applied to the African context. As William Pinar (2005) notes, Aoki leads us "into the inner layer, a layer he characterises as a journey on the way to understanding teaching as a mode of being" (p. 16). Aoki challenges teachers to transcend the traditional, technocratic approach to education and embrace a more holistic, empathetic stance. He urges teachers to "break away from the attitude of grasping, and grasping, and grasping," instead seeking a genuine orientation to the essence of teaching, allowing them to attune to the true calling of their practice (Pinar, 2005, p. 17). For Aoki (2005), teaching is a practice deeply attuned to the space where care resides—a place of gathering and belonging where the mutual presence of care from both teachers and students fosters a shared sense of indwelling. In the African context, this Aokian description "of what teaching is" is crucial in order to compel teachers to acknowledge and to turn towards this call and act to irradicate the shadow burdens that still subjugate many African learners.

Complementing Aoki's notion of care as a virtue, Jan Patočka's (1996) concept of "caring for the soul" emphasises authentic engagement with the world through reflective, lived experience. Patočka's emphasis on a deep, existential form of care aligns with Aoki's view of teaching as an ethical and relational practice, where the teacher's role is to cultivate meaningful, lived connections with learners and the world. This perspective shifts the focus from mere intellectual development to nurturing care as a way of being and becoming for the learner.

It is important to distinguish this understanding of "care" from Nel Noddings' (1984) "care theory," which posits care as expansive and relational, created, and sustained through interactions with others. While Noddings emphasises the reciprocal nature of care, Aoki's notion, rooted in his Japanese heritage (of *Katei*), focusing on the inherent qualities or virtue of the teacher to act with compassion, kindness, and a moral sense of responsibility toward learners, is not contingent the learners' acknowledgement or reciprocation to that care.

The integration of Aoki's and Patočka's philosophical perspectives offers a powerful framework for reimagining education and curriculum as well as research in post-apartheid societies. This approach calls for a curriculum that adopts pedagogical strategies aimed at addressing the shadow burdens through genuine care for the child's holistic development. Moreover, it demands a fresh perspective on how we conduct research in African schools and universities, emphasising the recognition of both learners and research participants as complete human beings.

It is crucial that we first acknowledge and discuss the historical and economic context of poverty as a shadow burden in Africa, particularly in South Africa to appreciate the urgency of this approach. This will be followed by an in depth exploration of trauma theory to understand the effects of the shadow burdens on the cognitive development of the African learner. Finally, we will chart a new way forward to pedagogically address the lingering effects of these shadow burdens still subjecting the lives and school context of African learners on a daily basis. This examination suggests a foundation to formulate a more holistic and empathetic approach to education that genuinely cares for the soul of the African child. This approach not only addresses the immediate challenges that learners face but also works towards healing generational traumas and set up classrooms as spaces for authentic engagement and transformation in African education systems.

The Shadow Burden of Poverty: Economic Realities of the Modern-day African Child

The shadow of poverty casts a deep and pervasive darkness over the lives of the majority of African people in South Africa. This burden, deeply entangled with the lingering effects of colonialism, apartheid, and racism, continues to shape the nation's economic landscape long after the end of formal segregation. South Africa as discussed in Chapter 4 stands as one of the world's most unequal societies, with wealth still disproportionately concentrated in the hands of a minority white population.

The extent of this inequality is starkly illustrated by the Gini coefficient, a measure of income inequality ranging from 0 (perfect equality) to 1 (perfect inequality). Alarmingly, this indicator has worsened from 0.660 under apartheid to 0.696 in the post-apartheid era (World Bank Report, 2018; Statistics South Africa, 2017), signalling that the dream of economic liberation remains elusive for many Black African people. This inequality is not an abstract concept but a harsh daily reality for millions of African children.

The depth of poverty in South Africa as discussed in Chapter 4 is profound, with 55% of the population living below the poverty line, and those closest to it subsisting on a mere R992 per person per month. Even more concerning is that 76% of those above the poverty line live under constant threat of falling into poverty, underscoring the precarious nature of economic stability for the majority of the population (World Bank Report, 2018). The reliance of 61% of poor households on meagre child support grants (R500/month) further illustrates the depth of economic vulnerability (Koopman & Koopman, 2024; Statistics, 2017). Moreover, recent studies reveal that 20.4% of the population (7.8 million people), particularly in African communities, are socially vulnerable in terms of food security (Statistics South Africa, 2017).

The educational landscape mirrors this economic disparity, bearing witness to the intergenerational transmission of poverty. According to a 2016 International Literacy Report on South African learner performance, 8 out of 10 Grade 4 pupils cannot read proficiently. International assessments consistently place South African learners at the bottom of global rankings in mathematics and reading. The Trends in International Mathematics and Science Study (2019) reveals that a staggering 63% of Grade 5 children perform below the low international benchmark in mathematics, a figure that may rise to 76% due to the COVID-19 pandemic, during which children lost 25% of contact time over two years when the country was placed under hard lockdown. In reading, the situation is even more dire, with projections suggesting that up to 88% of Grade 5 pupils may score below the low international benchmark (Mullin, Martin, Foy and Hooper (2017) these authors wrote the PIRLS 2016 report).

These statistics paint a grim picture of a generation of African learners struggling against the tide of historical injustice and contemporary neglect.

The shadow burden they carry is not just one of material deprivation but of thwarted potential and stunted dreams. It is a burden that weighs heavily on their young shoulders, shaping their worldview, their sense of self-worth, and their prospects for the future. This ongoing cycle of poverty and educational underachievement based on the statistics listed in the previous paragraph serves as a stark reminder that the legacy of colonialism and apartheid continues to exert a powerful influence on the lives of African learners, demanding urgent and sustained intervention to break the chains of intergenerational disadvantage (Koopman & Koopman, 2024).

In light of these challenges, Ted Aoki's (2005) vision of teaching and curriculum as an existential endeavour takes on new significance. For South African learners and teachers, teaching is not only about acquiring knowledge but also about reclaiming identity, dignity, and the right to self-definition in the wake of historical oppression. To fully grasp the depth of this challenge, we turn to Franz Fanon, a philosopher, scholar, psychiatrist, and decolonial thinker who understands the psychological impact of oppression on the human soul and the need for caring as a restitutive process.

Frantz Fanon's (1967) incisive observations reveal how colonialism—and systems like apartheid—were crafted to empty the native's mind of all substance, distorting, and destroying the oppressed people's history and cultural identity. Fanon insists that if we genuinely care for the soul and well-being of black people, we must reclaim and reaffirm the cultural identities and practices systematically devalued by these forces. This perspective challenges us to radically reimagine how we view the child as a learner and, especially, the education they receive. Present educational approaches often mirror Western preferences, perpetuating cultural superiority while ignoring or erasing the trauma inflicted on African bodies and psyches.

Here, Aoki's emphasis on the importance of lived experience in education aligns with the need to transform such a system. For South African learners—particularly those facing vulnerability and poverty—their lived reality is not a series of isolated moments. Rather, it demands an engagement with the entirety of their experience, recognising how historical trauma and current economic hardship shape their educational encounters.

In this vein, Jan Patočka's (1996) concept of "caring for the soul" takes on new meaning. For Patočka, this care is inseparable from "care for death," implying a deep recognition of life's finitude and its impact on the soul's development. For many South African learners and teachers, the presence of death—be it psychological, cultural, intellectual, or emotional—due to poverty or deprivation is an ongoing reality. By embracing this reality, rather than avoiding it, education can become a transformative practice that supports individuals in confronting and transcending their challenges, fostering a more authentic engagement with life.

Caring for the soul in South African education is not a luxury but an imperative. It requires a commitment from teachers, researchers, and policymakers to move beyond traditional Western paradigms and engage with the complex realities of post-apartheid South Africa. By embracing Aoki's vision of care as the essence of teaching and Patočka's emphasis on authentic engagement with the world, we can begin to address the deep-seated challenges in South African education.

This approach calls for a fundamental shift in how we conceptualise education and research. It demands that we view learners and teachers not as isolated individuals but as bearers of complex histories and lived experiences. By caring, we open up possibilities for healing, transformation, and the creation of a more equitable and just society. In doing so, we can work towards an education system that cares for the souls of all children (as well as when conducting research), fostering authentic engagement, critical reflection, and the realisation of human potential in the face of historical and ongoing challenges.

Trauma Theory: The Enduring Impact of Colonial Violence on African Learners

The violent encounter between Africa and Europe through imperialism and colonialism fundamentally reshaped the African continent, creating what Serequeberhan (2013) termed the "dark continent" within the modern world (p. 55). This history of lived violence continues to reverberate through African societies, particularly in education, where the trauma of colonialism remains an underexplored discourse. Said (cited in Serequeberhan, 2013, p. 57) captures the essence of this violence insightfully:

> Imperialism was the theory, colonialism the practice of changing the uselessly unoccupied territories of the world into useful new versions of the European metropolitan society. Everything in those territories that suggested [difference] waste, disorder, uncounted resources, was to be converted into productivity ... You get rid of most of the offending human and animal blight ... you confine the rest to reservations, compounds, native homelands where you can count, tax, use them profitably and you build a new society on the vacated space ... Thus was Europe reconstituted abroad its 'multiplication in space' successfully projected and managed ...

This colonial violence—its displacement, erasure, and systemic dehumanisation—as discussed in this quote and in the previous sections, continues to cast a long shadow over the lives of African children. Trauma theory provides a framework for understanding the profound psychological and educational impact of this historical trauma, as well as the counterviolence it provokes in response to these deep scars.

Fanon (1967), in "The Wretched of the Earth," powerfully argues that the trauma of imperialism and colonialism extends far beyond those who directly experienced these violent historical events. He posits that this unresolved trauma becomes a form of psychic inheritance, passed down through generations, manifesting in the lives of descendants who continue to live under the shadows of oppression, exploitation, and dehumanisation. Even if future generations did not experience colonial violence firsthand, they remain profoundly affected by its lingering presence in societal structures, cultural identity, and interpersonal relationships. The violence of the past, Fanon emphasises, leaves scars on the collective consciousness, perpetuating cycles of alienation, inferiority, and internalised oppression.

Returning to Freud's (1959) concept of transference, which we introduced and discussed in Chapter 1, we can now examine its specific manifestations within educational contexts shaped by historical trauma. While the Chapter 1 outlined the basic mechanisms of transference and countertransference in therapeutic relationships, these dynamics take on particular significance in classrooms where histories of racial oppression and poverty intersect with teaching and learning. The unconscious redirection of feelings from past to present, previously discussed in our analysis of transference, manifests uniquely in the classroom. Here, learners may project their internalised experiences of historical trauma onto their teachers, while teachers' countertransference—influenced by their own cultural backgrounds and biases unknowingly—can create complex patterns of interaction that echo and sometimes reinforce historical wounds.

Building on our discussion of Freud's (1959) characterisation of teaching as an "impossible profession," we can now see how the "return of the repressed" specifically impacts educational environments. This understanding adds new dimensions to Bibby's (2011) advocacy for therapeutic education, though we must move beyond viewing this approach as a simple solution to systemic inequalities.

Lacan's (1949/2006) theory of the "mirror stage," which we touched upon in Chapter 1, provides additional insight when applied to the classroom contexts shaped by racial oppression, particularly in settings like apartheid South Africa. The systematic othering creates what we might call an educational mirror stage, where learners encounter distorted reflections of themselves within institutional spaces. This process, combined with what Fanon (1967) terms epidermalisation, reveals how educational environments can either perpetuate or begin to heal the psychic wounds inflicted by systemic racism.

Foucault's (1975/1995) insights into how political systems shape people's psyches further underscore the deep-seated nature of this trauma. His assertion that "the soul is the effect and instrument of a political anatomy ... the prison of the body" reminds us that the psychological make-up of individuals is influenced by political forces (p. 30). In the context of colonial and post-colonial societies, these forces have created psychological prisons that continue to shape the reality of learners and teachers alike.

The ongoing impact of this historical trauma, as described by Caruth (1996), is not confined to individual experiences but circulates within society as a shared cultural and historical reality. The legacy of racial segregation, dehumanisation, and exploitation has created lasting psychological wounds that continue to manifest in contemporary education. Learners growing up in conditions of poverty and systemic social injustice are often grappling with deep-seated emotional and psychological pain that shapes their ability to learn, engage with content, and form meaningful relationships with their teachers and peers.

This understanding of the pervasive nature of trauma in educational contexts brings us back to the crucial importance of Aoki (2005) and Patočka's (1996) philosophies of care in education. Their emphasis on authentic engagement with the world through reflective, lived experience offers a pathway for addressing the complex psychological dynamics at play in classrooms affected by historical trauma. Aoki's vision of teaching as an act of care takes on new depth when viewed through the lens of trauma theory. It calls for teachers to be attuned not just to the cognitive aspects of learning, but to the deeper psychological forces that shape learners' experiences.

As Bibby (2011) suggests, teachers must turn to psychoanalysis to understand the child in their fullness, recognising that what happens outside the classroom—the historical, social, and cultural forces—deeply influences what happens inside it. For many learners and teachers in post-colonial contexts, the reality of historical trauma and its ongoing manifestations is a constant presence. By confronting this reality rather than shying away from it, education can become a transformative process that helps individuals confront and transcend their psychological wounds, leading to a more authentic and meaningful engagement with life and learning.

The application of trauma theory to the educational experiences of African learners reveals the profound and lasting impact of colonial violence. By integrating insights from psychoanalysis, critical theory, and phenomenology, we can develop a more nuanced understanding of the psychological dynamics at play in post-colonial educational settings. This interdisciplinary approach not only illuminates the challenges faced by learners and teachers but also points towards potential pathways for healing and transformation through education grounded in care, authenticity, and critical awareness.

Shattering the Shadow Burden: Towards Education and Research as a Caring for the Soul

As we now reflect on the contributions within this book, William Pinar's (2005) words drawing on Aoki's thinking describe how education as an academic discipline is under "savage attack by politicians" (p. xvi), echoes through my mind (p. xvi). It is evident, from the preceding discussions in earlier sections of this chapter that the situation has only intensified over the last twenty years. This assault as a result of the shadow burdens has not only persisted but intensified, morphed into a new attack in the form of neoliberalism thrust on the African child with multinational corporations, tech-oligarchs, university leadership and management joining politicians, with their curriculum architects in reshaping education according to market-driven ideologies, prioritising performance metrics, the promotion of digital utopianism at the expense of pedagogical wisdom and the holistic development of learners. In light of the challenges facing our disciplines, Pinar (2005) like Fanon, reiterates (drawing on Aoki's curriculum wisdom), we—talking to the academic community—must return and reaffirm our dedication to the intellectual foundations of education by deepening our engagement with curriculum theory and history. This renewed focus on the theoretical and historical underpinnings of our discipline is crucial not only for preserving our professional integrity, but also for equipping us to critically engage with and shape the future of education in an increasingly complex world. Therefore, in the question of how to we move forward and extend the boundaries of knowledge for education in

South Africa I return to the deep insights and shared emphasis of Jan Patočka and Tetsuo Aoki on the notion of *care*, offering us a compelling framework which we can use to understand the deeper purpose of education and research. Why are the work of these two scholars relevant for a time such as this to address the lingering effects of the shadow burden? We'll start with Aoki first.

Pinar in the foreword to the book titled "Curriculum in a new key: The collected works of Tetsuo Aoki's" describes Aoki as follows:

> Ted's greatest gift was, and remains today, his ability to call out of each of us deeply felt teaching and learning concerns that are transformed through penetrating inquiry. He is a pedagogue of pedagogues, and because his pedagogy is so profound, it lingers with us as we go forward and teach. The genealogy of his powerful pedagogy is the legacy that Ted leaves in the minds and hearts of countless curriculum scholars, particularly in Canada. (p. xxi)

William Pinar reminds us that true pedagogy transcends mere instruction, instead awakening within us a perpetual state of inquiry that transforms not only our understanding of curriculum, but our very being as caring teachers. Aoki's enduring influence challenges us to continuously excavate the depths of our educational experiences, fostering a lineage of critical, compassionate, and deeply reflective practitioners who carry forward his vision of teaching and learning as a transformative, existential journey. Pinar's description of Aoki, which he himself claims resonates deeply with the ethos of phenomenological inquiry (although in his work he draws on poststructuralism and critical theory in many other parts of his work). Aoki's philosophy and vision for curriculum and teaching has always been to dwell humanly with the child. To "dwell together humanly", Aoki suggests, means to create spaces of mutual respect for human engagement, understanding, and care, transcending historical wounds. This "dwelling together" Aoki (2005) argues must be beyond empathy. He draws on the anthropologist Magorah Maruyama who states that, "Empathy is a projection of feelings between two persons within one epistemology." (p. 219) For understanding in a trans-national or trans-cultural situation, what we need is trans-spection, which is a trans-epistemological process. He continues to interpret Maruyama's and echoes that "trans-epistemological process" to mean a way of bridging two ways of knowing. Simply put, this trans-epistemological process means to converse and listen with care. He then draws on a powerful quote of Oakeshott to show what the nature of the engagement should be in a space where two ways of knowing meet, especially when they both come from different walks of life, or worlds when he writes:

> As civilized human beings, we are the inheritors of a conversation, begun in the primeval forests and extended and made more articulate in the course of centuries. It is a conversation, which goes on both in public and within each of ourselves. It is the ability to participate in this conversation, and not the ability to reason cogently, to make discoveries about the world, or to contrive a better world, which distinguishes the human being from the animal and the civilized man from the barbarian. Indeed, it seems not improbable that it was the engagement in this conversation (where talk is without a conclusion) that gave us our present appearance, man being descended from a race of apes who sat in talk so long and so late that they wore out their tails. Education, properly speaking, is an initiation into the skill and partnership of this conversation in which we learn to recognize the voices, to distinguish the proper occasions of utterance, and in which we acquire the intellectual and moral habits appropriate to conversation. And it is this conversation which, in the end, gives place and character to every human activity and utterance (Aoki, 2005, p. 202).

In this generative-conversational space, Aoki wants us to see how teaching and learning is essentially and initiation into a participation in a shared dialogue. This is the space in which learners and teachers learn to listen, speak, and understand each other as they co-create the intellectual and moral foundations necessary for respectful coexistence and mutual growth, despite historical divides or cultural disparities. This Aokian perspective suggests that teachers should prioritises the holistic well-being and growth of students and learners over the mere transmission of information or rigid adherence to curricula, as we see in his depiction of Miss O, "who listens to and is attuned" to "the care that calls for the very living with her grade 5 pupils" (p. 15). Through invoking Miss O, we revitalise not only Aoki's vision of this generative-conversational dialogue, but also accentuate care as a prerequisite for authentic in education. Pinar (2005) notes, that care and empathy transcends the conventional boundaries of pedagogy, inviting teachers to engage with their students on a more fundamental, existential level. But what does the word caring in the context of education and curriculum mean?

In an attempt to answer this question, we will turn to the philosophical ideas of Jan Patočka, a Czech philosopher student of Husserl and Heidegger, who was forbidden to teach and publish in universities in his country of birth and unknown to many scholars outside of Europe. Let us then first introduce Patočka than his thinking. Patočka's concept of "caring for the soul" emerges from a life marked by intellectual rigor and political resistance. As a phenomenologist trained under Edmund Husserl and influenced by Martin Heidegger, Patočka developed a unique philosophical stance that bridged classical Greek thought with contemporary existential concerns (Patočka, 1996). His work on "being in the world" not only critiqued but also expanded upon the ideas of his mentors, offering a fresh perspective on human existence and education. Patočka's philosophy was forged in the pressures of 20th century European turmoil. His commitment to academic freedom and intellectual integrity led him to clash repeatedly with authoritarian regimes. During the Nazi occupation of Czechoslovakia, Patočka was banned from teaching, a fate that would be repeated under the subsequent communist regime (Tesar, 2013). These experiences of oppression and silencing deeply shaped his philosophical outlook, particularly his emphasis on the importance of living in truth and resisting ideological conformity. The concept of "caring for the soul" in Patočka's work is not merely an abstract philosophical notion, but a call to action in the face of societal and political pressures. It advocates for a form of education that goes beyond the transmission of knowledge to nurture the whole person, encouraging critical thinking and moral courage. This approach resonates strongly with contemporary concerns in education, particularly in post-colonial societies like South Africa, where the ghosts of colonialism and apartheid continue to shape education and continue to haunt us. These ghosts will not rest, cannot find peace as they continue to wander and seek vengeance on those who disrupted and destroyed them. Therefore, South Africans will not find rest until we have been restored and authenticated to our true selves and banish these ghosts to Hades forever.

Patočka's philosophy offers valuable ideas for reimagining teaching and learning in contexts marked by historical trauma and ongoing social challenges. His emphasis on authenticity and lived experience aligns with calls for curricula that could assist in addressing the "shadow burdens" that many learners carry. By encouraging teachers to focus on "caring for the soul," Patočka provides a philosophical foundation for a more holistic, empathetic approach to teaching and learning. It is this "caring for the soul" that is a prerequisite for the evocation and restoration of authentic lived experiences and identities as legitimate with dignities.

Hence, Patočka's (1996) philosophical concept of "caring for the soul" and Aoki's notion of care, are not only complementary but conjoined, as it helps us to understand part of the complexity of the soul. Patočka drawing on Plato's *melete thanatou* from the *Phaedo* and Heidegger's notion of *Sorge* (care) that describes *the soul* as the being of *Dasein*, in which he perceives the soul as that "substance" in the human being which alone is capable of truth. Patočka (1996) explains this cogently when he writes:

When thinking begins, the most it is possible to say is that on one side here stands the world, like a collection of everything which is, on the other side stands the philosophizing man with his ability to understand that which is the world. This ability to understand, this is called soul, in the Greek conception. This is the original understanding, that, on the basis of which man has the ability of truth and of individual truths (p. 13)

For Patočka, the soul is our fundamental capacity to comprehend and engage with the world around us, serving as the bridge between our individual consciousness and the vast expanse of existence. This unique ability to understand and to seek truth is what defines us as thinking beings, allowing us to not only perceive the world but to actively participate in uncovering its meaning and our place within it. To "care" for th(is)e soul like Aoki, Patočka helps us to understand that true caring is all about moving human life with truth. Findlay (2002) explains this eloquently when he writes:

The soul acts on us in those moments when we must decide, when we encounter the possibility of exerting control on our own fate by refusing to give in to the weight of events as they come at us. It acts on us by recognizing truth, and by differentiating between good and evil. This, however, is not a given characteristic. It exists for us as an inherent possibility, one available only if we pursue it. It comes, also, at a price, for the decision to act based on recognition of good and evil is the decision to accept the burden of a life that is no longer simple and instinctive, but problematic. (p. 63)

According to Patočka, the soul should not be thought of as an object or a thing, but rather as the space where we reflect on and understand our own existence. In this sense, the soul is not a fixed part of us, but something dynamic, constantly moving and evolving based on our experiences, choices, and reflections. It is through the soul that we engage with life in a meaningful way, discerning right from wrong and making choices that either lead us toward growth or, alternatively, cause us to regress. This movement of the soul is fundamentally connected to ontology, which is the philosophical study of being. Patočka (1996) argues that caring for the soul is about nurturing this movement toward growth, which he associates with the pursuit of "good." When we care for the soul, we make deliberate choices to advance in our understanding of ourselves and our place in the world. This growth is not just intellectual but deeply existential, touching on every aspect of what it means to be human. In contrast, neglecting the soul or making harmful choices can lead to a "loss of being," which Patočka, drawing on his lived experiences, equates with moral and existential deterioration—what he refers to as evil.

Patočka poses an essential question, asking why we should care for the soul, particularly when doing so forces us to confront difficult questions about good and evil? The answer, he argues, lies in the soul's connection to being. Our soul is the means by which we engage with the most fundamental aspects of existence—what it means to live a meaningful life. Caring for the soul allows us to grow, not just as individuals, but in our capacity to understand life in its fullest sense. This act of caring helps us move beyond mere survival and toward a deeper engagement with life's ethical and existential questions. Patočka (1996) believes that while this caring might seem to complicate life, as we are constantly forced to reflect and make difficult choices, it is the essence of being human. Contradistinctively, to live unreflectively, without caring for the soul, would mean to live without purpose, direction, or moral grounding. By choosing to care for the soul, we accept the challenge of discerning good from evil, and in doing so, we engage in the ongoing process of becoming fully human or as Aoki (2005) might call "to dwell humanly" together. Caring for the soul, therefore, is an existential task that requires us to reflect on our actions, make moral decisions, and strive for a deeper understanding of what it means to live well. This care, rooted in ontology, is essential for leading a meaningful life, even as it complicates our experience by forcing us to confront the realities of good and evil. Ultimately, the soul's movement toward growth is what allows us to fulfil our potential as human beings.

Using Patočka's philosophy as a guiding principle for teaching it should inspire the teacher to nurture each learner's innate potential for self-discovery in search of truth and meaning making, fostering a learning environment where learners are empowered to actively engage with the world and carve out their own unique place within it. In Patočka's world, a caring teacher is concerned about guiding learners towards an authentic self-promoting and reflective engagement with their everyday lived experiences of what it means to a morally just human being. In this way the teacher creates opportunities for students to question, reflect, and connect their learning to the deeper truths of their existence. Just as Patočka's phenomenological approach challenges researchers to be active participants in uncovering the essence of human experience, the teacher's role becomes one of fostering this same level of reflection and truth-seeking in the classroom following Aoki's notion of trans-epistemic dialogue. The notion where the teacher encourages learners to see education not as a passive process of receiving knowledge but as a transformative journey where they develop the courage to engage with the world, discover truth, and speak it, is what Patočka might call *parrhesia*, or the act of speaking truth without fear of risks and/or favour.

For Patočka, to be "caring for the soul" challenges teachers to view their roles metaphorically, as travel agents helping students live more authentically by cultivating their capacity for understanding and self-realisation. The classroom is then transformed into a space where learners are not only taught facts but are encouraged to live truthfully, reflect on their experiences, and develop as whole, engaged human beings.

Pedagogical and Research Principles for Transcending Historical Burdens of African Children

We unlock a powerful framework for expanding the boundaries of knowledge and addressing the lingering effects of apartheid, colonialism, poverty, and racism that continue to influence many African learners today when we combine Aoki's (2005) notions of "caring" and "dwelling humanly together" with Patočka's philosophy of "caring for the soul". These notions constitute principles that challenge teachers and academics to reconsider their approaches to teaching, learning, and educational research with African children. Those who pursue these principles will be compelled to banish mechanical or hierarchical models for those that centre on human subjectivity, embodied, dignity, and lived experience.

Aoki's metaphoric vision of lingering on the bridge comes to mind here, in which the teachers finds herself in deep contemplation, and meditation seeking newness and becoming to dwell humanly with her learners while emphasising deep care, respect, and a shared responsibility for nurturing each learner's potential. The classroom is perceived as a space where the teacher and learner share a mutual journey—one that honours the uniqueness of each person's cultures, welcoming the voices of learners while fostering a sense of togetherness. This Aokian approach disrupts dominant ideological narratives and hegemonies while embracing instead of erasing the multiple voices, cultures, personalities as a process of being and becoming. They question their own histories and cultural values with an open mind as a transitionary space. Patočka's notion of the soul, as the locus of understanding, similarly calls for a pedagogical practice that focus on the deeper task of guiding learners toward a reflective and authentic existence. To care for the soul of African learners is to help them navigate not only their intellectual growth but also their personal and existential development, ensuring they move beyond the inherited traumas of colonialism, apartheid, and systemic inequality. They are given a space in the classroom to give expression to their fears, pain and suffering as part of the healing process, while the teacher listens with her heart and not her mind with a deep sense of empathy and care to untangle those difficulties.

In practical terms, applying these philosophies to shatter the shadow burdens requires teachers to create learning environments that acknowledge and validate the lived experiences of African learners. This might involve incorporating local knowledge systems and languages into the curriculum, fostering critical dialogues about historical injustices, and encouraging students to explore their cultural identities. Teachers can implement Aoki's concept of "dwelling humanly together" by creating collaborative learning spaces where students' voices are heard and valued, promoting a sense of belonging and shared responsibility for learning outcomes.

Patočka's emphasis on "caring for the soul" can be realised through pedagogical approaches that encourage self-reflection and critical thinking. Teachers might introduce contemplative practices, journaling, or arts-based methods that allow students to explore their inner worlds and connect personal experiences to broader societal issues. In this way teachers can help learners develop resilience and a sense of agency in the face of systemic challenges.

Furthermore, these philosophies call for a reimagining of assessment practices. Rather than focusing solely on standardised measures of achievement, teachers can develop holistic evaluation methods that recognise personal growth, critical consciousness, and the ability to navigate complex social realities. This approach aligns with both Aoki's emphasis on the human dimension of education and Patočka's focus on authentic engagement with the world.

Teachers can create transformative educational experiences that not only address academic needs but also contribute to healing historical traumas and fostering a new generation of empowered, critically conscious African learners by integrating these philosophical approaches.

When we apply these principles to research, this phenomenological framework offers a way of looking deeply into the soul of research participants, just as a teacher looks into the soul of her learners. Like the learners in Miss O's classroom in Aoki's work, research participants must be treated with the utmost respect and care, recognising their stories and experiences as sacred. Fieldwork, through this lens, becomes a mutually enriching process of discovery and self-reflection, rather than a one-sided data collection exercise. Researchers are not mere observers but active participants in a shared dialogue or what we want to call an inter-epistemic open conversation. Simply put, researchers should not view their role as distant authorities but as partners in their learning-life journeys.

This approach to educational research, grounded in Aoki's (2005) concept of "dwelling humanly together" and Patočka's philosophy of "caring for the soul," transforms the research process in several significant ways:

1. The traditional hierarchical relationship between researcher and participant is reimagined as a collaborative partnership. Researchers engage in what van Manen (1990) calls "hermeneutic conversations," where both parties contribute to the co-construction of meaning. This aligns with Aoki's (2005) vision of the classroom as a space of mutual engagement and shared responsibility.
2. Phenomenological research emphasises methods that allow for deep, rich exploration of lived experiences. In-depth interviews become opportunities for participants to reflect on and articulate their experiences in ways that may be transformative for both the participant and the researcher. Observational techniques shift from detached notetaking to engaged participation, mirroring the way a caring teacher is fully present in the classroom.
3. The process of analysing phenomenological data becomes an exercise in "caring for the soul" of the research. Researchers engage in what Gadamer (1975) terms a "fusion of horizons," where they seek to understand the participant's world while acknowledging their own positionality (as discussed in Chapters 1 and 2). This requires a level of reflexivity and openness to being changed by the research process, much as teachers must be open to learning from their students.
4. The ethical dimensions of research are heightened when viewed through this phenomenological lens. Confidentiality and informed consent become more than procedural requirements; they are expressions of deep respect for the participant's dignity and lived experience. Researchers must constantly reflect on the potential impact of their work on participants, considering not just potential harm but also possibilities for empowerment and transformation.
5. In line with the phenomenological emphasis on lived experience, research findings are often presented in ways that preserve the richness and complexity of participants' stories. This might involve using

extensive quotes, narrative forms, or even artistic representations that capture the essence of the phenomenon being studied. The goal is not just to report findings but to evoke in the reader a sense of what it means to live the experience being described.

The ultimate aim of phenomenological educational research, viewed through the lens of Aoki and Patočka's philosophies, is not just to generate knowledge but to contribute to understanding the lived world and consciousness of African learners with lingering historical burdens to help improve educational practices and policies. Research findings are disseminated in ways that speak not just to academic audiences but to practitioners, curriculum developers and policymakers to provide guidance in shattering shadow burdens. This approach has the potential to produce research that is not only rigorous and insightful but also deeply ethical and transformative.

Conclusion

Aoki and Patočka's work challenge us to reconceptualise teaching and learning and educational research as a means of cultivating an authentic existence—an approach where both teachers and learners confront the deeper, existential questions of life. The freedom to explore one's identity, the pursuit of understanding, and the courage to speak truth without fear or favour are central to this transformative process. This philosophy aligns with the central themes explored throughout this book, where each chapter grapples with the complexities of education—whether in the context of creativity through music (Chapter 3), the challenges posed by artificial intelligence (Chapter 4), entrepreneurial learning (Chapter 5), the lived experiences of a black South African principal in leading the school towards becoming a learning organisation (Chapter 6) or the existential struggles of African pre-service teachers navigating identity, self-worth, and race (Chapter 7).

By grounding our educational practices and research methodologies in phenomenological principles that honour both Aoki's care for the child and Patočka's care for the soul, we open new possibilities for meaningful engagement and transformative learning. This approach helps dismantle the residual effects of apartheid, colonialism, and systemic injustice and allows African learners to reclaim their full humanity and engage authentically with their education. It is in this shared space of care, reflection, and human dwelling that true transformation can occur, breaking free from the oppressive systems of the past and moving toward a future where all learners can thrive.

In each of the chapters in this book, phenomenology serves as a philosophy and/or a method to reclaim the essence of education, one that aligns with Aoki and Patočka's vision of education as a profound, life-giving activity. While Chapter 1 highlighted the value of phenomenology in education research Chapter 2 begins by addressing researcher positionality and reflexivity, reminding us that teaching and research is as much about self-awareness as it is about imparting knowledge. This self-reflective stance is crucial in maintaining the integrity of phenomenological inquiry and in fostering authentic educational experiences. Chapter 4 delves into the tension between lived experience and the increasing presence of AI in education, echoing Aoki and Patočka's concern for preserving human capacity for reflection amidst rapid technological advancement. As we navigate the integration of AI into educational settings, their philosophies remind us of the irreplaceable value of human interaction, empathy, and care in the learning process. Each of these explorations reinforces the importance of grounding educational practices in the richness of human experience and subjective meaning-making. Throughout the book, we observed a consistent return to the fundamental questions posed by phenomenology: *How do we experience the world? How do we make meaning of our experiences?* And *how can education and research honour and illuminate these processes?* By engaging with these questions, the contributors to this book demonstrate the enduring relevance of phenomenological approaches in addressing contemporary educational challenges.

Although the contributors to this book do not draw on Aoki and Patočka's work explicitly, they weave together these various phenomenological insights, resonating with Aoki and Patočka's vision of curriculum and education as the care for the soul. It is through this care—this deep, authentic engagement with the self and the world—that education and research can truly fulfil their transformative potential. Each chapter moved beyond mere technical proficiency to foster deeper human engagement with the world, to open up possibilities for education and in particular curriculum that is truly meaningful and life-affirming. By grounding education and research in lived experience and reflective practice, they call for a renewal of teaching and learning—one that honours the complexity, subjectivity, embodiment, reflexivity, and richness of the human condition. As we face the challenges and opportunities of the 21st century, the insights offered by phenomenology, as exemplified in the work of Aoki, Patočka, and the contributors to this book, provide a valuable compass for navigating the ever-evolving landscape of education and research. In essence, this book serves as both a celebration of phenomenological inquiry in education and as an invitation to teachers, researchers, and learners to embrace a more holistic, care-centred approach to knowledge and understanding. This chapter introduced and unpacked the notions of care in teaching and learning and educational research but also explained why is it crucial that these notions in a country like South Africa which has a long legacy of historical burdens. It is our hope that the ideas presented here will inspire continued reflection, dialogue, and innovation in the pursuit of truly transformative educational and research experiences.

References

Aoki, T. (2005). Towards understanding curriculum: Talk through reciprocity of perspectives. In W. F. Pinar & R. L Irwin (Eds.), *Curriculum in a new key: The collected works of Ted T. Aoki*. New Jersey: Lawrence Erlbaum Associates, Publishers

Bibby, T. (2011). *Education - an impossible profession: Psychoanalytic explorations of learning and classrooms*. New York: Routledge.

Caruth, C. (1996). *Unclaimed experience: Trauma, narrative, and history*. Johns Hopkins University Press.

Fanon, F. (1967). *Black skin, white masks*. (C. L. Markmann, Trans.). Grove Press.

Findlay, E. F. (2002). *Caring for the soul in a postmodern age: Politics and phenomenology in the thought of Jan Patočka*. New York: State University of New York Press.

Foucault, M. (1995). *Discipline and punish: The birth of the prison* (A. Sheridan, Trans.). Vintage Books. (Original work published 1975)

Freud, S. (1959). Repression. In J. Strachey (Ed. & Trans.), *The standard edition of the complete psychological works of Sigmund Freud* (Vol. 14, pp. 141–158). Hogarth Press. (Original work published 1915)

Koopman, O., & Koopman, K. J. (2024). Towards a phenomenology of the broken [South] African body as the site for research. *Journal of Education*, 94, 127–145.

Lacan, J. (2006). The mirror stage as formative of the I function as revealed in psychoanalytic experience. In B. Fink (Trans.), *Écrits: The first complete edition in English* (pp. 75–81). W. W. Norton & Company. (Original work published 1949)

Mullis, I. V. S., Martin, M. O., Foy, P., Kelly, D. L., & Fishbein, B. (2020). *TIMSS 2019 International Results in Mathematics and Science*. Boston College, TIMSS & PIRLS International Study Center. Retrieved from https://timssandpirls.bc.edu/timss2019/international-results/

Mullis, I. V. S., Martin, M. O., Foy, P., & Hooper, M. (2017). *PIRLS 2016 International results in reading*. Boston College, TIMSS & PIRLS International Study Center. Retrieved from https://timssandpirls.bc.edu/pirls2016/international-results/

Noddings, N. (1984). *Caring: A feminine approach to ethics and moral education.* California: University of California Press.

Patočka, J. (1927/1996). *Heretical essays in the philosophy of history* (J. Dodd, Ed.). Chicago: Open Court.

Pinar, W. (2005). "A lingering note": An introduction to the collected works of Ted T. Aoki. In W. F. Pinar & R. L Irwin (Eds.), *Curriculum in a new key: The collected works of Ted T. Aoki.* New Jersey: Lawrence Erlbaum Associates, Publishers

Serequeberhan, T. (2013). *The hermeneutics of African philosophy: Horizon and discourse.* New York: Routledge.

Statistics South Africa. (2017). *Poverty trends in South Africa: An examination of absolute poverty between 2016 and 2015.* Pretoria: Statistics South Africa

Tesar, M. (2013). Lessons of subversion: Ethics and creativity in neoliberal academia. In M. A. Peters & T. Besley (Eds.), Creative education (pp. 111–118). Rotterdam: Sense Publishers.

World Bank Report. (2018). *Overcoming poverty and inequality in South Africa: An assessment of drivers, constraints and opportunities.* https://documents1.worldbank.org/curated/en/530481521735906534/pdf/Overcoming-Poverty-and-Inequality-in-South-Africa-An-Assessment-of-Drivers-Constraints-and-Opportunities.pdf (Accessed 16 June, 2024)

BIOGRAPHIES OF AUTHORS

Oscar Koopman is a Senior Lecturer in the Department of Curriculum Studies at Stellenbosch University. His main research focus is on the application of phenomenology in education research. He has published two sole-authored books: "Science Education and Curriculum in South Africa" (Palgrave Macmillan, 2017) and "Science Education and Pedagogy in South Africa" (Peter Lang, 2018). Additionally, he has co-authored two books with Dr Karen Koopman, these are "Phenomenology and Educational Research: Theory and Practice" (Whale Coast Academic Press, 2020) and "Decolonising the South African University: Towards Curriculum as Self-Authentication" (Palgrave Macmillan, 2023). Oscar Koopman has also published articles in international and continental journals and contributed chapters to various books.

Karen Joy Koopman is a Senior Lecturer in Commerce Education in the Department of Educational Studies, in the Faculty of Education, at the University of the Western Cape in South Africa. She completed her PhD at Stellenbosch University on the lived experiences of Accounting teachers. Her research mainly focusses on phenomenology and curriculum studies. Dr. Koopman has published both locally and internationally. In 2020 she published a co-authored book with Dr Oscar Koopman titled *Phenomenology and Educational Research: Theory and Practice*. In 2023, she published *Decolonizing* *the South African University: Towards Curriculum as Self Authentication* with Dr Oscar Koopman.

Jeff Beyer is an Ecopsychologist with a B.A. in Philosophy, a B.S. and M.A. in psychology, and a PhD in Existential Phenomenological Clinical Psychology. He has spent the past fourty years in clinical practice, supervision, and teaching in community hospital systems, private practice, and at Carnegie Mellon University in Pittsburgh, Pennsylvania. He has delivered numerous papers at the National Conferences of the American Psychological Association and contributed articles to professional journals and books on depthful human relating, ecopsychology, and the essential interconnectedness between psychological and ecological health and well-being. Lately he can be found with his hands in the dirt of his Pittsburgh community working with volunteers to nurture local human/nature ecosystems toward a more healthy, diverse, and sustainable trajectory.

Russ Walsh, is a licensed clinical psychologist with over thirty years of experience working with adolescents, adults, couples, and families. He earned his Ph.D. from the University of New Mexico, and his research has focused primarily on phenomenological and hermeneutic methodology. He has served as Director of Clinical Training, Psychology Clinic Director, and Department Chair, and has overseen more than twenty-five dissertations involving the elaboration of qualitative research methods. For the past several years, his research has focused on two distinct areas. First, following from his active participation in Duquesne's study abroad programmes, he has (with Monica Walsh) conducted qualitative research exploring students experiences of, and perspectives on, learning while studying abroad. Secondly, he has worked with his colleague (and Duquesne alumnus) David Danto examining the resilience of particular First Nations communities in Canada, as well the indigenous land-based interventions carried out in those communities.

Chatradari "Chats" Devroop, a research professor at Tshwane University of Technology, is an internationally acclaimed music performer with a diverse background in various genres. His academic interests stem from exploring his own musical practice, which now takes priority in his research, integrating the fields of music, philosophy, and music technology. As a widely published author, Devroop's recent focus has been on artistic research, aiming to formulate a South African perspective on this approach. His unique blend of practical experience and academic pursuits has sparked his interest in this emerging field.

Suriamurthee Maistry is a Full Professor in the school of Education at the (University of KwaZulu-Natal.) He is a critical curriculum scholar whose work is inspired by critical political economy, Anti-Blackness Theory and Unapologetic Black Inquiry (UBI). His transdisciplinary phenomenological work intersects with Critical University Studies (CUS) to critique historical, systemic and structural anti-Blackness continuities under contemporary neo-liberalism. He currently leads a National Research Foundation-funded project titled *"Higher Education Curriculum and Pedagogic Responsiveness in the Context of Innovative Artificial Intelligence (AI)"*. His previous projects include *"The South African Textbook Research Project"* and the *"Decolonising Postgraduate Supervision Project"*.

Gosaitse Ezekiel Solomon is a PhD candidate (in Social Science Education) at the University of Kwazulu-Natal. He holds a BBA and PGDE from the University of Botswana, and a Master of Science in Business and Marketing Education from the University of Wisconsin-Whitewater (USA). He currently teaches pedagogy in Business Education at the University of Botswana. Gosaitse is deeply interested in researching entrepreneurship education at secondary education level particularly focused on students' experiences of reflective learning in experience based entrepreneurial activities. Methodologically, he leans on pragmatism oriented hermeneutic phenomenology to investigate entrepreneurial learning from a processual and holistic perspective.

Keith Long, a retired principal, recently completed his PhD focusing on the application of phenomenology in investigating the lived experiences of school principals as they lead their schools towards learning organisations. Throughout the course of his doctoral studies, Dr. Long discovered his niche in research, which he now confirms is phenomenology.

Juliana Smith, a former Deputy Dean in the Faculty of Education at the University of the Western Cape, currently holds the position of Professor Emeritus within the same faculty. With an extensive background in graduate education, Prof. Smith has successfully supervised numerous doctoral students to completion. She has also made significant contributions to her field through the publication of book chapters and journal articles in both national and international journals.

Clive Jimmy William Brown is a lecturer and the Intermediate Phase Teaching Practice Coordinator and Chairperson of the Faculty of Education Transformation Committee at the Cape Peninsula University of Technology (CPUT), South Africa. He collaborates on several local and international education projects and researches Initial Teacher Preparedness, Teaching Practicum Models, and Early Teacher Professional Development. Brown recently earned his PhD from the University of KwaZulu-Natal, where he studied the lived experiences of student-teachers in diverse South African schools. His work uses a critical phenomenological framework to explore how strategically student-teachers from various backgrounds navigate their teaching practice

Sarasvathie Reddy is an Associate Professor in the discipline of Higher Education Studies and Academic Leader of the Education and Development Studies Cluster at the School of Education, University of KwaZulu-Natal. Her research and teaching focusses on diversity in higher education, curriculum development and design, doctoral education, academic staff and student development, and the assessment of learning in higher education contexts. She has graduated ten Masters and seven PhD students to date and has published more than thirty peer-reviewed publications. In 2019, she received the UKZN College of Humanities Teaching Excellence Award and the School of Education Teaching Excellence Award.

INDEX

A
African child – 159, 150, 151, 152, 157, 163
Alterity – 69, 70, 72
Ambiguity – 38, 39, 40, 41, 42, 43, 49, 51, 54, 55, 56, 84, 87
Anderson, J.R. – 47, 56
Annamalai, N. – 48, 56
Antunes, S. – 37, 38, 56
Aoki, T. – xx, 17, 18, 150, 151, 153, 154, 156, 157, 158, 159, 160, 161, 162, 164, 165, 166, 167, 168, 169
Apartheid – xii, 17, 18, 73, 126, 127, 128, 129, 132, 135, 139, 140, 142, 144, 145, 146, 149, 152, 153, 154, 156, 160, 163, 164, 166
Arpiainen, R. L. – 84, 85, 98

B
Barrett, J.R. – 46, 57, 51
Bayne, S. – xv, xx
Beck, C. T. – 90. 98
Betti, E. – xi, 14, 24, 34

Bibby, T. – 155, 156, 168
Biesta, G. – 87, 98
Brady, M. S. – 97, 98
Bristow, W. – 39, 57
Burbules, N. – 87, 98

C
Castro-Alonso, J.C. 43, 57
Chaplin, A.D. – 40, 57
Churchill, S. – 23, 24, 34
Cilesiz, S. – 50, 53, 57
Clearing (Lichtung) – 28
Coetzee, M.-H. – 38, 57
Colaizzi, P. – 23, 26, 27, 24
Cope, J. – 83, 84, 85, 86, 88, 96, 97, 99, 101
Corporeality – 84, 90, 92, 94
Cowart, M.R. – 51, 57
Crawford, R. – 52, 57
Creech, A. 47, 57
Creely, E. – 41, 57
Cromleigh, R.G. – 39, 57

D
Dasein – 87, 109, 118, 119, 120, 130, 131, 145, 160
Davidson, J.W. – 44, 45, 57
De Beauvoir, S. – 11, 19
Deleuze, G. – 73, 74, 75, 79
Devroop, C. – 38, 41, 58
Dewey, J. – 16, 43, 48, 86, 87, 101

E
Elpidorou, A. – 86, 99
Epidermalization – 155
Epoché – 9, 14, 22, 25

F
Fanon, F. 153, 155, 156, 157
Feenberg, A. – 72,79
Fletcher, D. E. – 84, 87, 101
Foucault, M. – 156, 168
Frascheri, S. – 88, 97, 101
Freeman, L.- 86, 99
Freud, S. – 2, 3, 5, 19, 155, 168

G
Gadamer, H. – 14, 24, 28, 30, 34, 165
Gilbert, A.S. – 39, 58
Giorgi, A. – 11, 14, 22, 26, 27, 28, 31, 32, 33, 34
Goldie, P. – 97, 99
Grier, J. – 39, 58
Guattari, F. – 73, 79

H
Harari, Y. N. – 64, 79
Harris, A. – 107, 123
Heelan, P. – 11, 19
Heidegger, M. – 2, 6, 9, 11, 14, 15, 16, 17, 19, 25, 28, 34, 40, 41, 58, 68, 86, 99, 105, 108, 109, 110, 113, 118, 119, 120, 121, 122, 123, 130, 131, 132, 144, 159, 160
Higgins, D. – 83, 84, 99
Hinchman, T. – 39, 58
Hjorth, D. – 84, 87, 99
Holder, E. – 39, 42, 58

Husserl, E. – 6, 7, 8, 12, 11, 14, 17, 19, 22, 27, 30, 35, 40, 41, 57, 58, 68, 75, 76, 79, 105, 108, 109, 110, 113, 114, 121, 123, 130, 131, 132, 145, 160

I
Ihde, D. 65, 68, 69, 70, 71,76, 79, 80

J
Juntunen, M.-L. 43, 48, 59

K
Kassean, H. – 83, 88, 100
Käufer, S. – 40, 58
Kolb, D.A. – 49, 58
Komulainen, K. J. – 87, 98
Kools, M. – 104, 106, 107, 108, 123, 124
Krishnan, K. – 38, 58
Kurczewska, A. – 83, 85, 87, 88, 99
Kyrö, P. – 87, 88, 100

L
Lacan, J – 2, 19, 155, 168
Lackéus, M. – 85, 98, 100
Lähdeoja, O. – 44, 58
Lee, S. – 12, 13, 67, 80
Lefebvre, H. – 11, 19
Levinas, E. – 67, 80
Locke, J. 39, 58, 75
Lopez, K.A. – 108, 110, 123

M
Magrì, E. – 87, 100
Mamlok, D. – 65, 69, 78, 80
Maruyama, M – 158
Masethe, M.A. – 37, 58
Maurer, A. – 39, 59
McKay, T. – 38, 59
McQueen, P. – 87, 100
McQuillan, D. – 64, 80
Merleau-Ponty, M. – 6, 7, 9, 11, 16, 19, 32, 35, 40, 41, 57, 59, 62, 66, 75, 77, 80, 86, 87, 131
Mitchell, M. – 64, 80, 83, 99, 100
Morris, S.L. – 41, 59, 133, 146

Muhamba, D. – 40, 59

N
Nijs, L. – 43, 44, 46, 59
Nilsson, N. J. – 65, 80
Noddings, N – 151, 169

O
Oakeshott, M – 71, 80, 158
Olivier, A. – 50, 59
Omoeva, C. – 51, 59

P
Patočka, J. – 18, 150, 151, 153, 154, 156, 158, 159, 161, 160, 162, 163, 164, 165, 166, 167, 168, 169
Pinar, W – 150, 157, 158, 159, 169
Pittaway, L. – 83, 84, 85, 101

Q
Quong, T. – 103, 123

R
Ricoeur, P. – 11, 19
Rose, J. – 51, 58, 59, 68
Rosenberg, R. – 68, 69
Rousseau, J.-J. – 39, 59
Roy, M. – 39, 59
Rubin, D. – 39, 59

S
Saevi, T. – 48, 59
Said, E. – 154
Saint Aubert, E. – 77, 80
Salner, M. – 23, 24, 26, 30, 35
Sanger, C.S. – 49, 59
Sartre, J-P. – 6, 11, 19, 57
Schiavio, A. – 46, 59
Schutz, M. – 44, 45, 59
Scott, P. – 60, 72, 80
Seaman, J. – 78, 80
Secomandi, F. – 67, 76, 77, 80
Sedley, D. – 38, 59
Selden, P. – 84, 87, 101

Senge, P.M. – 17, 104, 106, 107, 108, 109, 110, 113, 118, 119, 120, 121, 122, 123
Serequeberhan, T. – 154, 169
Silverman, M. – 45, 60
Smith, D.W. – 19, 27, 35, 38, 56, 60, 90, 99, 100, 101, 123
Stark, J. – 43, 60
Stoll, L. – 104, 106, 107, 108, 122, 124
Suleyman, M. & Bhaskar, R. – 65, 81

T
Temporality -12, 41, 84, 101
Testa, S. –, 88, 97, 101
Thompson, N. A. – 97, 101
Thorburn, M. – 62, 76, 81
Thrownness (Geworfenheit) – 118, 120, 121, 132
Trauma theory – xxi, 18, 151, 154, 157, 156

U
Unready-to-hand (Unzuhandenheit) – 25

V
Valentine, K.D. – 53, 60
Van Manen, M. – xx, xvi, xix, 12, 75, 126, 146, 165
Van Zijl, A.G. – 44, 60
Vass, E. – 44, 60
Verbeek, P. -68, 69

W
Waldenfels, B. – 75, 81
Walker, A. – 103, 123
Walsh, R. – 28, 29, 30, 32, 34, 35,172
Watts, G. – 84, 85, 96, 97, 99
White, R. – 59, 60, 127
Willis, D.G. – 109, 108, 110, 123

X
Xu, Y. – 41, 60

Z
Zahavi, D. – 39, 60, 125, 130, 147, 145

COMPLICATED
A BOOK SERIES OF CURRICULUM STUDIES

Reframing the curricular challenge educators face after a decade of school deform, the books published in Peter Lang's Complicated Conversation Series testify to the ethical demands of our time, our place, our profession. What does it mean for us to teach now, in an era structured by political polarization, economic destabilization, and the prospect of climate catastrophe? Each of the books in the Complicated Conversation Series provides provocative paths, theoretical and practical, to a very different future. In this resounding series of scholarly and pedagogical interventions into the nightmare that is the present, we hear once again the sound of silence breaking, supporting us to rearticulate our pedagogical convictions in this time of terrorism, reframing curriculum as committed to the complicated conversation that is intercultural communication, self-understanding, and global justice.

The series editor is

Dr. William F. Pinar
Department of Curriculum Studies
2125 Main Mall
Faculty of Education
University of British Columbia
Vancouver, British Columbia V6T 1Z4
CANADA

To order other books in this series, please contact our Customer Service Department:

peterlang@presswarehouse.com (within the U.S.)
orders@peterlang.com (outside the U.S.)

Or browse online by series:

www.peterlang.com

www.ingramcontent.com/pod-product-compliance
Lightning Source LLC
Chambersburg PA
CBHW052021290426
44112CB00014B/2330